Hancock

Freddie Hancock and David Nathan

Freddie Hancock was born in London and educated at Kendrick High School for Girls, South Hampstead High School for Girls and Regent Street Polytechnic.

She worked for two years for the Holland America Line, learning the public relations trade. She then became Assistant Head of Publicity, Universal Film Corporation of America, UK Division. She later formed a limited PR company and was responsible for much of the promotion for the foreign film industry in England. She closed her business when she married Hancock, at his request, and due to her distress following Hancock's death, did not reopen it until five years ago. In the interim period she acted as consultant and adviser to a number of companies. She now lives in America – though she frequently visits England for consultations – where she represents, amongst other companies, *Screen International* and Chattanooga Corporation.

David Nathan was born in Manchester, and after joining the *News Chronicle*, Manchester, at fifteen, went on to work on many regional and national newspapers. He was part of the regular writing team for *That Was the Week That Was* and subsequent Saturday-evening shows, and he has written plays for both radio and television. His books include *The Freeloader*; *The Laughtermakers*; *Glenda Jackson*; *John Hurt, An Actor's Progress* and *The Story so Far.*

He is the assistant editor and theatre critic of *The Jewish Chronicle*, and is married and has two sons.

HANCOCK

BY FREDDIE HANCOCK
AND
DAVID NATHAN

ARIEL BOOKS
BBC PUBLICATIONS

Published by BBC Publications
A division of BBC Enterprises Ltd
35 Marylebone High Street, London WIM 4AA

First published 1969 by William Kimber and Company Ltd
Paperback edition published 1975 by Coronet
This edition first published 1986. Reprinted 1986

© Mrs Freddie Hancock and David Nathan 1969, 1975, 1986

ISBN 0 563 20461 3

Typeset by Phoenix Photosetting, Chatham
Printed in Great Britain by Mackays of Chatham Ltd

Contents

Picture Credits

First section Hancock and Cicely at the seaside, Popperfoto; Hancock and Cicely in a Piccadilly café, Popperfoto; Hancock in 1956, BBC; Hancock with Galton and Simpson, Radio Times/Don Smith; Hancock in 1959, Photosource/Fox Photos; *Hancock's Half Hour* cast, BBC; Hancock with 'Funniest Man of 1959' TV award, Photosource/Keystone; Anthony Aloysius St John Hancock, BBC; Hancock in 'The Missing Page', BBC; Hancock with Sid James, BBC; Hancock with Sid James and Hattie Jacques, Photosource/Keystone.

Second section Hancock in 'The Radio Ham', Radio Times/Don Smith; Hancock in 'The Blood Donor', Radio Times/Don Smith; Hancock shaves in 'The Bedsitter', BBC; Hancock reads philosophy in 'The Bedsitter', BBC; Hancock on the phone in 'The Bedsitter', BBC/Philip Glassborow; Hancock on *Face to Face*, BBC; Hancock as office clerk in *The Rebel*, Kobal Collection; Hancock with George Sanders in *The Rebel*, Kobal Collection; Hancock as successful artist in *The Rebel*, Kobal Collection; Hancock with movie camera, Kobal Collection; Hancock at Cannes with David Nathan and others, Robert Penn/David Nathan; Freddie Hancock, Peggy Leder; Hancock with Bernard Delfont, Popperfoto.

Third section Hancock wearing jumper and jacket, Photosource/ Keystone; Hancock, with folded hands, Photosource/Keystone; Hancock with John Le Mesurier in *The Punch and Judy Man*, Kobal Collection; Hancock with Mr Punch, Philip Glassborow; Hancock with photographers, Popperfoto; Hancock with Freddie at wedding, Photosource/Keystone; Hancock with Freddie, Popperfoto; Hancock looking belligerent, Photosource/Keystone; Hancock with cigarette, Kobal Collection; Hancock with Galton and Simpson, BBC Hulton Picture Library; Hancock in 'The Croupier' sketch for ATV, Popperfoto; Hancock rehearsing in Australia, John Fairfax and Sons Ltd.

Preface

When Tony Hancock played Jolly Jenkins in *Red Riding Hood* at the Theatre Royal, Nottingham, in 1950, there were some nights when he braced himself with a tot of rum like a sailor about to face the cannon's roar, and ran on stage to deliver the factory song or the pig song, muttering and moaning up to the very moment when he warmed the audience with his smile and beamed at the children he would shortly lead in the dreaded chorus.

The despair was self-mocking for he knew he needed the regular, well-paid work, and it was tinged with truth for he truly hated what he was doing. I was there on many an evening in the three months or more that the panto, which starred a fifteen-year-old Julie Andrews, was in town for I had struck up a friendship with this extraordinary man whose eyes would light up and dance when – as frequently happened – the idea that something was funny hit him. He could not wait until he offered it to you, diffidently, like something he had just cooked up, which, in a sense, he had, for what was funny was the way he looked at something, far more than the thing itself.

A little later both of us reached London. In the years that followed there were meetings in dressing rooms and elsewhere, the occasional interview and, under his expert guidance, sessions with the bottle which were excessive even in Fleet Street and for which I soon realised I had neither the stamina nor the stomach.

One of the happiest occasions was a meeting at the 1960 Cannes film festival at which I engineered a joint interview with Tony and Trevor Howard in which they both expressed boundless admiration for each other and swore that one day they would work together in a television comedy.

Freddie was a friend from another part of my professional life. One of London's top show business PR experts, she was a familiar figure in the film and theatre circles in which I increasingly worked. She was more respected than most for she told the truth about her clients and, if that was not always possible, she at least did not invent stories to get publicity for them. Later, of course, I found out that she had, with increasing distress, to lie desperately to protect Tony from adverse attention.

When she and Tony came together I remember vaguely thinking that what with Tony's drinking habits and Freddie's determination they were in for some interesting times together. Just how interesting and how traumatic I did not know until I came to write this book which now, seventeen years later, goes into its third edition. This is less a boast than a tribute to the extraordinary talent we have tried to celebrate, the immortal part of a mortal man blessed with the rare gift of giving laughter, not only to his own generation, but to people who were unborn when he died.

Death has also claimed some of the people whose recollection and insights were invaluable in putting this book together in the first place. Among them was Sean Kenny (June 1973), a great personal loss for he was a marvellous companion; Ralph Reader (May 1982) and J. B. Priestley (August 1984), who recommended this book to *Sunday Times* readers as an honest account of Hancock's struggles, his triumph and his fall.

Where they appear in the book I have largely left them to speak in the present tense, for it would distort the text if they were presented as being dead when, in fact, they were all so vibrantly alive when the book was first written and published.

I have corrected a couple of facts which were wrong in the original – the location of the sanatorium in which Galton and Simpson first met and the authorship of 'The Crooner' sketch. Material from the Written Archives of the BBC, not available in 1969, has provided some interesting, perhaps illuminating, glosses on incidents in Hancock's career and further conversations with Ray Galton and Alan Simpson and other sources have provided others. The additions have been incorporated in the text, or appear as notes at the back of the book.

To all those who helped with the original book I must add the names of Neil Somerville and his colleagues at the BBC Written Archives Centre, Caversham; Sheila Hamilton, Marketing Manager of BBC Enterprises, Rene Goddard of BBC Audience Research, my perceptive editor, Sheila Ableman of BBC Publications, Chris Bumstead of the Tony Hancock Appreciation Society, Wendy Gresser of Harvey Unna and Stephen Durbridge Ltd., and Jim McManus. And, once more with feeling, Ray Galton and Alan Simpson.

David Nathan, October 1985

Introduction

The biographer's dilemma in writing about the life of a great but controversial talent can be immense.

To tell the whole truth, particularly where the truth hurts, often diminishes a much-loved image, angers a vast and devoted public unwilling to be robbed of their illusions.

I sympathise with this, not merely because I loved Tony Hancock and married him, but because I shared with the millions a tremendous admiration for his genius, total identification with the lovable character who became perhaps the first authentic idol of the television screen.

But if the quality of genius is a love of truth so, too, must be the essence of a biography. And Tony himself, who loathed sham publicity and false sentimentality, would want nothing less than the truth.

That truth is warm, rich, and wonderful. It is also chill, brutal, at times hateful. Here was a man who achieved the ultimate triumph of being known only by his surname – in such distinguished company as Garbo, Chaplin, Fernandel, Laurel and Hardy.

Yet behind that unique, sombre smile was a tortured and tormented existence, into which I too was slowly drawn and by which I was almost destroyed.

It is because of this deeply personal involvement in which my life swung violently between ecstasy and despair that I could not, alone, attempt an objective account of Tony's life.

For this reason I asked the writer, David Nathan, who knew the man as well as anyone alive today, to collaborate with me – in fact to write the book with the compassion it deserves, but with the objectivity it demands.

If the book achieves a greater understanding of the secret torments of a clown, the interminable agony of making the millions laugh, the project will have been worth while.

But I hope it will do more than that.

What I pray for is that this complex, unhappy but richly-endowed character will emerge into a kinder and warmer light than the hasty and pártisan obituaries conferred upon him.

The genius of Tony Hancock will rise above the innuendoes and half-truths which distort and often corrode a much-loved public figure.

I hope this book, despite its uncomfortable revelations, will show that a gem, though flawed, can still be priceless.

Freddie Hancock, 1969

Chapter One

Anthony Aloysius St John Hancock was a comic fiction who lived in an imaginary place called East Cheam and had total reality for millions of people. Anthony John Hancock, clown, was not content with this and searched for more reality, and more truth until he finally lost himself in a fantasy world.

From the moment the perfection of the creation was achieved the clown struggled to free himself from it. It was like watching a man trying to lose his own shadow.

Hancock deeply and bitterly resented carrying the burden of other people's images. The tragedy is that those images were basically true. Hancock could never see himself as others saw him.

Successful comedians are, to some extent, love objects. They arouse powerful proprietorial feelings among their audiences and they know that their first business must be to be liked. To some it comes naturally and gracefully; others have to work at it, planning their moments of pathos with the skill and dedication of a hospital sister laying out surgical instruments. Their armoury includes the little-boy-lost look, the disarming gesture, a glimpse of premeditated panic in the eyes, a note of helplessness in the voice and an unthreatening belligerence. They smile invitations of love to a crowded theatre and, even off-duty in a roomful of approving people, they will seek out the one man who withholds affection and retire hurt if they cannot win him over.

It is a form of self-abasement that was particularly despised by Hancock. 'It's comedy according to cookery-book recipe,' he would snort – 'mix the ingredients, add a soupçon of sentiment and top with a sprinkling of pathos. Very nasty.'

But then he had no need of it. Pathos is a short-cut to love and Hancock needed no artificial sweetener to make his personality palatable to the public. He was born with the gift of being loved as others are born with curly hair or a natural talent for singing. It could be measured, charted, drawn like a line on a graph as it grew deeper and rose higher until, at the period of his greatest popularity, 33 per cent of the adult population of the United Kingdom sat in front of their television sets for half an hour a week loving him and laughing at him.

Audiences are frequently perceptive but they do not see everything. There is at least one cuddly comedian who proves that it is possible to be held in high regard by an audience and deep loathing by acquaintances; a man with undetectable friends.

Hancock's friends were many and their degree of love can be measured by their high, though not total, rate of forgiveness. As he grew more and more panic-stricken in his search for some ultimate unattainable truth in comedy he grew more and more wounding.

Those he loved and those who loved him deepest were not spared. His marriage to his first wife, Cicely, foundered in violence and alcohol after fifteen years. Nor did the fifteen years that his second wife Freddie gave him in professional and personal devotion avert ultimate disaster, although she struggled valiantly to free him from his need for drink and fought hard to get his career back to its former splendour.

There was a ruthless streak in him which allowed him to cut out of his life all those who had contributed to it but were considered to be of no further use. Eventually, he decided that he himself was of no further use and the ruthlessness turned inward and destroyed him.

It was a visible progress, watched by a public as baffled by it as he himself was and holding him in an extraordinary amount of tenderness even after the laughter had died.

Canio in *I Pagliacci* would have got much more sympathy from his audience – particularly a British audience – if they had read about his personal problems in the papers or watched him in a revealing television interview. There is no longer much of a private life for public performers. The newspapers do not actually create the deep concern millions feel when things go wrong for the favoured few; but they mirror it and, to some extent, the rawness of the exposure keeps the healing process at bay.

Hancock's life was summed up by Spike Milligan, another clown who has had troubled times, when he said: 'One by one he shut the door on all the people he knew; then he shut the door on himself.'

But before that happened there was a great deal of laughter and a lot of fun. No man with Hancock's transforming smile could have led a wholly depressing or morose life.

There were times when he fell about laughing even more than

his audiences did. Indeed, in one way or another, there was a vast amount of laughter in the man.

At any rate while the doors were opening.

Anthony John Hancock, public man, round shoulders hunched over the microphone, round eyes holding the audience transfixed, delivers his stuff, his good old reliable and blessedly safe stuff, and the words flow smoothly as a stream, broken only by pauses dotted like deftly placed stepping stones leading to the final haven of desperately-needed applause.

He is foreman of a gang of navvies and 'would like to thank you all for your support, ladies and gentlemen. Next week we will be appearing at the corner of High Street and Station Road with Cecil on pneumatic drill and Percy on shovel. We look forward to your continuous support . . .'

Anthony John Hancock, private man, bent shoulders hunched over a record player in the corner of the room, round eyes dancing with delight, eager to spread his enthusiasms, saying, 'Just listen to it, listen! She's got every bleeding violinist in the world there. Or it's Max Jaffa and a couple of his mates.'

Anthony John Hancock, drunk, round shoulders sagging, round eyes bleary, red and dulled, having sailed to desperation and back on a sea of vodka, makes amends for last night's beating of the second Mrs Hancock by ordering six dozen red roses which fill the room with enough sweetness to drown the taste of tears and overwhelm the fumes of alcohol.

Anthony John Hancock prised his way into the world on 12 May 1924, the second son of Jack and Lily Hancock of Hall Green, Small Heath, Birmingham. Small Heath, sixty years ago, was a respectable middle-class area filled with the houses of moderately substantial citizens. Part of it was quite smart and part of it was sliding slowly into seediness.

Jack Hancock was a convivial man, who managed a shipping office though he was more interested in his semi-pro work as an entertainer at clubs, smokers and masonics. His wife frequently accompanied him at the piano.

Birmingham's only legacy to Hancock was an accent he could slide into at will, for the family left the city when he was three years old and made for the more genteel air of Bournemouth where his father had acquired a laundry.

Bournemouth was insulated from the worst effects of the depressed thirties. In the winter the town slept, its stillness broken only by the slow saunterings of the elderly retired as they took the air on warmer days. In the spring the town woke slowly to discreet activity as the tide of entertainers flowed in. The small, thin, round-shouldered boy grew to anticipate the sights and sounds of summer-season show business. He watched the sand sculptor smoothing his huge and beautiful horses out of damp sand, and heard the music and laughter that floated up from the concert parties. Frequently, sometimes with his elder brother Colin, who, seven years older, was to be killed while serving with the RAF during the war, he watched the Punch and Judy show, half fascinated, half horrified at the unbridled violence and cruelty of Punch.

Punch was to stay with him for a long, long time and even the sand artist would spring to life on film long after his art had drifted away.

Back at home, the laundry had given way to a pub, the Railway Hotel, and Jack Hancock was enlarging the number of his semi-professional engagements.

Once with a friend called Peter Read he was travelling to an engagement in a hired chauffeur-driven car. There was a prop basket on the floor of the car. Suddenly, Jack Hancock said, 'It's gone again.'

'It hasn't, has it?' said Peter in great alarm.

'It has,' said Hancock. 'Quick, get the flute and play it. Quick, otherwise we'll never get it back in the basket.'

The driver went white and tried to keep his eyes on the road and look around the car at the same time. Finally, he pulled up. 'Either you get that snake into the basket or we don't budge another inch,' he said.

It took a long time for the two laughing men to convince the driver that there was no snake.

Jack Hancock was an elegant entertainer, an early Terry Thomas who wore a monocle and a top hat. He had a polished line of patter and a winning way with a song.

Informed opinion at the clubs, masonics and golf club dinners, the annual licensed victuallers' ball at the Pavilion and other important social functions, was that Jack Hancock was as good as most professionals and better than some.

He was friendly with a number of real professionals and many of them dropped in at the Railway Hotel or even stayed there during their visits to the town to play at the Pavilion Theatre. The young Tony was fascinated by them. Clapham and Dwyer, 'In a Spot of Bother', Elsie and Doris Waters 'Gert and Daisy', the

Houston Sisters 'The Irresistibles' and the slightly surrealist Stainless Stephen 'Semi-colon' would, he recalled later marvelling at their extroversion, go into an act at the drop of a hat.

They were not at all like the stars of today who, off-stage, frequently worry about the state of the country or demand to know what Life is all about – a question Hancock himself came increasingly to ask.

They were exotics – 'different from any other kind of people I had ever met in my young life; they seemed to get so much more out of simply being alive,' he said years afterwards.

But these were mostly holiday encounters. Running a pub edges in on the business of running a family and in addition, when Tony was seven, a younger brother, Roger, was born.

Tony was sent off to Durlston Court, a boarding school in Swanage.

He was happy there, being good at games if not academically outstanding. He was a useful footballer, a better than average seam bowler and despite a physique more related to swotting than sport, a fair boxer.

'I was an odd-looking character, ugly-looking feller,' he said later. 'I felt that people laughed at me.'

He was particularly conscious of his rounded shoulders and, in a forlorn effort to straighten them out, used to hang from a bar until his arms ached and he was forced to drop. He gave it up as hopeless after catching sight of his shadow.

'I looked like a bloody great bat,' he growled.

Durlston gave him – or tried to give him – his first stage experience. During holidays he had stood often enough in the wings at the Pavilion Theatre watching his father's friends and now he had the chance to go on and do it himself.

The advantage for schools of doing Gilbert and Sullivan is that there is an almost unlimited number of small parts requiring little or no talent. So much so that there are frequently more boys on the stage than in the auditorium. This pleases both the boys and the parents. Tony's part in *The Gondoliers* was not huge but at least he had a line to say which was more than many of the others. He had to come on leading a train of nobles and announce with great dignity, 'My Lords, the Duke!'

'I held myself in reserve at the rehearsals,' Hancock recalled later. 'I didn't see any point in burning myself out. Then came the dress rehearsal and I decided to really throw myself into the part.

'Trembling with excitement, I waited in the wings with my company shuffling and fidgeting behind me. Then came the cue.

With a slow, measured tread I led my nobles on to the stage. With dignity we halted in the middle. My hand came up in an impressive gesture of introduction. My mouth opened. It closed and opened again. But the only thing that came out was a strangled gargle.

'The master in charge of production took it rather well.

'"Go off and come on again, Hancock," he said.

'Disconsolately, the train trooped back into the wings. With much shoving and barging we took up position. Once more the slow measured tread . . . the flowing gesture and this time . . . a mouselike squeak.

'My jaws were working but my voice wasn't. Not one other sound could I raise.

'"All right, Hancock," said the master, "you've had your moment of clowning" . . . so he gave me a 15-second walk-on part for a crowd scene.'

The adult Hancock was also the victim of excruciating tensions before any kind of public appearance, whether on stage or television. Most performers have first-night nerves. Hancock had every-night nerves, and was often sick in his dressing room before facing the audience or the cameras.

Laughter is a form of approval. It is sought in every saloon bar and every dinner party; it is a driving need that is part of the make-up of every comic who has ever tried to wring it from a reluctant audience.

Hancock, as a boy and man, needed it as much, possibly more, than most. He must have done in order to endure the agonies of nerves he suffered every time he stepped on the stage in search of it. He comforted himself with the thought – correct as it happens – that every artist suffers some degree of nerves and that if the nausea ever ended, so too would the artistry. It was no more reason to give up performing than Nelson's frequent sea-sickness was cause for him to join the army.

But at Durlston all Hancock was aware of was acute disappointment and the need to try again. The next production was *The Pirates of Penzance* and he auditioned and was accepted for the chorus. Tragedy struck again. His voice began to break.

The music master stopped the pianist and sat with his head in his hands. Then he took Hancock aside and, very confidentially, whispered, 'What I really wanted was a very good stage manager.'

'On looking back,' Hancock recalled, 'I must have sounded like a cross between Paul Robeson and Lily Pons.'

An iron determination and inflexible will were ever Hancock's weapons against both his own nerves and other people's obstinacies and they were more than a match for the music master. He was allowed to join the chorus on condition that he opened his mouth and thwacked his thigh but did not, under any circumstances, sing.

It was during one of his school holidays that he made his first visit to the South of France which later became his haven from the strain of work and, later still, his hiding place where the wounds healed or, at least, hardened.

For some reason, he was kept in the heat of the Riviera in his school uniform of black pinstripe trousers, black jacket and Eton collar.

Staying at the same hotel was the great comedian Sidney Howard who was clearly fascinated by the sight of this strange, sweltering boy. Howard and his wife fussed over him trying to keep him pin bright in his pinstripe, seeing that all was spotless. One day the great man saw an obtrusive piece of white cotton on the boy's lapel.

'Mustn't go out looking a wreck, must we?' he said as he pulled the cotton away . . . and away . . . and away.

The other end of the reel was in the boy's pocket.

'You'll go far, sonny,' said the great man.

Back home in Bournemouth, the Railway Hotel was given over in favour of a small private hotel called Durlston Court after the boy's prep school at Swanage. It gave Jack more freedom for his entertaining, the directors of the Railway Hotel not appreciating the need for his frequent absences in the evening. It did not lessen the demands made on Mrs Hancock's time.

'None of us,' Hancock recalled, 'my brothers, mother or my father, enjoyed a family life as it is customarily understood – it is quite impossible when you are involved in running a hotel.' He was often lonely. His mother told an interviewer, 'Tony once asked why he couldn't have a home life like the other boys. But it was impossible of course. I was busy with customers all the time.'

'When everybody was too busy to talk to me,' he later said, 'I resorted to the simple solution of dipping into the hotel petty cash and taking myself off to the pictures. I saw so many, many pictures during those years, just before my early teens.'

When he was home for the holidays Hancock's job was to write out the daily menu. There was a permanent basic soup stock which allowed him scope to exercise his gift for the pompous which later became so important a part of his clowning. Calling upon his geographical knowledge, he would describe the soup one day as *Crème d'Alsace*, another time it would be *Potage Luxembourg* or *Consommé Italienne*. Even for the young Hancock there would be no Brown Windsor.

Tony was eleven years old and returning home when he saw the ambulance start away from outside the hotel and turn the corner of the street. He never saw his father again.

All that summer, the gay and debonair Jack Hancock lay in hospital and, eventually, he died. The boy had not been allowed to see him. It was a shock that would have outraged the least sensitive system. Later in life Hancock had dreams and nightmares about his father and, waking, talked of the little he remembered with deep regret. But he always looked on hospitals with a more than ordinary loathing.

Six months later Mrs Hancock married again, becoming Mrs Robert Walker, and Tony graduated from prep school to Bradfield College, Berkshire.

Again, he enjoyed himself in sport and got through the academic side without attracting much attention or acquiring a public-school patina. It was just as well – it would have been a sore handicap in the kind of comedy he was to develop.

Years later when John Freeman asked him on television to define his rung on the social ladder, Hancock replied: 'Lower middle class.' But as the resident of Railway Cuttings and later Earl's Court he assumed a manner of speech suitable for someone who, though upwardly immobile, desperately aspired to higher social status.

Hancock's ordinary speaking voice was warm and gentle, untainted by affectation, unmarked by any obvious regional identification. When a funny idea struck him he would imperceptibly slide into character and either drop his aitches or signal that he was taking great pains to avoid dropping them.

Possibly Hancock avoided picking up a public-school accent because he did not stay at the school long enough, deciding to leave, without apparent opposition from his family, at fifteen, the earliest possible legal age.

There followed a series of jobs it is difficult to imagine Hancock in. Of course it was wartime and labour was scarce, but all the same, it was employment which hindsight at least boggles at.

The boy who became the man who could make a suit crumple just by looking at it, had ideas of sartorial elegance far above his reach. Armed with a vision of advancing elegantly on distinguished customers, tape measure on arm, bowing from the waist, he joined a local branch of the multiple tailor, Hector Powe.

He arrived, neat blue double-breasted pinstripe immaculately pressed, and was shown the broom cupboard. After sweeping out the shop he was asked to make tea.

Two hours and thirty-five minutes later he left.

He liked the Durlston Court Hotel, liked studying the old ladies who were resident there. No doubt he exaggerated slightly when he said they used to set out for the dining room at 11.30 and get there just in time for the gong at one o'clock. But he was probably right when he noticed that they marked their marmalade jars.

However, his mother, a formidable lady with little time for idle boys, 'told me politely that it was necessary that I should find another job and get into the habit of going regularly to work.'

The next unlikely job for the boy who, as a man, was to become agitated at the sight of a form, was as a Civil Servant. The Board of Trade had moved from London to the Carlton Hotel, Bournemouth, and the young Hancock was told at the Labour Exchange that they were looking for staff.

He wore the same suit that had landed him the job at Hector Powe's but this time he carried a rolled umbrella. The post he was applying for was as Temporary Unestablished Assistant Clerk, Grade Three.

He asked about the prospects.

'Surely, Mr Hancock,' replied the interviewing officer, 'it is not necessary for me to outline prospects. This is the Civil Service. The prospects are obvious.

'We can arrange,' he said after studying the form Hancock had filled in, 'for you to start next week.'

'I can't decide right at this moment,' the boy told the astonished official. 'There are several other irons in the fire. I'll drop you a line in a day or so.'

After a week, the other irons having melted away, he wrote saying that he could start. He was not a success.

All this time he was gathering material for an act. Perhaps a better word would be 'stealing'. There was hardly a comic of the day who appeared in Bournemouth or who was heard on the radio who did not, in some way, contribute.

When he left Bradfield his mother had made him attend commercial classes in order to learn shorthand and typing. Later he would drive secretaries crazy by telling them that they had put down a wrong outline. At the time it came in very useful in building up material. Max Miller, a comic who by perfect timing could get away with material of a blue to make painters envious, was a favoured if unknowing contributor. Tony did not know much about timing then.

He spent a week's Civil Service wages – £2 10s. – on a pair of Max Miller brown-and-white co-respondent's shoes and a Max Miller curly-brimmed hat and, one wartime night in a church hall in Bournemouth, 'Anthony Hancock . . . the Confidential Comic' slid down the slipway of his professional career and for a modest fee of ten shillings launched himself on the waiting world. He did not, in all honesty, make much of a splash.

Certainly, engagements came, mainly at smoking concert level, stag affairs with unshakeable, unshockable audiences whose organisers were unwilling to pay more than ten bob a time for the privilege of strolling down memory lane with the confidential comic.

Mother decided to help out. She went to see George Fairweather, a former postman who had been helped by Jack to take the big stride from semi to full professional and was then running shows for the troops at the Theatre Royal.

'Tony's a chip off the old block,' she said, 'and he's dying to have a go.'

Tony's basic act was reinforced by Cyril Fletcher type material and he could knock off an odd ode in less than an hour.

George Fairweather recalls: 'I gave Tony a little spot in a show for the troops. He was terrible. He just stood there and said the material and did an impression of Cyril Fletcher which was quite good. But the stuff he had written himself was all about Goebbels getting plastered and Hitler being a bastard and I told him that he would never become a comedian as long as he thought of dirt.'

But he couldn't get it over to him. 'The troops laugh, don't they?' said Hancock.

'Of course they laugh,' George told him. 'Put four or five hundred soldiers in a hall and they'd laugh if you came on and said arseholes. But it's not artistry.'

One night Tony came and said to him: 'You don't think I've got it but I've got a date on my own.'

It was in a Catholic church hall. The show was made up of semi-pros and amateurs and he was the lead comic.

Sure of himself, he strode on stage, leaned over the footlights and told a joke about a commercial traveller and a blonde. The audience stirred uneasily. Then he gave them one about a sergeant-major and an ATS officer. Mums looked at dads and dads avoided looking at mums. The landgirl and the farm labourer joke was altogether too earthy and caused a sudden outbreak of nervous coughing. Hancock ended on the bishop and the actress joke and the audience rose to him – and walked out. He left the stage to the worst sound a comedian can hear as he makes an exit – his own footsteps. He was paid his 10s. 6d. and asked to kindly leave the hall. He told George in tears the following day that the church authorities had said they wanted to fumigate the place.

Barely seventeen at the time, he had little idea of what he had been saying. Seventeen-year-olds then were not as knowing as they are today. He never told another dirty joke in his life. Nor did he like listening to them, though he had to bear his fair share of the comedian's burden – the saloon-bar shoulder-slapper who says, 'I know you can't use this one in its present form but you'll be able to clean it up a bit' and then, eyes gleaming, a laugh on his lips, tells a story that would have had the citizens of Sodom sending for the police.

The third job came when he decided that he was leading too sheltered a life in the Civil Service and needed to meet more people. Once more his mother came to the rescue and spoke to Peter Read who now ran a pub called the Pembroke.

'Yes,' he said, 'I'll fix him up: we need a new potman.'

Hancock's mother knew her son and was doubtful.

'I don't think Tony would be very keen to be a potman,' she said.

'All right,' said Peter, 'we'll call him something else.'

A few days later Hancock joined the staff as Domestic Manager. His duties were those of a potman. He rehearsed his act in the cellar to stacks of crates and rows of barrels, building in his imagination the responses he needed.

Real audiences, however, were different. Before he faced them he shook and sweated and paced and muttered his lines. When he got on the stage he did not know what to do with his hands. His left hand in particular stroked the lapel of his jacket in a rapid up-and-down movement.

'You must stop it,' George told him one night just as he was about to go on. 'It's too distracting. If you can't think of anything else put it in your trousers pocket at least.'

Hancock walked on stage, left hand in trousers pocket, and started his patter to an audience which contained about 250 servicewomen. George, watching him from the wings, became alarmed and then horrified. True, the left hand was in the pocket but the up-and-down movement that had once threatened to wear out the lapel was still there. It looked very bad indeed.

'Take your hand out of your pocket,' hissed George. But Tony didn't hear him.

'Take your bloody hand out of your pocket,' bellowed George.

Later he commented: 'That was Tony's first experience of gestures.'

Back at the Pembroke, Peter Read must have been a very easy man. Once, when his domestic manager went off suddenly with a bad chill, he received a telegram hastily scribbled by Mrs Walker as she looked after her son and her guests and given to someone else to take to the post office. It read: 'TONY HAS HAD CHILD STOP MANY THANKS FOR ALL YOUR HELP.'

Another time he sent Tony to siphon some port. The boy was sent home by taxi helpless. It was time to look for another job.

He became secretary of the Bournemouth War Services Organisation which arranged shows for the unsuspecting troops. His first camp concert was a disaster.

He was working a confidential Tommy Trinder routine which involved a brisk, cheery strut to the front of the stage, a foot on the footlights showing an expanse of loud sock, a lean forward, then a string of gags.

The stage was in the camp canteen and had been erected only a few hours before the concert began. The footlights collapsed as soon as he touched them. At all service shows the seating arrangements were invariably the same, probably still are and are no doubt laid down in King's Regulations.

Officers occupied the front rows with the C.O. sitting dead centre, servicewomen filled the other seats immediately behind them and then came the other ranks.

Hancock was pitched into the C.O.'s lap.

'I had the presence of mind,' he recalled later, 'to lift my hat.'

'You're a clot,' the C.O. snarled.

Hancock tried to get back on to the stage, slipped and fell on to the C.O.'s wife.

He picked himself up and tried to squeeze between the front of the stage and the row of officers' knees. There was not enough room. The whole of the front rank of officers had to file out into the gangway and stand there as, muttering thanks, Hancock squeezed past and climbed on stage to continue his act.

He had to wait though until the hysterics in the rear ranks had subsided. On the way home he puzzled why his carefully selected sure-fire gags never got the response that his accident received.

The only time his nerve failed him completely at this stage was when he was compèring a show and his first entrance was greeted with dead silence. All subsequent announcements were made from the wings.

It was about this time that BBC producer Leslie Bridgemont visited Bournemouth to audition for a half-hour talent show. Hancock read a monologue for him entitled 'The Night the Opera Caught Fire'. Bridgemont said he thought he would be worth a few minutes on the broadcast and would arrange for a contract to be sent.

Fame was clearly beckoning. When the contract came Hancock read it carefully, no one was going to pull anything on this old pro.

One paragraph he noted with particular care said that a copy of the script must be sent to the producer three days before the performance.

The script was duly prepared and then taken to a Bournemouth printer. Two days later Bridgemont received a printed copy in heavy Gothic type, elaborately bound in thick paper.

When Bridgemont returned to Bournemouth to arrange the show, he was very suspicious, thinking that he was the victim of some complicated leg-pull. He listened to a halting explanation and then observed: 'A typewritten copy would have done.'

'I wish I had realised it,' said Hancock later. 'Ninety per cent of my fee went to the printers.'

As a performer, he was no doubt improving, learning to select material with more care, if not with more regard for copyright. But as an organiser he was less accomplished.

After he and ten members of the concert party had waited for two hours in the cold for a coach he had forgotten to order, he was asked to resign.

He would have had to leave anyway.

Chapter Two

The war in 1942 was not going well. Britain stood embattled and the Nazi hordes were triumphant in Europe. Someone had to stop them. They sent for Hancock. He had already volunteered for the RAF and, with visions of becoming a fighter ace, he travelled to Weston-super-Mare.

It was not the rounded shoulders, the concave chest, or the sunken cheeks that prevented him from flying. The reason he himself decided was that his arms were not the right length for a pilot. He was sent to the RAF Regiment, a body of fighting men created for the purpose of defending airfields against ground attack. There was, of course, an assault course over which Hancock had to charge at regular intervals, plunging his bayonet into straw-filled sacks while emitting the regulation blood-curdling yell. It was not his style.

'From this hell,' he recalled, 'I was rescued by the formation of a camp concert party.'

He had impressed the C.O. with an account of his professional experiences and, because of coincidental rehearsals, missed the progressive route marches which started off at one mile with full kit and lengthened with every successive march. When the concert party was disbanded Hancock was plunged straight into a fifteen-mile hike. It is true that he eventually found his feet in the RAF but that was not until some time later.

The RAF Regiment decided that they did not need him and sent him to another base to re-muster. He was assigned to a Canadian unit. At Bournemouth. For a time it was idyllic. He had all the swagger attached to being one of our lads in uniform and spent most of the time at home or with his concert party friends. This was not what war was about.

Hancock was transferred to Stranraer in Scotland or, as he called it, the Las Vegas of the North. Here he was given a post of special responsibility suited to his talents. His job was to look after the coal dump and see that innumerable fires were lit in the Nissen huts.

In letters home his job was described as Deputy Fuel Controller.

For other men, the war was measured in sand or salt water, bombs and bullets, barbed wire or battles. Hancock measured his war in coal. He could see mountains of it stretching ahead as far as the mind could see in an endless glistening black and most unholy mass; whole pitfuls of coal to be heaped in truck-loads on his hut doorstep to be shifted, carted, humped and ultimately burnt to drift away in smoke over a landscape where, he once said, you were delighted if the sheep moved because it made some sort of joke.

Clearly even an ENSA concert party was preferable to this and he travelled to London for an audition. The following day he travelled back to Scotland furious with himself.

No sooner had he opened with 'Ladies and Gentlemen', than his voice dried up through nerves.

He tried again, this time for the Ralph Reader Gang Show.

Before the war Ralph Reader had led the Boy Scouts into show business in a great burst of healthy high spirits extolling the virtues of comradeship and what it meant to have a pal. Now as Squadron Leader Reader, he was doing a similar job for the RAF.

He remembers the audition.

'Tony was very slight, very thin, very small,' he said, 'and I asked him what he did. He said he did most things but he wanted to be a comedian. I asked him if he had any comedy material and he rolled off about a dozen jokes. Apart from one, I hadn't heard any of them before.

'They were not real jokes but mostly service situations. This was fine because we wanted people who could play in sketches. The one thing that struck me more than anything else was that he stood there so completely at ease.'

At ease! Hancock was petrified! But he contemplated the alternatives and steeled himself. On the one hand were the waiting audiences ready to roar with laughter at his quizzical view of this crazy old world we live in; on the other the waiting coal heap, silent and brooding.

A few weeks later Hancock was on a troopship bound for Algiers, one of the Gang. On board was another Aircraftsman Second Class, the most junior rank in the most junior service, called Bob Moreton. Later, he was to charm radio audiences with his Bumper Fun Book. Later still he was to end his life in a gas-filled room in Australia. He confided to Hancock that he had brought his white dinner jacket with him in case there should be a dance on board. He proved it by bringing it out when they un-packed, three decks below water level.

Hancock thought he would fill the role of a jaw-jutting, stiff-upper-lipped Englishman and cut along to the NAAFI to buy himself a pipe and some tobacco. Carefully, he filled the bowl and lit it, then leaned over the rails and gazed into the Atlantic distances in the dedicated manner of one who had avidly watched Jack Hawkins in all the wartime naval films. He took one puff and the bowl dropped off into the ocean, leaving him with the stem clenched tightly in his teeth. Hancock never smoked a pipe again. He knew when to accept defeat.

There were a dozen men in each of the fifteen Gang Shows and they did everything themselves from singing a sentimental song to building a makeshift stage.

They wore uniforms – on stage – of grey shirts and trousers and red scarves and would open the show by singing with enormous heartiness, 'We're Riding Along on the Crest of a Wave.'

There was always a pianist who would usually double on piano-accordion, one singer, a couple of comics and a number of char-acter men for sketches. The second half would open with one of Squadron Leader Reader's more heart-rending numbers such as 'Keep the Memory of Home Right With You' for which the cast would line up, their hands on each other's shoulders, and look misty-eyed into a spotlight. It is difficult not to get misty-eyed while looking into a spotlight. This song would touch the heart of the toughest soldier.

There was a flight sergeant in charge of each unit but the rest were airmen. There was a request by one unit that they should all be made sergeants which would at least mean that they would not have to queue for meals after travelling all night and preparing the show. This was turned down on the grounds that if a bunch of singing sergeants and comic non-coms turned up it would be thought that they were a crowd of soft-job seekers and would lose a great deal of sympathy.

Number Nine Gang Show in which Hancock worked travelled around North Africa and Italy for a while and, in 1945 in the period between the defeat of Germany and the capitulation of Japan, was merged with Number Four Show. In this way, Hancock met Graham Stark. It was a relationship which started with warmth and years later was to chill in the sudden withdrawal of Hancock's friendship. But at the time they were just two airmen-comics in search of a laugh.

In fact Hancock, by then, was getting accustomed to the heady triumph of having a huge audience hanging on to every word and begging for the fun never to stop. It is a feeling full of power. But it is power stripped of corruption and bathed in a great glow of benevolence. Nothing fortifies a performer more, and to the dedicated comic a taste of it will cure everything from unpaid bills to unrequited love.

Of course, service audiences are always fairly easy, as George Fairweather had pointed out in the Bournemouth troop show days. But there is the ordinary reaction of pleasure given out by any bunch of good-natured men glad of some relief from boredom, and the special, highly-charged joy which on rare occasions lights up audience and performer alike and becomes a joint and long-treasured experience.

It happened to Hancock and Stark in Gibraltar when they were doing a sketch about two old air force officers before an audience of 2000 sailors. Laughter filled the Rock Theatre until it reverberated. It was prolonged and helpless and rang with approval.

In the middle of the sketch Hancock looked at Stark and licked his lips. It was a time to savour.

Ten years later the two comics were working a sketch written by Galton and Simpson in a radio show called *Star Bill*, broadcast from the Garrick Theatre on Sunday evenings. Suddenly they felt these huge waves of laughter beating down on them from the audience. When the sketch was over Hancock whispered to Stark, 'Remember Gibraltar?'

At Gibraltar they had been quartered in a Nissen hut at the sea end of the runway. They were ordered to fly back to England at six o'clock one morning. Aircraft had been coming in all night long 15 feet above their heads and Hancock stayed in bed until the last minute. Hastily he stuffed his things into the old, non-issue brown suitcase he used. They were flying in a Stirling bomber which stood nearby and as Hancock ran to it, the pilot revved up his engines. The clasp on the suitcase broke and all his underwear soared away into the Mediterranean. Mechanical things were never on Hancock's side.

Peace broke up the Gang Shows and Hancock spent his last few months in the service taking care of costumes and props with another airman called Peter Sellers.

'We were allowed to wear civilian clothes,' Hancock recalled, 'and we called ourselves Mr de Sellers and Mr le Hancock, pretending to all the boys coming from the stations to hire gear to stage their own shows that we knew everybody who was anybody in the business.'

Sellers said, 'He wandered around and kept saying, "How long are we going to be stuck here?"'

In their parallel careers Sellers ran second to Hancock for a long time. His radio reputation was as a member of a team – the Goons – and he made no inroad on television at all. But suddenly he overwhelmed Hancock, achieving the kind of international stardom, basically because he had the good sense to leave a lot of the groundwork to others, that Hancock desperately sought and never found.

It was Sellers, Hancock always claimed, who inspired his Hunchback of Notre Dame bit, 'I found him one day in the prop store acting Jekyll and Hyde like mad to two WAAFs sitting on a skip. He was doing it for real . . . the clawed hand, the twisted mouth, the snarling voice. Those poor girls were terrified.'

On 6 November 1946, Hancock was released from service about the same time as Sellers, Harry Secombe, Michael Bentine, Alfred Marks, Frankie Howerd, Jimmy Edwards, Morecambe and Wise and a number of other ambitious comedians.

Hancock was given a grey chalk-striped demob suit which he christened 'the railings' and a £60 gratuity.

He did not even consider going back to Bournemouth except for a visit and, as released servicemen could be demobilised anywhere they wished, he chose London.

His first stop was a room to himself in the Union Jack Club opposite Waterloo Station where he stayed for two weeks. Then he moved into a bed-sitter in Baron's Court.

He told George Fairweather during a visit to Bournemouth that he was 'going to have a bash' at it even if he starved.

'I think he practically did,' recalls Fairweather. 'He looked pretty dreadful – not that he ever looked robust. He always had a sort of grey pallor about him even when he got fat. I think it was nerves.'

Graham Stark recalls how, having been released about the same time, he and Hancock would spend days in the NAAFI Club until he himself evolved a cheaper way of life.

'I moved into a chocolate-brown basement in Holland Park with a barred eye-level window through which you could see the feet of passers-by. I bought a great sack of oatmeal and stood it in the fireplace and I discovered that if you mixed some of it with water you had a plate of porridge and it filled you up. Hancock came down and said, "I've got to get you out of here. You'll die in this room if you don't get out."'

But he was not able to help – then.

Hancock himself at the time felt that all he could offer to agents was his name and address; that stuff which had gone down well in the forces was very different from what was wanted outside.

'I spent most of my time in bed,' he said, 'living on very heavy sausage. It tasted like hell but you ate it and if you had a couple of glasses of water each day for about three days following you felt full.'

Occasionally, his mother came to see him in London and they had tea at the Regent Palace Hotel, sometimes with Stark. She used to slip her son a fiver under the table so that he would not be embarrassed.

'My mother,' Hancock said, 'for some extraordinary reason thought it would work. She gave me immense support. Initially, she thought that everything I did was great. It was only when I was settling down that she started to become critical. She was clearly very successful at hiding her doubts.'

For the most part though, it was the sausage, with an occasional tin of baked beans as a luxury item.

The strength was sapped from his confidence as well as his body. Each day he would take the tube train to the West End, intending to call on every agent in London.

Then he would drink a coffee, and tell himself he needed to look at the papers just to keep in touch. By then it was lunch-time and after that he usually went to the pictures. All his life the cinema was a place of refuge. He must have seen more films than a projectionist.

Hancock shared the general habit of postponing difficult or unpleasant situations but of course took it to excess. Letters would remain not just unanswered but unopened (at least until Freddie took charge of correspondence) and any severe problems would be dealt with simply by going to bed and pulling the covers over his head. It was a system that frequently worked.

The £60 gratuity was quickly running out.

One day he forced himself up the flight of stairs to an agent's office. He burst in announcing: 'I am Anthony Hancock, comedian, I wonder if you've got anything . . .'

The man behind the desk rose and Hancock moved forward hand outstretched. He stepped on a rug and it slid from underneath him. His feet skidded forward and his body went backwards halfway through the doorway.

He scrambled to his feet, muttered, 'Good morning, thanks' and rushed down the stairs.

And spent the afternoon at the pictures.

It was a time when variety was experiencing a brief boom, particularly in the provinces. The Sunday trains were full of ex-servicemen travelling to Bradford with shows that attempted to revive the camaraderie of the war years and, at the same time, capitalise on the new-found freedom from discipline by sending up traditional service concepts.

The shows were called everything from *Stars in Battledress* – which included Harry Secombe and Spike Milligan on guitar – to *Soldiers in Skirts* which had enough drag acts to keep a dress manufacturer happy.

Hancock's first professional stage job was in a Ralph Reader/ Air Ministry production called *Wings*, a mammoth Gang Show which toured the country for months.

There were about 300 ex-RAF men in it and Hancock was deeply grateful for this second 'call-up'. One of the items in which he took part was, in fact, a drag act. It was the only time, apart from playing an ugly sister in pantomime, that he ever climbed into skirts.

He was seen more as himself in a gag which would be depended upon to raise a howl of glee. He would slop across the stage in the most ill-fitting uniform imaginable to be stopped by the roar of a passing Warrant Officer.

'Where do you think you are?' the W.O. would bawl. 'Just look at your trousers! Look at your jacket! You are a disgrace to the service! How long have you been in the Air Force?'

Hancock would look up, pause – his timing was improving – and say slowly and with immense resignation, 'All bloody day.'

He also sang another of Mr Reader's songs called 'I'm a Hero to my Mum' which always touched a deep chord in the memories of the audiences. It was all about an airman who spent his whole war peeling potatoes and scrubbing floors and the song closed with the line: 'I don't care tuppence 'cos I know darn well I'm a hero to my mum.'

He sang it dead straight.

He was paid £10 a week during the run of *Wings*.

One of the places the show visited was Oxford and after another period of unemployment he found himself back there for the winter of 1947–8 playing an ugly sister in *Cinderella*.

In one scene he sat on someone's shoulders and together they would lurch down a flight of stairs. Always a seeker of more and bigger laughs, Hancock, on the third night, had the bright idea of throwing his skirt over his carrier's head.

Blinded, the 'horse' staggered across the stage, wavered over the footlights, then fell, Hancock on top of him, into the orchestra pit. Hancock climbed back, bitterly remembering the night he had fallen into the C.O.'s lap at the troop concert and with much the same sort of laughter ringing in his ears.

But he enjoyed Oxford. For one thing he had met one of the chorus girls and they decided it would be cosy – as well as cheaper – if they rented a caravan. They heard of one going for £1 a week and closed the deal dreaming of luxury and privacy.

The caravan, all flaking paint and rust, stood in the middle of a field. In the early hours of the morning, which is the middle of the night to anyone in the theatre, they were woken up by the caravan shaking and trembling. They were surrounded by a herd of cows all rubbing themselves against the peeling caravan. He took up the matter with the farmer.

'Them cows,' he was told, 'always go round that 'van first thing in the morning. Always have done. They sharpen their horns on it.'

Clearly there was nothing to be done – they were not in a position to criticise the demands of nature and a herd of cows was infinitely preferable to the average theatrical landlady.

Hancock got to know these landladies in the years to come.

He was fascinated and repelled by the seediness of a lot of theatrical digs and would go into long parodies in a 'refained' landlady-like voice.

'I've got some nice bread and margarine and some black pudding and ham and some boiled hake and a nice cup o' tea with some more nice bread and marg,' he would say, adding, 'And that was for breakfast.'

Once he was in town with another comedian who was given a newly-killed chicken by some people he knew. They took it back to the landlady at the digs and Hancock gave her the chicken and said, 'Would you cut this up, mince it and boil it for four hours.'

'Yes,' said the landlady.

'I thought you bloody-well would,' said Hancock.

He loved to tell the story of the landlady who gave him the bill and said, 'That'll be four pounds twelve.'

Hancock gave her one of the old white five-pound notes, and said, 'Take it out of this.' She looked at it and said, 'We don't take cheques.' It was the same woman who asked him if he was Jewish. He said he wasn't.

'Only we don't like that sort of thing round here,' said the landlady.

Actually Hancock was always attracted to the idea that way way back in the family tree there might have been some Jewish strain. There is no evidence for this and it was probably due to his general feeling that if there were any hard times around he was not going to be deprived of his fair share of them.

Among the more obvious contradictions in the Hancock character were that he hated squalor but frequently lived in it, enjoyed good and expensive food and could, in his more wretched times, eat salmon out of a tin.

But if he were given a dirty glass in a pub he would never simply ask for a clean one but beckon the waiter, point to the mark, and say: 'Do you think you could go away and put some grease, some lipstick and a few more fingerprints round the edge and make a proper job of it?'

He was a very oblique man.

After *Cinderella* he was asked to stay on for one more week as they were mounting a production of Noël Coward's *Peace in Our Time* which required a large cast. Hancock, in fact, played three roles. One carried one line, 'Good-night, Mrs Shattock', which he tried to say with infinite variations. In another he was a drunken German soldier in a pub. The landlord says: 'What will you have?'

'Bitte?' asks the fuddled German.

'Sorry, bitter's off,' the landlord says. 'You'll have to have mild.'

The most important role was that of a brutal Nazi officer.

'This is straight acting,' the producer said, 'a most unsympathetic role.'

But when the play opened the loyal rep audience remembered his ugly sister and laughed.

Their attitude was not helped by the fact that in order to disguise himself he had borrowed a pair of rimless bifocals from a friend. He had to pick up a glass with a ruthless gesture.

There were five attempts before he made contact, the bottom half of the bifocals being as thick as bottle glass. Olivier himself could not be ruthless under those circumstances, nor squash the titters.

After he returned to London things began to look truly desperate. The general idea then was that a comedian should tell stories, should stand in front of a microphone in a smart suit and tell smart jokes. Another way was to stand in front of a microphone in a funny suit and red nose and tell daft jokes. Hancock, though he had a private passion for limericks, could not tell jokes of any kind. If Bob Hope's team of gag-writers had fed him with a year's output he would have just stood there looking helpless.

His idea of comedy was to stand in front of a microphone and work himself into a situation. He did imitations, not in the meticulous manner of an impersonator, but in the style of a clown imitating an impersonator, the funny thing being not the accuracy of the mimicry but the fact that he was doing it at all. In this way he could impersonate people his audience had never heard of and though at the start of his career there were many who were familiar with George Arliss, he was still in the repertoire twenty years later and still picking up laughs.

George Arliss was a monocled English actor with a long upper lip who appeared in a number of pre-war American films, most notably as Disraeli. He died at the age of 77 in 1946. Hancock's only concession to the passing years was eventually to introduce this item by saying, 'And now here's one for the teenagers.'

He did impersonations of Robert Newton as Long John Silver and Charles Laughton as the Hunchback of Notre Dame for which he was able to push his left eye into the corner and whirl it around. Whenever in doubt about an audience he would mutter, 'I'll give 'em the eye; that's what I'll do. That'll fix 'em.' The Hunchback and his Captain Bligh of the *Bounty* made no concessions either to death or time. He would usually finish his act with a recitation of 'The Bells' which ended with a cry for sanctuary. 'Sanctuary! Sanctuary! Sanctuary!' he would storm, reeling around the stage in a lather of acting. Then the acting would abruptly stop and a half-apologetic smile would appear from nowhere. 'Sanctuarymuch' he would say, and walk off.

He also used to do impressions of a noted nature impressionist who specialised in farmyard noises. Very deliberately he would do them very badly. 'And now, as we close the gate, we meet Rover, Woof, Woof.'

George Fairweather's act in Bournemouth was nearly all impressions. He even did George Arliss, though it was at a time when it was fairly appropriate. A lot of Hancock's act was Fairweather's material hammed up. Fairweather never minded.

This then was the kind of humour Hancock was trying to sell without much success when he got a blessed week's work in Sidmouth, performing in a local cabaret.

The fee was £10 plus food and bed for the week. But he had only five shillings. He borrowed £2, just enough for the return fare, and set out.

This was going to be the week the luck changed.

By the time the train reached Sidmouth, Devon, 163 miles from London, he was confident enough to take a taxi in order to arrive at the hotel with a flourish.

In the hall, near the reception desk, was a poster advertising the coming week's cabaret attractions. His name was not on it.

He stared at the bill.

'Yes, sir? . . . what can I do for you?' said the receptionist.

Dumbly he pulled out his letter and showed it to her. She pointed at the date. He had arrived a week too early.

He dragged himself back to the station. The next train to London was slow and he had to change at Micheldever where there was a two-hour wait. He was ravenously hungry. There were two pennies and a halfpenny in his pocket and opposite was a café. The bill of fare was chalked on a blackboard, 'Tea . . . 2½d.'

Inside there were plutocrats calling for sausage and mash, egg and chips. Hancock sipped his tea.

In London, he had to walk from Waterloo Station to Baron's Court. It is a long way.

When he was turned forty and lost and panic-stricken in Hollywood during a fiasco of an attempt to make a film for Disney, Hancock, talking to Freddie Ross, the woman who was to become his second wife, recalled his early struggles.

There was a special chumminess among the young comics – Sellers, Sykes, Milligan, Bentine and many others who had finished their war stint and didn't quite know where they were going. Morecambe and Wise were also in the gang and Harry Worth was around – a young ventriloquist with an improbable-looking doll and an absent-minded manner.

As long as one worked the others survived. They met daily at a pub in Archer Street opposite the Windmill Theatre, the peak of their immediate ambitions. If one of them picked up a masonic concert or a couple of days' work at the Nuffield Centre, he would rush round to the pub with his advance salary, buy a round and hand out a few shillings.

Hancock used to tell the story of one comic who despaired, composed a tragic-comic note of farewell in which he punned that in future there would be one less feed to feed, sealed the door and window of his bed-sitter, turned on the gas and lay down on the floor.

After half an hour he got up. No gas. The meter had run out and he did not have a shilling. The only thing to do was to go to the Archer Street pub and tell the story.

Eventually, Hancock got his turn at the Windmill.

In the days before nude shows were more commonplace in Soho than coffee-houses, the Windmill Theatre was the sexiest place in London. Actually, it was about as sexy as a Julie Andrews' picture. The girls who moved, talked or sang wore slightly more clothing than can be seen these days on a warm day on Frinton or Southport beaches and those who were nude had, by order of the Lord Chamberlain, to stand absolutely still, no quiver or shiver being permitted.

The girls were pretty and most of them spent a great deal of the time knitting pullovers or scarves for their husbands and boyfriends.

Next to the Athenaeum, it was the most respectable place in London.

Like the Athenaeum it was death to comics. However, they used a lot of them between the acts to give the girls a rest as the show was non-stop, starting at 12.15 p.m. and finishing just before midnight. When other theatres shut at the beginning of the war, the Windmill remained open. Its slogan, in fact, was 'We Never Closed' which many comics used to – and still, alas, do – convert into 'We Never Clothed'.

The audiences, mainly men, kept both eyes glued to the stage and yet somehow managed to spot the slightest preparation to leave made by anyone sitting in front of them. Immediately the seat was vacated there was a mad scramble for it.

They closed in on the stage like cricketers on a nervous batsman and they treated the comic turns as breaks between overs. Sometimes they munched sandwiches and it was not unknown for them to fill in their pools coupons or read the evening paper by the reflected light from the stage.

Later a myth arose that Vivian Van Damm, the owner, was some kind of genius at spotting potentially great comics. Certainly, there was eventually a roll of honour listing the names of the comedians who had started there while still unknown. But while the girls often stayed for years, the customers seemingly never tired of their faces or whatever it was they were looking at, the Windmill consumed comedians like an old car uses petrol and got very little mileage out of any of them. Some of them were bound to succeed eventually: those who did not are forgotten.

Hancock was not working alone when he was booked for the Windmill. A few weeks before he had been at a party with Derek Scott, a pianist who is now musical adviser to a commercial television company. Hancock and Scott whipped up a double act.

It seemed successful; people laughed. They polished it up and went for their audition with Vivian Van Damm. The basic act was made up of impressions of a seaside concert party.

Hancock's friends tried to smarten up his crumpled clothes and poured whisky into him.

They warned him that he would have to impress old Vivian Van Damm himself. 'Act the pro,' they said. 'Show that you know the business. Call him V.D. the way everyone else does.'

It was something that Hancock could never bring himself to do. He settled for 'sir'.

Van Damm signed them up for five weeks and offered them £25 a week between them for six shows a day, six days a week.

'Not enough,' said Scott to Hancock's horror.

It was upped to £30.

'Mind you,' recalled Hancock, 'although it was a princely sum to share out in the pub afterwards, it was a 70-hour week and it worked out at 4s. an hour, not counting rehearsal time. At these rates, no wonder they never closed.'

But the experience was good, almost worth paying for. No audience in the future could ever be quite so indifferent as that first house at the Windmill.

The two o'clock show was worse. 'If they didn't like you in the first show,' said Hancock, 'they positively hated you in the second. It taught me to die bravely.'

At 3.30 things were a little better as the pubs had closed and the audience was more relaxed.

Occasionally, very occasionally, the word took over from the flesh and the comics got the attention and response they craved.

The concert party act was also used at the Nuffield Centre, a place where servicemen could get free entertainment. There were still a lot of servicemen around. Tuesday and Friday nights were specially put aside for acts by returning servicemen. It was a good showplace. One of the people who saw Hancock there was Dennis Main Wilson who was in charge of auditions for the BBC.

Hancock and Scott got themselves a BBC audition[1] where he was seen by Phyllis Rounce. Both Main Wilson and Miss Rounce were to play major roles in the career that was just beginning to open. Miss Rounce's mother lived in a pleasant middle-class London dormitory suburb called Cheam.

Chapter Three

Still on the Windmill conveyor belt, Hancock and Scott were wowing them a little bit, six shows a day. Miss Rounce, one of Hancock's earliest admirers, braved the disbelieving stares of the early show patrons and sat among the raincoated men to see him.

Miss Rounce, one half of the partnership which makes up International Artistes Representation, afterwards went backstage. Hancock would hardly believe there had been a woman out front or that she wanted to represent him. She became his agent.

With Miss Rounce he rose from half a double act at £15 a week to £500 a week in a West End show. In all his written recollections of the time she does not exist.[2]

Miss Rounce says: 'We were trying everywhere to get Tony a job in comedy and nobody wanted to know. They all said, "Come back when he is on £600 a week and we'll book him." So we said, "How do we get him to £600 a week if you won't book him now?" and they said, "Well, that's your worry isn't it, ta-ta."

'The variety scene was going down then and the person who first gave us a chance with Tony was a man called B. C. Hilliam of Flotsam and Jetsam. B. C. was running a show at Bognor Regis in the summer and I went to him and begged him to give Tony a job because, I said, we believed this fellow had got so much. B. C. eventually gave him the job at £27 10s. a week and was wonderful to him and taught him a lot. Tony always said this.'

'He helped me enormously,' said Hancock later.

Hancock left the Windmill with one memory he never tired of recalling. It is a story that represents the kind of theatrical tradition – a mixture of dedication and desperation – that Hancock loved. The other kind, the self-regarding, no-business-like-show-business, good old trouper who's gotta-smile-when-he-is-low kind, disgusted him.

It seems there was a magician at the Windmill who needed the whole ninety minutes between his performances to prepare his eight-minute act. He had about thirty different tricks concealed about his person and walked on stage stooping under the weight of all the gear secreted in a maze of pockets in his special frock coat. Each illusion was activated by the pulling of a strand of cotton.

With noble exaggeration, Hancock used to say, 'He walked on a fat dwarf and came off slim and tall.'

After a few weeks of non-stop preparation and performance the magician became very nervous. Breaking-point came when somebody accidentally knocked over his tray of tricks in the dressing room. He burst into tears. Hancock and Scott rallied round, packing him with rabbits in one pouch, doves in another. There were flags to go in his shirt and collapsible flowers up his sleeve. There were cards everywhere and lighted cigarettes in his specially lined rear pockets.

Then they pushed him on stage just in time. Unfortunately in their haste and the magician's distress, not all the illusions were stowed in their correct places. The magician was more baffled than the audience who did not know that when he pulled out a dove he had intended to produce a rabbit. Even if they had it was unlikely that they would have had any strong feelings about it.

But the final leave-'em-gasping trick was a paper-tearing act which magically would unfold to spell out the exact time.

'The time ladies and gentlemen,' said the magician, producing the torn paper with a great flourish, 'is twenty to four.'

The paper spelled out half past eight.

The tragedy of the story, and no doubt the bit that appealed strongly to Hancock, was that no one noticed. The magician went off to his usual spatter of applause. The only kind of time the audience were interested in was the time the nudes reappeared. And they were on next.

BBC auditions paid off in the form of a couple of *Workers' Playtime* broadcasts. This was a daily half-hour of song and patter held in factory canteens all over England. It was the BBC's contribution to industrial peace and high productivity and if you had only to say arseholes to the troops to get a laugh, you had equally only to mention the foreman to the factory hands to have them falling about in hysterics.

Every comedian at one time or another got a *Workers' Playtime*. It was a kind of initiation rite into the higher mysteries of the craft. It was not the kind of show that Hancock had ambitions to do regularly.

Cabaret was another matter. If the workers were undemanding might not the rich be inspiring? All the same it was just a well to be on the safe side as far as material was concerned. Most comedians dislike trying out new material, Hancock was terrified of it.

For Churchill's Club in New Bond Street, he chose an opening he had always considered, to use his own term, a stone-bonker cert. It was the one about a pub with a stag's head on the wall with the observation that it must have hit the other side at terrific speed to get lodged there like that.

The audience were, if anything, even more indifferent than at the Windmill. Whatever their reason for going to a night club, it was not to listen to stories about stags' heads.

Not that they actually heard any. Looking around at the bored unwelcoming faces, Hancock's nerve went and the story got so mangled that it appeared as if the landlord's head had gone through the wall. Not surprisingly, there was no laughter except from a drunk in the corner and a choking giggle from Derek Scott at the piano, behind him. Scott never laughed at Hancock when he was being funny, but he found Hancock's mortification at an indifferent and unresponsive audience irresistibly hilarious.

Hancock babbled through a bit more business and then got off quickly. He was not paid and the loss of the £5 fee rankled for years. Even when he was earning thousands of pounds, he would grumble about the fiver. It was the only place in London he would not on principle enter for a drink.

The only other cabaret he ever did apart from an appearance at the London show spot 'Talk of the Town' much later in his career, was at an election night ball held in Claridge's as the results of the 1950 polling were coming in. It was not a socialist party.

The ballroom at Claridge's is very grand, all chandeliers, mirrors and gilt chairs. The red-coated toastmaster, who would not have been able to tell someone the time without prefixing it with a thunderous 'My Lords, Your Excellencies, Ladies and Gentlemen . . .', did not help matters by announcing Hancock as 'Mr Hitchcock'.

Hancock and Scott made their way forward to no visible or audible signs of enthusiasm from the audience. Hancock began with his impression of the Hunchback of Notre Dame – really, all his impressions were impressions of a bad impressionist doing impressions. The audience were unimpressed. All the same, Hancock battled on and was in mid-crouch when the toastmaster held up his hand like a policeman stopping traffic. Hancock, bent like a child playing a game of statues, kept perfectly still while the toastmaster announced the full details of five election results. Then he indicated that the show should go on and Hancock started hopping out again, beating himself in anguish and crying, 'I'm so *ugly*, I'm so *ugly*.'

For the most part, the audience sat there and ignored him.

'The bells,' bellowed Hancock.

'Pity about old Cavendish-Clodpole losing his seat by such a narrow margin,' observed the audience, one to another.

'Sanctuary,' appealed Hancock.

'Those Labour fellers seem to be doing well,' said the audience, shaking a collective head.

The only person laughing, in fact, was Derek Scott who was nearly falling off his piano stool.

Hancock ended with his montage of athletes in action from the opening sequel of the Gaumont British Newsreel. He had time to notice that television and newsreel cameras were in the room, recording the event for posterity. It occurred to him that if, in a few hundred years, someone dug up the film they would wonder about the raving lunatic beating himself to death and being studiously ignored in the far corner of the room. Perhaps, he thought, it would be put down to some obscure political rite.

On his way out he saw his agent, Phyllis Rounce, and her partner, Bill Alexander, sitting in full evening dress at a table.

Hancock did not get paid for that cabaret either. It was what the business calls a prestige date.

He always said that it marked the point at which he became a socialist.

There was also the occasional week's variety in the provinces. One such week was in Blackpool out of season. With him on the bill was Harry Secombe. 'We used to commiserate with each other because we weren't doing very well,' said Secombe. 'Blackpool out of season is not exactly a mark of success.

'It was the week my first baby was born and we agreed that, for once, we would live it up. Only we couldn't find anything open and finished up on fish and chips and Tizer.'

Later, Secombe was to figure in the bizarre episode when Hancock disappeared without warning and for four weeks the BBC announced, 'This is *Hancock's Half Hour*, starring Harry Secombe, Sid James . . .'

It was time for experiment in humour. On radio, Secombe, Sellers, Spike Milligan and Michael Bentine were about to launch the Goons and Frank Muir and Denis Norden were already in full cry with their inspirational *Take it from Here* which launched Jimmy Edwards into orbit.

Hancock's closest friend at the time was a fair-haired high-complexioned ex-commando officer called Larry Stevens who contributed a lot of material to the Goon Shows. Stevens and

Hancock shared flats all over London from Bayswater to Primrose Hill. At one stage Hancock tried to make his fortune by starting a bookmaking business.

This was not only highly illegal but very risky. The theory was that Hancock would be able to earn enough money to pay any debts he incurred. According to Spike Milligan, he had to change his address very quickly – and very quietly.

Stevens was writing a lot of Hancock's material and Milligan recalls sitting with them in a pub when they decided to do a script about the landed gentry of England and build up a mythical family background for the Hancocks. Describing the ancestral home Stevens said, 'In 1883 they built a West Wing, the following year they added an east wing and the year afterwards . . .'

'The year afterwards,' broke in Hancock, 'it flew away.'

Milligan got so fond of that joke that he frequently uses it himself.

Milligan: 'Larry and Tony were like brothers. I don't know how or where they met. They seemed to have come from nowhere. They shared the same digs and the same women and they both drank. They both liked to laugh at the human race and they'd have hysterical laughing bouts. Sometimes they didn't go to bed all night and I'd come in in the morning as I was writing a script for someone with Larry and there would be this hysterical laughter and the floor littered with newspapers and the two grotty tumblers and it was hurting their heads to laugh.

'Once Larry was in a car with me and we had a crash and he hurt his leg and had to go to hospital. I telephoned Tony and told him. There was this hysterical laughter and I said, "It's serious, he might have broken his leg," but he couldn't stop laughing.

'I went round to the flat in Craven Hill Gardens and he asked what had happened. I said, "We were just on our way to see you in this car and we had a crash and Larry is in hospital." Then I said, "He was reading the *Daily Express* at the time." I thought Hancock was going to die, he was laughing so much.'

Hancock had a rich, rippling laugh which he called the family chuckle. It was a quiet laugh that seemed to begin at his boots and then scurry upwards to the ceiling. He described it as a kind of 'climbing up the wall' laugh. It was totally infectious.

Hancock, Stevens and Milligan used occasionally to go to a café in Chalk Farm so that Hancock could have the sweet pleasure of saying, 'We'd like three boiled rice with three raspberry jams.' Not that any of them would eat the stuff. Hancock found some words and phrases very funny. He used to say them with relish until they took an almost physical shape. 'Fulcrum,' he would say in his act, letting it hang there while he inspected its peculiarities. 'It's a word,' he would reassure the audience.

The Chalk Farm café had a notice on the wall announcing that the owner would give a free dinner to all his regular customers the year Fulham won the cup. If Fulham ever had won the cup, Hancock would have raced off to Chalk Farm to demand his free meal. He loathed seediness so much so that it fascinated him and it sometimes seemed as if, not finding it, he would create it himself in order to have something to react against.

Hancock went off to *Flotsam's Follies* in Bognor Regis for the summer of 1949 with instructions to provide five acts. He got four of them together and B. C. Hilliam let him off the fifth. A lot of props were required. Hancock always depended on the visual for his laughs but had not yet realised that his best prop was his face.

At that time, he exaggerated, 'I found that to get an act on stage I needed 15 flying ballet dancers, 78 trumpeting elephants and anything else a scrounging stage manager could lay his hands on.'

When the season ended he took what he thought were the best bits out of the four acts and welded them together as one act. With one or two variations they were to serve him in his solo performances for the rest of his life. Derek Scott had gone off to write music and Hancock was on his own as a performer.

The big show for the individual comic was *Variety Bandbox*. It was a Sunday-night programme at peak listening time, and was a great showplace for rising young comics like Frankie Howerd, Derek Roy and Arthur English. Hancock made a disastrous début in it.

'Tony was petrified,' says Phyllis Rounce, 'and the broadcast was a shambles. The producer said, "Never bring that man near me again. He is awful."'

But Phyllis and her partner, Bill Alexander, pestered and pestered until, two months later, Hancock was given another chance. This time there was more preparation and a greater understanding of the medium. This time he clicked and established the important fact that he could be funny without being seen.

There had, in fact, been a couple of appearances on television but it was very much a minority service and they contributed little to the advancement of his career.

'I was never really satisfied with myself,' Hancock said later, 'never quite sure what was coming over on the screen. So I ducked out.'

That winter he was happy to play pantomime in Woolwich for £35 a week. Even though he hated pantomime.

There was also an all-important breakthrough with Cissie Williams, the formidable lady who arranged all the bookings for Moss Empires.

She had been prevailed upon to accept Tony for the Brixton Empress, the Chiswick Empire and the Chelsea Palace. Monday night at Brixton, Hancock went on and, like many other good comics before him and since, died the death.

Miss Williams was not concerned about the lack of audience enthusiasm but was furious at the sight Hancock presented.

She stormed round to the dressing room where International Artistes Representation were sitting with their dejected client and asked how dare they let him go on with those filthy shoes and dirty shirt.

Quickly, the shirt was cleaned up and the shoes polished and then the client, who by now was refusing to go on second house, was taken to the pub opposite the theatre and talked round. Second house went well and Miss Williams was mollified both by his improved appearance and better reception.

A living was being made. Not a fortune but a living. No longer had Hancock to eat sausages and drink water for his supper; no longer had his mother to slip him a fiver under the tea-table at the Regent Palace.

In fact, Hancock was now in a position to slip someone else the occasional fiver himself. One went to Spike Milligan.

'I had been in a psychiatric ward,' said Milligan, 'and he sent me a letter through Larry saying that he wanted a script and that they seemed to have dried up. I wrote what I thought was a very funny script about Father Christmas and Tony gave me £5 for it. Later I asked him if he had ever used it and he said no, it was all nonsense. He was always generous to people worse off than himself.'

It was about this time that, for some totally unaccountable reason, Hancock and Stevens went ice-skating at a Bayswater rink. Probably it was a good place to bump into girls. As it happened Hancock bumped into the girl who very quickly was to become his wife.

Cicely Janet Elizabeth Romanis, daughter of a Harley Street surgeon, was, at the age of 20, a willowy auburn-haired girl who was a highly successful model in the days when they were called mannequins. She was one of the first English girls – and she was a very English girl – to work for Lanvin in Paris for a season. She was bright and athletic, strong and gay. She handled a car with the finely controlled fury of a racing-driver and she laughed a great deal.

They were married a few months after meeting on 18 September

1950, at Christ Church, Kensington, with her parents and Tony's mother and stepfather in attendance and with Larry Stevens as best man.

Hancock was principal comedian in summer season at Clacton at the time and on his way to his wedding called in at his agent's office near Leicester Square.

'How do I look?' he asked Phyllis Rounce. 'Do I look good?'

'There is only one thing that spoils it,' said Miss Rounce after a brief inspection. 'You are wearing the jacket from one suit and trousers from another.'

Quickly she rang up Moss Bros. and got her client kitted out properly. Then sent him off to his wedding.

His profession, he stated in the register, was 'actor'.

His father-in-law, Dr Romanis, somehow gained the impression that Hancock had been a radio officer during the war before transferring to the obviously more suitable work of entertaining.

Immediately after the wedding he had to dash back to Clacton and Cicely was booked for a fashion show in London. She joined him at Clacton that evening and left early the following morning for another London fashion show. They were glad when autumn came and they were able to lead a more settled life. They lived in a top-floor flat in Knightsbridge and the climb up five flights of stairs used to leave Hancock breathless. It never bothered Cicely.

The broadcasts were becoming more frequent and there was an occasional trip out of town for a week's variety. One week was in Bournemouth.

Hancock had dropped a line to George Fairweather telling him that he was married. They arranged to meet for tea at four o'clock. Fairweather had a hairdressing salon and was busy cutting hair at 3 p.m. when the telephone rang.

'I'm Cicely,' said a voice at the other end. 'I haven't met you but I'm looking forward to it.'

She told him she was at Bournemouth station. 'Tony didn't say you were coming down,' said George. 'No,' said Cicely, 'he doesn't know. But he went off and left me without any money. I had just enough to come to Bournemouth.'

When she arrived at the shop she had twopence in her pocket. 'You know Tony,' she said. 'He's done it again. He just went off with a "cheerio ducks, see you Sunday".'

George took her to his teatime appointment with Tony who merely said, 'What are you doing here?'

When she explained he said, 'Sorry, kid' and the three of them went off to the theatre. In the dressing room they found that

Hancock had forgotten to bring any clean shorts, socks or tie. George dashed home and got some for him.

When the week ended he went back to London – taking the shirts and things with him.

'Cicely didn't have any hysterics about being left with no money like that,' reported George later. 'She was very placid, very easy.'

That winter there was a better class of pantomime altogether. It was in Nottingham with Julie Andrews as principal girl. Hancock played a character called Jolly Jenkins.

For the most part he was extremely miserable. He hated Jolly Jenkins, hated the factory song he had to sing in which he frantically imitated a machine, hated above all the pig song with the lyric that started, 'Every little pig has a curly tail . . .'

The show ran for three and a half months so Cicely gave up her modelling to stay with him. She never seriously took it up again. From then on she had a full-time job looking after her husband.

Cicely was a splendid cook and Hancock – helped also by the beer he was putting down in ever-increasing quantity – began to assume the shape that eventually led to his being called 'Tub' by his Railway Cuttings intimates. There were fierce and sporadic attempts to slim but no matter how many pounds he lost, he was essentially a round man.

The year he gained a wife was also the year Hancock suffered a great, if impersonal, loss. Sid Field died.

He was forty-five, a superb clown who drowned an unknown pain in drink. Hancock adored him. He went to see him in *Harvey*, a fantasy in which Field was partnered by the invisible rabbit of the title, three times in one week. He knew every line of Field's sketch material and used to quote from it at length.

'And now' – this was Field's classic feed Jerry Desmonde in the golf sketch – 'And now you must address the ball.'

'Dear ball,' said Field with the greatest affection.

Hancock became helpless with laughter at the very recollection of it and there grew a total, and ultimately dangerous, identification with Field. Eventually it led Hancock to justify his own drinking by reference to Field's.

Hancock never met Field, being always too shy a novice to go backstage and introduce himself. It would have happened, would have been inevitable, had Field only lived a little longer. Hancock was gaining in strength, style and confidence and was earning more money.

There was more regular work on the radio. Derek Roy had his

own hour-long show called *Happy Go Lucky* which ran fortnightly. It was not the happiest or luckiest of shows.

The show had a running sketch about a scout patrol called the Eager Beavers. Hancock was the scoutmaster and the scouts were Bill Kerr, Peter Butterworth and Graham Stark.

'I'd come back to London, after nearly four years working in rep,' says Stark, 'and I was starving. One morning, Tony telephoned and said I'd be great for one of the scouts. I told him I'd never done a broadcast in my life but all he said was to get down to Roy Speer's office that afternoon at three o'clock. Speer, the producer, was charming but he didn't know me from Adam. I got the job all the same. It literally started my whole career.'

Speer became ill and Dennis Main Wilson took over the show for the four programmes that were left. The first thing he did was to throw out the next Eager Beaver sketch.

'It was all about them going on board ship with some sea scouts,' said Main Wilson, 'and it was ten minutes of sea-sick jokes. When I cut it out, Hancock came up to me and nearly kissed me because I'd saved him the embarrassment of having to do the thing. With four more shows to go I fired all the writers on the spot and Derek Roy and his wife and myself wrote the next one. Then I consulted Gale Pedrick who was script editor and asked him if he had any young writers he wanted to get experience for. He showed me a script that was a knock-out. It came from two boys who had started writing together when they met in a sanatorium in Milford, Surrey. I liked the script so much that I said they should do the remaining shows.'

The two 'boys' were Galton and Simpson.

In October 1951 at the Paris Cinema, a BBC studio in Lower Regent Street, Alan Simpson and Ray Galton met Tony Hancock for the first time.

They had not spoken on the first show Galton and Simpson wrote, but during rehearsal for the second, Hancock was slumped in a seat in the auditorium. 'Did you write that sketch?' he asked them as they walked past.

Simpson said, 'Yes.'

'Very good,' said Hancock and continued slumping.

After the Derek Roy show had finished Hancock asked Galton and Simpson to write something for him for a *Workers' Playtime* broadcast. They talked about a fee. Hancock said he had no idea what he should pay and eventually suggested: 'I'll give you half of what I get. How's that?' 'That' to Galton and Simpson was, to use their own estimate, 'fantastic'.

Indeed it was. Hancock's fee for *Workers' Playtime* was £50 and Galton and Simpson were accustomed to getting eight guineas between them. With £25 to split they too were on their way to the big time.

They met again later with a show, also produced by Dennis Main Wilson, which went through a series of permutations, starting off as *Forces All Star Bill*, becoming *All Star Bill* and ending up as *Star Bill*. It was from this that *Hancock's Half Hour* grew.

But Hancock became a radio and stage star long before that. *Educating Archie* was one of the most popular shows on the air. Archie was a wooden dummy and his reality sprang from ventriloquist Peter Brough's larynx and manipulative ability. As far as the listeners were concerned he might just as well have stayed in his box. As it happened he was present at all broadcasts in all his wooden cheekiness for the benefit of the studio audience. For Hancock playing a tutor trying to instil a bit of his own shaky culture into Archie's unreceptive head, it was necessary for Archie to attend rehearsals as well.

'I can't make the script live,' he told Brough, 'unless he's here.'

Brough recalls Hancock's ultimatum with admiration tinged with anguish.

'Standing there with my leg up like a stork used to give me gyp and at that time I had a lot of trouble with varicose veins. But no matter what I said Tony always used to insist. "I can't make it work unless I work to him," he would say. "Now come on, let's do it properly."'

By January 1952 the BBC's Listener Research organisation were reporting that Hancock was considered by a number of listeners to be the star of the show.

The critics had already been kind. Clifford Davis wrote in the *Daily Mirror*:

Tony ('Flippin' Kids') Hancock shoots to star billing in his first outing with the Archie team. This man is funny. A slick script and smooth production marks this a winter winner as usual . . . Verdict: Flippin' fine.

Collie Knox in the *Daily Mail* said:

It has revealed in Tony Hancock a comedian of immense verve and personality. With his split-second timing and his 'Flippin' Kids' Tony makes me laugh more than anyone on the air. If Mr Val Parnell is searching for a successor to Sid Field – and of course he must be – he might well find him in Hancock. For this artiste, like the ever-lamented Sid, is a comic second and an actor first.

It was the kind of praise that Hancock must have viewed with mixed feelings. First of all, despite the evocation of his beloved Sid Field, he was in no mood for reincarnation. He was his own man, unique. Under the nerves, the tension and the occasional panic lay an unquenchable faith in himself as clown. Whatever humility he had was not as a performer but as an earner. When, about this time, Phyllis Rounce told him that she had booked him for a Sunday engagement at a fee of 200 guineas his first reaction was that they must be raving mad to pay him that much. Once he had enough he never bothered about the money he was earning though it often gave him some anguish to pay out the money he owed. He rarely carried any about with him and his minor borrowings – a pound or three here and there – became a sore point with some of the people he worked with.

He rarely paid back the small sums but could be extraordinarily generous with the big ones.

Collie Knox's use of the word 'artiste' would have amused him. Occasionally, he used it himself with a special kind of mocking distaste. He thought it was very archaic, very pretentious. 'Artist' was a different word altogether. He would not have minded that one little bit.

Educating Archie was written by Eric Sykes and he and Hancock found instant *rapport* when Hancock asked Sykes how to say one of his lines.

Sykes was writing a lot of fantasy at the time and one sketch he did was set in hell with Hancock as the guide. It was a period in world affairs when the Russians were being extremely awkward, and one of the best-known words in the English language was *Niet*.

The sound of marching feet tramped past the microphone and Hancock's line was 'All from Russia'.

'How would you like me to say it?' asked Hancock.

'Say it,' said Sykes, 'as if you are tapping the ash off a cigarette.'

Give Hancock a reply like that and he would love you for life.

That winter *Educating Archie* transferred from the air to the stage, reaching the Prince of Wales Theatre as *Archie Andrews' Christmas Party*. In addition to Brough and Hancock there were Hattie Jacques, Peter Madden and Ronald Chesney from the regular broadcasting team. They were reinforced by a clown who doubled on drums, a magician, a pair of trick roller-skaters and a man who made shadow pictures with his hands.

Above: Hancock at the seaside with his first wife, Cicely
Below: Cicely and Hancock dining out at a café in Piccadilly. Hancock found restaurants a source of fun, whether they were seedy or grand

Hancock in 1956 – the year in which some of the best Hancock's Half Hour *radio shows were transmitted*

Hancock with Alan Simpson (left) and Ray Galton (right). The writers based the Hancock character on many aspects of Hancock's own personality

Above: Hancock with the 'Funniest Man of 1959' television award
Above left: By 1959 Hancock was the best-loved comedian in the United Kingdom
Left: Hancock recording for the radio Hancock's Half Hour *series with (left)*
Kenneth Williams, (right) Bill Kerr as the inarticulate Australian and (far right) Sid
James as the crooked, pragmatic twister

Hancock as Anthony Aloysius St John Hancock in his Homburg hat and the coat with the astrakhan collar. The Hancock character was belligerent, yet petulant, suspicious but easily taken in. He inspired enormous affection in the British public

Above: Hancock in 'The Missing Page'. This show from the television Hancock's Half Hour *series displays Hancock's brilliant talent for mime*
Below: When Hancock's Half Hour *transferred to television in 1956 the successful relationship established between Hancock and Sid James was confirmed*

Hattie Jacques appeared only occasionally in the television series. The break with Sid James did not occur until 1960

The first show was at 11 a.m. and the second at 2.30 p.m. Val Parnell then asked Hancock to join the cast of *Peep Show*, a revue running in the same theatre in the evenings. So he had a third performance at 6.15 p.m. and a fourth performance at 8.30 finishing at 11 p.m.

'Do you know any night-club that wants a good cabaret act?' he asked Brough one day. 'And I could do with a few Sunday concerts as well. I'm wasting my time you know – I actually have moments when I've nothing to do but sleep.'

He found time, however, to do his first Royal Show. Brough for many years organised the cabaret at the Windsor Castle Christmas Party and in 1951 he invited Peter Sellers, Kitty Bluett, Tony Hancock, Peter Madden and Hattie Jacques.

Later, Brough reported: 'The success of the evening was undoubtedly newcomer Tony Hancock. He made Princess Margaret laugh so much that she was in danger of ruining her make-up.'

At the Prince of Wales and later on tour with the *Archie Andrews Show*, Hancock was naturally frequently surrounded by children.

Once, after meeting a lot of children from an Archie Andrews fan club, Brough told him, 'It was nice of you to be so patient with that little boy. He really loved meeting you.'

'Before, I was an idol to him,' said Hancock. 'Now I'm just an ordinary bloke.'

But Hancock had no time for 'stars' who were just ordinary blokes. 'A star,' he defined, 'is someone who is out of reach.' Hancock wanted to be a star.

Meanwhile he was doing fine. Wherever he went people used to grin and say 'flippin' kids'. It was one of those catch-phrases that are a short-cut to instant identification, instant laughter.

Once established and taken into public favour they become a lifeline by which many a comedian has hauled himself to safety in the deathly calm of an unresponsive audience. Some comics spend years fruitlessly searching for a good catch-phrase.

Hancock despised them. He called them crutches.

'It was obvious that I would have been typed if I had stayed on as Archie Andrews' schoolmaster, so I left,' he said.

One memory he took with him was of a glimpse of the dummy hanging on a hook behind a door. It gave him occasional nightmares.

The friendship with Sykes had developed to such an extent that when Sykes got married in February 1952 Hancock arranged for the couple to hold their reception in his parents-in-law's flat in London. Afterwards Sykes heard that Hancock, knowing the bridegroom's passion for brass bands, had arranged for the brass section of the BBC Variety Orchestra to play them off at the airport on their honeymoon flight to Jersey. Unhappily it was the day that King George VI died and the plan had to be abandoned. All the same, it was a nice, quirky thought.

Hancock was on a variety tour when the call came. Nat King Cole was top of the bill and Hancock was the lead comic. In Glasgow he had, like every worthwhile English comedian, been ignominiously rejected, and in Birmingham, his home town, he had a rousing reception.

Jack Hylton, the tough little Bolton-born bandleader-turned-impresario, was in something of a fix. He had a show called *London Laughs* which starred Jimmy Edwards and Dick Bentley, the two stars from the Muir and Norden radio programme *Take It From Here*. Bentley left the show following an argument on billing.

Hylton wanted to replace him with Hancock and was offering £500 a week. A release from the rest of the variety tour was arranged and *London Laughs* opened at the Adelphi Theatre in London on 13 April 1952.

There was a real waterfall.

'Mr Jimmy Edwards,' reported *The Times* the following morning,

is supported by Mr Tony Hancock – the well-meaning man who attracts to himself whatever troubles may be about.

Hancock began in awe of Edwards and they finished up close friends. Hancock was a socialist, Edwards a Tory; Hancock was earnest and quiet, Edwards bluff and breezy with a strong tendency to roar good-humouredly at people. Above all, Edwards was an ad-libber, a comic capable of roaming round his lines like a jazz musician improvising on a theme. Hancock was helpless if anyone deviated from the script.

The lighthouse sketch written by Muir and Norden is for a stand-up comic who gets all the funny lines and a straight man. Hancock was quite happy to play the stooge to Edwards in this sketch and would not have dreamed of trying to steal laughs from him.

But after a few weeks doing the same lines twice nightly, Edwards got a bit bored and started to ad-lib. Hancock just shut up and stood there with his straightest face. The more Edwards ad-libbed, the straighter Hancock's face became and the more the audience laughed – at Hancock.

Later Edwards was to say, 'I love him because he's not trying to take it off me. He just doesn't know when to bloody well shut up.'

The Hancock mouth might have been closed, but the eyes, the set of the mouth and the hang of the jowls were more eloquent than anything Edwards could think up and he had the generosity and the grace to admit it.

That November Hancock was in the Royal Show with Gracie Fields, Bud Flanagan, Jimmy Edwards and Gigli. George Fairweather was with him in his dressing room at the Adelphi when he was notified of his selection.

'He was very emotional, very thrilled,' Fairweather recalls. 'He said, "Oh, if only Dad could have been here."'

'He will be with you in spirit,' said Fairweather.

'I wish I could feel like you,' Hancock said.

'He made me promise,' said Fairweather, 'with tears running down his face that I would be there in his father's place at the Royal Show. Well, of course I was very touched by this and I agreed.

'He also said that he hadn't even got a photograph of his father and didn't know if one even existed. I went back to Bournemouth and remembered that there had been one in the *Bournemouth Echo* with Jack's obituary notice. It was a picture of him shaking hands with Charlie Coborn, the Man who Broke the Bank at Monte Carlo. I went to the paper and they searched their archives and found the right issue but they didn't have a print. They photographed it again and blew it up. I paid three guineas for it and was pleased to get it. I sent it to Tony with a message saying: "Here's your good luck token for the night." And I never heard another word.

'I thought that was the end, that he had done it on me too many times, but he came down again just as though nothing had happened. I said, "You're a right bastard," but he said, "You know me. I don't mean it," and within ten minutes you were pals with him because there was no harm in him. He was just like a naughty child.'

'What a lovely show,' said the Queen after that Royal Performance. She asked Ted Ray how he had found the troops in Korea and was told 'they are in fine heart'.

'The Duke,' said one report,

was particularly amused by Tony Hancock's fantastic story, accompanied by mimicry of the commander who had to swim for it when his submarine submerged.

Hancock was a very refined naval officer subject to sudden lapses. 'Put the kettle on, Harmsworth. Oh, I see you have. Suits you too.'

'One cannot leave the comedians,' said *The Times* critic,

> without mentioning Mr Tony Hancock's naval inventions which he points with the explanatory postures of a figure by Fougasse.

Hancock was not quite sure what was meant but, clearly, it was high praise.

On radio, Dennis Main Wilson was having trouble ringing the comedy changes week by week on his *All Star Bill*. He had his singers and his supporting characters like Graham Stark but the top comedy spot was getting increasingly hard to fill. He recommended that they should stop trying and get a resident comic – Hancock.

Early Galton and Simpson material did not show a piercing insight into the follies and foibles of the human race. That was to develop later.

'Call yourself a legionnaire?'

'Yes, sir.'

'Well, get your legionnaire cut.'

They don't write material like that any more.

Back at the Adelphi, Hancock was beginning to feel troubled about doing the same thing over and over again night after night. Perhaps he would have been able to cope with this better if he could have relaxed and ad-libbed a little. There is a great problem here which afflicts many performers. Millions of people do the same boring job day after day not just for a year, not just for a couple of hours a night, but day after day, eight hours a day for the whole of their working lives.

The performer counters this argument – as Hancock did – by saying that no one could expect an artist to paint the same picture over and over again. Which equates a Rembrandt painting with a West End commercial revue. This is not to doubt that Hancock was an artist, even a genius. But distinction must be made between the character of the man and the nature of much of his work. The work, in comedy terms, was frequently undemanding; the man always made the most stringent demands upon himself in carrying it out.

Every time he appeared in front of an audience, whether on stage or through television, he drained himself. He could banish marital crises, hangovers, disputes and a thousand small insecurities. Unlike many other performers who relax in their dressing room before their first entrance, Hancock would go on early to the wings where he would, if it was not already there, work himself up into a state of tension pacing up and down in the narrow space and muttering his lines to himself.

In a way his neuroses were necessary to him. It was partly bound up in his relationship to his audience. Rarely for him did their warmth enclose him protectively as it does with more relaxed performers. For him there was always something hostile out there despite long evidence of overwhelming affection. He once hazarded that there was a special place in the middle of Hyde Park where people met secretly before coming to the theatre and decided what kind of audience they were going to be. He visualised them as 'sitting there steaming in their plastic macs'.

It was while he was at the Adelphi that the drinking became heavier and more noticeable though it never affected his performance. It was a long time before that would happen.

But the strain was telling. There was what is always referred to as a 'nervous breakdown' in show business circles and can mean anything from a slight headache to delirium tremens. With Hancock it was more than the first and less than the second, but it was enough to move the normally immovable Jack Hylton to agree to release him for a few weeks' holiday.

He and Cicely went to the South of France. They had found a small pension in Antibes where the food was good, the people friendly and the atmosphere unpretentious. It was a place to relax in when things were going well and a refuge when they were going badly. There were times when he invited friends there, generously providing the air fare, and times when he slopped about alone and morose. Despite his awful French he became part of the local scene, playing *boule* with the old men, drinking *pastis* and *vin du pays* in the waterfront cafés and loafing around in an old shirt and slacks, looking indistinguishable from the natives.

It was a place where no one made demands on him of any kind.

So great was the success of *London Laughs* that despite the danger signs, Hylton jointly with George and Alfred Black booked Hancock, Edwards, Galton and Simpson, Muir and Norden for another show to take its place at the Adelphi the following autumn after running through the summer season at Blackpool.

At Blackpool, Freddie Ross entered Hancock's life.

Chapter Four

The new show had set pieces like 'Paris by Night' and 'The Gay Nineties'. There was a trio who balanced bedsteads on their feet while lying on their backs and the stars were Jimmy Edwards, Tony Hancock and Joan Turner, 'the girl with a thousand voices'.

In the spring before he went to Blackpool, Hancock's radio show *Star Bill* was getting exceptionally good listening figures and his own stock was steadily rising. The BBC's Audience Research files show that it had a listening public of 15 per cent of the adult population of the United Kingdom and that 55 per cent of these found 'exceptional enjoyment' in listening to him. Miss Turner was next, with 45 per cent showing exceptional enjoyment in her performance. Hancock's personal rating had increased in seven shows from 44 per cent to 55 per cent but throughout the whole series he was always top of listeners' lists.

For the stage show Galton and Simpson created a sketch which was to give him his biggest laughs since he fell into the C.O.'s lap.

It was called 'The Crooner' and, basically, was a take-off of American singers like Johnnie Ray who then dominated the British variety scene. His introductory music for the sketch was loud and brassy and off-stage there would be the announcement: 'Here is another singing sensation. You've heard of Johnnie Ray, now here's Britain's answer to them all – Mr Rhythm himself – Tony Hancock.'

Hancock would edge on to the stage in what used to be called a zoot suit of palest blue. With it he wore a string tie and shoes with crepe soles inches thick. He allowed himself to be admired for a few moments with an 'I'll kill 'em kid' look on his face. A few girls from the chorus would be planted in the audience and they'd scream and faint.

A comedian's business consists of tiny movements of the facial muscles – the wrong lighting can kill an act stone dead – gestures, a sudden slump of the shoulders, a cocky glint in the eye. It is a million things that would take a slow-motion camera to detect, and yet each one signals its own message clearly to the back row of the gods. Comedians themselves can demonstrate what they do, but they can't describe it.

After the uproar died down a little, Hancock would say: 'Now I'd like to introduce my pianist, arranger, composer and brother-in-law, Sam.'

And the stooge would walk on dressed in exactly the same clothes as the star.

Occasionally, he would break out of the act, look at his feet and confide, 'Cor, I don't know how they do an hour and a half at the Palladium – I've got toes like globe artichokes.'

He would assume a vile accent, Birmingham overlaid with American, and say, 'Now I'd like to sing you a little toon, a toon which we recorded over there and would like to bring over here from over there to over here [his eyes rolling], our latest record which should have been a hit but they forgot to drill a hole in the middle, a little toon . . .'

And the band would go into a fast tempo version of 'Knees Up Mother Brown'. It would always seem that Hancock would be unable to get the last three notes, but he always managed it.

The act lasted for 18 minutes and too many years. He was still doing it to audiences who hardly remembered what the crooners of the time looked like.

While in Blackpool, Hancock tried to master the motor car. He did not pass his test then and when he eventually did he rarely drove. He recognised that he was a danger to himself and others. In time he had to resign himself to the fact that he was unable to cope even with an electric razor or a motor mower. It did not really matter; Cicely did all the driving that was necessary and was always in attendance.

After only four weeks, despite rave notices in the local press and audiences who were captivated by him, despite the fact that it was only an 18-week run, he became restless.

He was in the process of changing agents – unknown to Phyllis Rounce – and his new man, Jack Adams, was with Kavanagh Associates. This was a sort of co-operative of writers run by Ted Kavanagh who had written the ITMA show. Muir and Norden were in it and Jimmy Edwards was one of the clients.

The first thing anyone at Kavanaghs knew about the crisis Hancock was suffering in Blackpool was an irate telephone call from Jack Hylton. It appeared that Hylton had received a medical certificate signed by a psychiatrist to the effect that if Hancock continued in the Blackpool show his health would be affected.

The psychiatrist had an address in Bolton, a small town in Lancashire on the outskirts of Manchester.

'I was born in bloody Bolton,' stormed Hylton, 'and you know what I'd give for a bloody Bolton psychiatrist. You just tell Hancock that if he tries any of this we will send up an independent doctor and I'll have him for breach of contract and everything under the sun.'

Hylton, it was known, was a man as good as his most litigious word.

'Our trouble,' said Denis Norden, recalling the incident, 'was that we had to support Tony. We were his agents and his friends whether he was right or wrong. Obviously we had to try to talk him out of it, but if he had made up his mind we had to try to help him.

'We wanted to get another psychiatrist to endorse this Bolton lad but Tony wouldn't come to London and, at that time, there weren't all that many psychiatrists around. In the end I rang up a Harley Street man, told him what the position was and asked him if he could help in any way. He said he couldn't go to Blackpool but if I came along and saw him we might be able to plot some kind of campaign.

'So I underwent a strange kind of once-removed analysis. I actually lay down on the couch and poured out someone else's problems. The most interesting thing we discovered was that Tony owned three cars but couldn't drive. This was right up the psychiatrist's alley. "Obviously there is some sort of problem there," he said.'

Whatever the problem was it was not rare or interesting enough to persuade the psychiatrist to go to Blackpool and Hancock resolutely refused to come to London. So he stayed in the show until the end of the run.

Freda Ross, called Freddie, sometimes Fred, was twenty-four years old and had emerged bright, eager and ambitious from a sheltered middle-class Jewish home in Hampstead. Her father was that social rarity, a quiet, shy bookmaker; her brother a solicitor, and her mother a mother. Her future involvement with Hancock would tax their understanding to its limit.

Equipped with an education at South Hampstead High School, topped with a commercial course at Regent Street Polytechnic, Freddie had worked in public relations for a shipping line and a film company and had just started her own publicity business. She was in Blackpool to do some advance publicity for the Ted Heath band.

Walking along the promenade one day in May, she was hailed by Dennis Main Wilson, 'Just going to see Hancock and Edwards rehearse their new show,' said Main Wilson. 'Why don't you come along.'

Freddie recalls the atmosphere: 'The day a show opens everybody has a kind of professional hysteria. Voices are an octave higher, people chatter, people laugh more than they normally do, people are on edge more than they normally are and, don't ask me why, they keep trying things on. Stars break nails, ladders appear in stockings, everything tends to be heightened and irritating.

'Against all this Tony stood apart, a giant teddy bear in what I later learned he called a quiet think. I first saw him from the back of the circle rehearsing "The Crooner" sketch. He was in a sweater, open shirt, baggy trousers and suède shoes. His hair was longer than it should have been and he looked as if he was carrying all the troubles of the world on his shoulders. We were introduced later and we talked. Tony always remembered my saying, "If I had a talent like yours I'd be proud, not worried." Years later he was often to remind me of it.

'We talked for a long time and then, before going off for a rest, he insisted that we should join him before the show. We went to his dressing room before the curtain went up and just as he was about to go on and I was going out to see the show, I said, "Oh, they're an awful audience tonight." He went out with that glazed look of built-in security which means, "I can only die on stage." And of course, it brought out the absolute best in him. He was a great sensation.

'After the show Dennis Main Wilson and I joined Tony and Cicely for a meal. Then they took us back to their furnished flat and we talked into the early hours of the morning. Tony was belligerent as soon as he found out that I was a publicity agent. The very words personified to him the kind of American publicist shown on the films – fast talking, quick-witted and glib with no ethics and no character. Someone who sold people as though they were pieces of meat.

'We argued. We never really stopped arguing, ever. He was an exciting personality. He did not smile all that often, but when he did it was worthwhile. His eyes smiled very often. He had a lasting effect on me from that moment.'

Freddie returned to London the following morning but visited Blackpool twice during the season. She went in to see Hancock between shows. He did not indicate, she says, that he would like to get to know her better, but he teased her a lot about her middle-class bourgeois Jewish background and was friendly. More important, though she did not realise it at the time, he allowed her to be around before and during his performances, a rare privilege that he granted to few women, even Cicely.

Even when he returned to London and *Talk of the Town* opened at the Adelphi – the theatre-restaurant of that name had not been created – he told her that the only kind of publicity an artist needed was a good notice.

'When I read the reviews,' said Freddie, 'I thought how right he was and I dropped him a note to say just that.'

The reviews were indeed excellent.

> The buffoonery [said *The Times*] is clean and gay. Mr Hancock comes into his own as a transatlantic music hall star passing to and fro between the portentous and the ridiculous.

The other critics were less restrained in their praise. Clearly, Hancock was overtaking Edwards. *Talk of the Town* opened on 17 November 1954. *Hancock's Half Hour* had started on radio on 2 November.

It is necessary to go back a little in order to shut a door or two.

After his introduction to radio through Hancock, Graham Stark was doing well. He had carried on under Dennis Main Wilson's banner and was, in BBC terms, 'resident' on *Forces All Star Bill* and *All Star Bill* when Hancock joined it as principal comic.

The show went on for two years and then suddenly out of the blue Hancock told Stark, 'We'll have a rest for a few weeks.'

'I got a message,' says Stark, 'to see Dennis and he said that there were going to be six more shows but that there had been some policy changes. I said, "You mean that I'm not going to be in it?" He said, "It's just that we . . ."'

'"We? What do you mean we? Do you mean you personally or Alan and Ray?" He said, 'No, Tony feels . . ."'

'"Tony," I said, "isn't the BBC. Here's a show that's been going for two years. We started it without Tony who was brought in. It helped to make him a star. And if I may say so, I contributed and you and Alan and Ray contributed."'

'He said, "I know, I agree," and went a bit pink. Then he said, "Don't worry, Graham, we'll do six more, the last six, and there's no question of you not being in them."'

'That was the first time the penny dropped. How could Tony do this to me? I couldn't understand it, we got on great, were a great combination and didn't compete. Suddenly, before I knew it, it was going to be *Hancock's Half Hour* and he'd recast it himself and, of course, I was not in it. It didn't worry me because I was booked for *Educating Archie*. But the rift was there. It upset me a bit at the time. I broke my heart because I thought we were great friends and I owed him a great debt which I'll never forget.'

Then there was Phyllis Rounce.

'I used to go down most nights to the Adelphi to see if he was all right,' she recalls. 'He got really frustrated about doing the same thing every night and was drinking a fair amount in the pub near the theatre. One night, to my utter astonishment, I was barred from his dressing room by the stage-door keeper. When I asked for an explanation I was just told that Mr Hancock said I was not to be allowed in.

'I was terribly upset. We'd been very close and he'd given me no indication. There had been no row – nothing. I came back to my office and – it was something I hadn't thought of at all before – I took the contract out and I found that that was the day it expired. It had never entered my head before that we were getting to the end of it. I thought we'd just go on.

'I went down the next night and insisted on seeing him and we had an extraordinary encounter. I was asking for an explanation and he just sat there like a great woolly bear and said nothing at all.

'So I said, "Oh well, cheerio." After five years of such great collaboration in every way it was like cutting off my right arm.

'I remember how he used to fall about laughing when I used to tell him that I must dash off to see my mother in Cheam. He would fall on the floor at the very sound of the place.'

On radio, *Hancock's Half Hour* got off to a slow start.

BBC Audience Research Report for Tuesday 21 November 1954, 9.30–10 p.m. Light programme:

Twelve per cent of the adult population of the UK heard the show. The previous week *The Al Read Show* at the same time was heard by 25 per cent.

Tony Hancock was given a great welcome by the vast majority of this sample audience who were delighted that he should have his own programme. Although the low appreciation index (52 as opposed to the average variety 'Gang' show of 62) suggests an unenthusiastic response to the show as a whole, there appears no doubt that its star enjoys widespread popularity.

Among points found worthy of favourable comment by the listeners were that there were no 'moaning crooners' no 'shrieking choirs' and no 'blaring dance bands'. The script was criticised.

Apart from the minor group who dislike Tony Hancock and had apparently not expected to find anything in the least amusing in the broadcast

the report went on,

there were many who were plainly disappointed. Some liked the first scene but felt the show deteriorated towards the end.

Several remarked that they could see nothing funny in the wrecking of Lord Dockyard's palatial home and thought it 'poor stuff' for adult amusement. There was a good deal of comment to the effect that Hancock and the cast worked hard to so little effect and a number expressed sympathy for them. 'Hancock is one of the funniest,' said an accountant, 'but even the best must have good material.' 'There were a few amusing moments,' wrote a clerk, 'but the script was generally pretty weak.'

It was a small beginning.

The same year Hancock made his first film, a dire comedy called *Orders is Orders* in which he played a military bandmaster. The cast included Peter Sellers.

'I sneaked into the cinema where it was showing,' Hancock once said, 'and asked if they had a seat in the circle. The box office girl said, "A seat? You can have the first fifteen rows."'

At the Adelphi he was beginning to wilt and writhe under the burden of what was clearly going to be another long run.

Freddie was 'popping in from time to time to say hello'.

'I was sitting one day in the small dressing room when he was making up,' she recalls, 'and above the wardrobe was a suitcase. I said, "What's in the suitcase?" and he said it was full of letters. "Fan letters?" "I don't know, I've never opened them."'

'That was alien to my tidy mind so I opened them and got a secretary from an agency and sorted them out.

'We worked on them for a solid week and a half at the Adelphi. There were about fifty or sixty that had to have his personal vetting before the replies were drafted so, after some cajoling, he arrived at 10.30 one morning. He drank one cup of coffee and two cups of tea, read a few letters and said, "That's enough – I think we had better have a staff outing."'

The secretary went off to do some typing and he and Freddie walked the half mile or so from the Adelphi to a workman's café in Whitcomb Street.

Inside he said, 'Lamb or beef?'

'Lamb.'

They were served with two hot lamb sandwiches. They were wrapped in greaseproof paper and he put them in the pocket of his navy-blue duffel coat – bought, incidentally, not at an army surplus stores but at Simpson's – and crossed the street to the Leicester Square Cinema. It was 1.20 p.m. and all the seats were the same price if bought before 1.30. Hancock bought two seats.

'Hang on for a minute,' he said and selected two bars of milk chocolate at the kiosk. 'Pudding,' he announced.

Freddie, a self-confessed cinematic coward who finds anything more powerful than a cowboy film too much strain on her nerves, found herself watching a picture about the Mau Mau in Kenya.

'I sat with the hot lamb sandwich in one hand and the milk chocolate in the other and wondered what on earth I had got myself into.'

After the film, Hancock said, 'That was nice,' and pushed off back to the Adelphi.

It was in this almost casual way that the relationship started. It would be five years before they became lovers.

At the time Freddie found Hancock more verbally than physically exciting. He was good to talk to. Professionally, she found it stimulating to have him on her list of clients. She was just building up her business – later to include such disparate characters as Harry H. Corbett and Max Jaffa – and Hancock was particularly interesting as he was poised halfway between success and stardom. Even when the backlog of letters had been shifted he found he needed her to arrange the interviews that were now frequently in demand. Freddie spent every evening at the Adelphi.

'He had a marvellous mind and was great fun,' she recalls. 'There were moments when he and Cicely were on the edge of a row but that happens with all married couples, especially in show business when so much of the time is spent in a state of nervous tension or reacting from it. Cicely and I got on fine together.'

Sometimes Hancock would take Freddie to Lord's to watch cricket in the afternoon; at others they would visit one of London's innumerable drinking clubs. Hancock was not drinking excessively; just regularly. Freddie would keep to Coke.

Early on, he asked her to marry him but she put it down to an off-patch with Cicely and laughed it off.

It is clear that the dependence grew on her side too. She asked his advice about a man she considered marrying and she occasionally had her dates pick her up at the Adelphi – 'to prove to him that I had another life'.

'There was a closeness,' she says. 'I can't fully explain why because he was a very difficult and unpredictable man always, yet I found him very easy to be with. It seemed that I could persuade him to do things when he was feeling bolshy. You had to suggest things to Tony so that the idea seemed to come from him. Later we talked about the things that had brought us together and decided that basically we had a similar sort of background. We both came from middle-class bourgeois families and though he often professed to hate middle-class ideas he understood them.

'He was an impossible, unpredictable, irrational man and as his illness took over he got more and more abhorrent. But during his early years he was lucid and logical and very perceptive about people. I found him the most exciting person I have ever met – to talk to. I wasn't physically attracted to him – at least I don't think so.

'We became more and more close to each other. I didn't agree with him all the time but the disagreements were not violent until we got married – or at least started living together.

'I would wander in and out of the Adelphi and at times he got very cross about this. I was taught very firmly that you knock on the door and don't come in until you're told to. He didn't really approve of comedians' wives and from the time I became his wife I wasn't allowed near the theatre.

'But at the time he would sit in his dressing room, often with nothing on but his pants, and chat away quite happily while he made up. He had terrible spots all over his body. They were dreadful to look at. They got better when I got him on a diet but this wasn't until we lived with each other.

'It was strange, but I once went with him to Coventry, purely professionally – we had separate rooms – and I knocked on his door and walked in and found him in his underpants exactly like I had seen him scores of times in his dressing room. But we were both terribly embarrassed.

'Gradually we got fonder of each other. He would start to see me home from the Adelphi and sometimes he'd be a bit drunk and we'd neck. It was very prim and pure really. He often talked about leaving Cicely and I was frightened of the whole situation. I was too worried about what people might say and that it might affect his career. I was frightened of the total personal commitment he demanded. Right the way through our relationship I was always sending him back to Cicely. And when we broke up for the last time and I started divorce proceedings I told one of his friends that he should go back to Cicely.

'He knew everything about me and I knew everything about him. He was the one person I trusted enough to talk freely to.'

The Hancocks' fifth-floor flat in Queens Gate Terrace was, by all accounts, pretty seedy. As Main Wilson describes it, 'There was an old leather club armchair with the stuffing coming out, a few other odd chairs and a put-u-up settee. There was an underfelt on the floor but no carpet. There was a mark where someone had been sick. There were piles of fan letters behind the lavatory pan. I looked into the bedroom one Sunday and there was a *Sunday Pictorial* from the previous week still sticking out of the bedclothes.'

It is something of a mystery why the smart and spirited Cicely who made her own clothes and was such a wonderful cook, who came from a comfortable and tidy home, tolerated such disorder. It is clear that while Hancock could be very generous to buskers and would invite his friends abroad without thought of expense, would buy rare wines and eat in expensive restaurants, he did not like spending money in large amounts. He would not even buy clothes or shoes for himself until the things he was wearing showed every indication of falling to pieces. For Cicely, it was always much easier to go with him than to go against him. She too had started to drink on the principle, she told a friend, that if you can't beat 'em you join 'em.

It was on to this domestic chaos that Freddie would descend aghast at the disorder, a tidy-minded whirlwind of industry, surreptitiously sliding her hand down the backs of easy chairs to salvage unopened letters to be briskly dealt with the following day.

Main Wilson says: 'Freddie came in dynamic, driving and a bit daunting. I told Tony: "You are now one of the greatest names in the business. You're going to earn a lot of loot. You need a publicity agent to take all the worries off your hands, to fix appointments, answer fan-mail." Within three weeks Freddie Ross had answered about two years' back fan-mail and Tony had got six new suits and a haircut. What Freddie was trying to do was to make Tony upgrade himself into the full responsible pro. Cicely was very happy about it.

'Freddie was around a lot and was clearly in love with him. I knew it would never work.'

Though Freddie was his publicity representative and general factotum, there were long periods when she did not work at all for him or see him. One of them lasted for eighteen months. Fear at what she was getting into was only slightly outweighed by his fascination for her. Several times she fought her way free, and thought that they would never meet again except by accident. Then, one day, she would return to her office to find him sitting there, impatient and annoyed that she had not been there to receive him.

Freddie says, 'He would say something like "I can't stay away from you", and I would get all conventional and say, "You can't pick me up and put me down whenever you feel like it."

'But it would all come to nothing. I had a weakness about him and that's all there is to it. I had a tremendous amount of pride but I could hold on to it for just so long. Then he would wear me down.'

When she was working for him she received a salary of £7 a week for most of the time.

Hancock was by now pleading with Hylton to be released from the Adelphi but Hylton was unco-operative. He was a man who could be difficult when he was in the wrong; when he was in the right he was unshakeable. Hancock grew to respect him and hate him and later he himself used the business methods he attributed to Hylton.

One of them was the cold telephone treatment. Basically, it is never to ring back, in reply to a message. Another was that if it is necessary to send an aggravating letter it should be timed to arrive on a Friday so that the weekend intervenes to allow the aggravation to take root. If possible send it to arrive just before a public holiday weekend. It is a system calculated to make the coolest man sweat.

Hancock sweated and strained and drank and at last went down with another nervous breakdown which necessitated five days in a London nursing home under sedation.

It was the sleep treatment given to patients in need of drying out, but Freddie believes it was genuine nervous strain and not drink on this occasion.

Despite the friction between the two men, Hylton invited Hancock to one of his parties. Hylton's parties were as long as they were lavish and Hancock, after two shows, thought that he had better take a pill to keep him awake. He obtained a Dexedrine tablet from a friend and put it into his pocket. Getting ready for the party after the second show he felt hot and nervous and pulled at his shirt collar. The button came off.

There was no time to change so he adjusted his tie to cover the gap and dashed off to Hylton's flat. It was a good party but about 2 a.m. Hancock felt his eyes closing. 'Ah,' he thought, 'time for the pill!' It worked almost at once. Suddenly he became the life and soul of the party. He was urged to further efforts by the laughter and applause of the other guests. He shone in the company of people who earned their living by shining. He floated, uninhibited and tireless. At 6.50 a.m. when everyone else had gone he was still playing snooker with Billy Ternent at £5 a frame. He got to bed at eight o'clock and woke about noon, feeling fine.

'That was a powerful pill,' he thought.

As he dressed, he remembered the missing button and felt for it in his pocket. He pulled out the pill.

'I was a raving success on a swallowed shirt button,' he recalled later. 'God knows what I would have been like if I had swallowed the bleeding pill.'

On the air *Hancock's Half Hour* was rapidly rising in popularity. By January 1955, with a topical script about Hancock taking part in the Monte Carlo Rally which used the voices of BBC commentators Raymond Baxter and Brian Johnston, it was reaching 10 per cent of the population and had an appreciation index of 69. It was moving to a greater reality, to a deeper comedy, to a time when public-house and theatre managers would claim that it affected business.

By February, the BBC found that most of their listening panel thought the scripts had a welcome freshness and originality and were ideally suited to Hancock's style. A Methodist minister said: 'This has been the funniest thing on radio recently. All good fun and no crooners or jazz. No rowdiness.'

These reports are confidential, officially only reaching producers. But they're permitted to show them to individuals involved in their shows. There is no doubt that Hancock saw them. He once, in fact, quoted from the first report.

Popularity marches in step with publicity. Hancock was suspicious and distrustful of newspapermen as a class but made friends with a number of individual journalists. He had a common attitude of ambivalence towards interviews and was both fearful and fascinated by the prospect of one.

He always started off by maintaining that he was not going to give another interview. Then Freddie would persuade him of its necessity and he would agree. When the journalist arrived in his dressing room, Hancock would usually gang up with him against Freddie. 'I don't suppose you want to interview me,' he would say, 'and I'm not all that keen. It's all the fault of that silly bitch there. Let's have a drink.'

Freddie would be told to go and Hancock, having demonstrated his general reluctance, would then talk freely. This way, everyone, even Freddie, was happy.

In one of his interviews, he told Herbert Kretzmer, now television critic of the *Daily Mail*, about his worries over his feet.

'They've been put on wrong,' he said. 'They don't join the ankle right. I can feel them flapping like a penguin's. When I cross the lounge of a swank hotel my feet come along with me. It is almost as though they were separate, not part of me at all.'

It was a theme he often referred to. Of course it was funny but it came to seem a little obsessive, especially as he had normal 8½ size feet.

'Dammit,' he told Freddie. 'They flap. I feel I've got the shoes on the wrong feet. Look at them – only useful for picking up nuts. Mark my words, girl, if they're against you, you've had it.'

'Who?'

'Yer feet. When I walk into the Dorchester they know I'm trying to impress somebody and they bloody well go off on their own. Feet are anarchists. But that's where the comedy starts – from the feet up.'

He was taken up by the intellectuals. J. B. Priestley writing in the *New Statesman* about the new crop of comics said, after dealing with Frankie Howerd, 'Another despairing but different type is Tony Hancock, a very clever performer owing more to art than nature. He comes on all smiles and confidence to recite, to sing, to dance, but is quickly reduced by the malice of circumstances aided by a strange blank stooge who is the very image of no enthusiasm, to a gasping, pitiable wreck, his gleaming, rolling eye pleading for our tolerance, for just another chance. This is all in a high tradition of clowning. Good clowns never try to be funny: they are very serious but eager and hopeful creatures lost in a hostile world.'

Priestley and Hancock met a couple of times and in 1968 Priestley published a novel which features an erratic highly disturbed comedian called Lon Bracton. 'Hancock was alive at the time,' says Priestley, 'so the physical description is different. All the rest is Hancock.'

The Hancock of 1954 was not the Lon Bracton of 1968. But was well on the way.

In 1954 the achievements were already immense and the prospects were limitless. The crowds were packing into the Adelphi in their thousands and tuning into the radio programme in their millions. A series was planned for commercial television to be written by friend Sykes. Love and money were pouring in in overwhelming amounts. Hancock was overwhelmed.

He told his agent, Jack Adams, that he did not know where his career was taking him. He was miserable and morose. And, though Adams says he never saw him drunk, there was no doubt that he was drinking far more than was good for him.

The show must go on must it? That was a load of old rubbish for a start. Hancock fled.

The second series of *Hancock's Half Hour* was about to start and Dennis Main Wilson took the script round to the Adelphi. The stage-door keeper said: 'If you're looking for the boy, sir, 'e's gone.'

'What do you mean, gone?' asked Main Wilson. 'He's got the finale walk down to do yet.'

All the same, he had gone. He had done his act, said something about the stage being too steep to climb and had gone.

After the show Main Wilson and Jimmy Edwards toured every night club in the West End without finding him. About 2 a.m., Main Wilson was telephoned by a friend in the Special Branch to whom he had given two tickets for the opening broadcast of the series.

'If,' said the Special Branch Officer, 'there is going to be a broadcast tomorrow what was Hancock doing on the last plane to Rome tonight?'

Through the unofficial use of Interpol, Hancock was traced to a pensione in Positano. He could not, of course, be brought home.

The first four episodes of the second series of *Hancock's Half Hour* were introduced by announcer Robin Boyle saying, 'This is the BBC Light Programme. We present [snatch of the theme music] *Hancock's Half Hour* starring Harry Secombe, Sidney James, Bill Kerr . . .'

When Hancock returned, reports Main Wilson, 'he never said thank you to Harry. He was like a little dog with his tail between his legs. He did not give any explanations and I didn't think I was entitled to ask for any.'

One of the BBC's many virtues is its way of dealing with awkward talent. Nobody, at any level, carpeted Hancock though he had clearly broken his contract.

Was Hancock's sudden disappearance, which could have wrecked his career completely, the result of unrelenting constant strain or was it caused by one particular incident?

A possible answer has its roots in a meeting four years earlier while Hancock was in a summer show in Clacton.

Frankie Howerd was then managed by Stanley Dale, a former Flight Lieutenant in the RAF who rejoiced in the nickname of 'scruffy' and had won the D.F.C. for sitting on an incendiary shell which had penetrated his aeroplane.

Howerd went to Clacton for a Sunday concert accompanied by

Dale. One of his gags depended entirely on a precision change in lighting which, in a normal theatre, would be controlled easily. At Clacton somebody would have to sit on a girder to do it. Because he could not climb up in the middle of the show, Dale was prepared to go up at the beginning and sit there throughout the whole performance for the sake of one gag.

This impressed Hancock and he saw a lot of Dale – who eventually became his agent and manager – when he returned to London. Dale formed Associated London Scripts with Eric Sykes, Frankie Howerd and Spike Milligan and was soon joined by Galton and Simpson. Their offices were above a greengrocer's shop in Uxbridge Road, Shepherd's Bush.

Hancock was fascinated by Dale's distinguished service career and often spent hours poring over his log-book. Gradually Dale began to make decisions for Hancock.

Dale's bank manager was in charge of the Middlesex Air Training Corps and asked him if he could bring along one of his show business friends for a ball they were holding in Hendon. There was, of course, no fee. Hancock agreed to go after his performance at the Adelphi and Dale called for him. Jimmy Edwards came into the dressing room just as they were leaving and asked if he could go along too, being an ex-RAF man. The trio went off happily to Hendon.

When they got there, the ball was rolling and everyone was delighted to see them. They were especially delighted to see Edwards. He was, after all, the bigger star, the better known face. They made quite a fuss. Hancock watched it with that rueful half-smile. He knew that Edwards was not taking the limelight consciously.

The following day he caught the night plane to Rome.

A bruised ego is a tender thing.

With the stage show finished, there was now the radio work and the first attempt at television comedy, a series of six written by Eric Sykes.

'We were similar in temperament,' says Sykes, 'but different in working methods. He had to have something down on paper, get hold of a line and rehearse it and rehearse it. I told him that he wrung all the juice from it before it ever got to the public.'

Scripts were usually ready by Monday with the programme going out live on Saturday. One Thursday Sykes wanted to change a line. Hancock said it should have been in on Monday and Sykes told him: 'I'm not writing classics, I'm writing comedy. It changes daily as we do.'

The argument boiled until Sykes walked off the set. The following Sunday he took a plane to Paris with his wife. They had not been there long when Tony and Cicely walked in to their hotel. 'I know a place,' said Hancock, 'where we can get some mussels.'

He led them to Montmartre but could not find the restaurant so they had a drink. At nine o'clock that night they still hadn't found any mussels but by that time they were laughing so much that it didn't matter.

Comedy on television was in its infancy. Live transmission not only carried the risk of unexpected snags but severely limited scope. Changes of scene or costume had to be kept to a minimum or masked by the intrusion of a song or dance. It was cumbersome and inflexible and full of traps.

The Hancock series, though not wildly successful, had its moments.

'Good evening,' Hancock opened. 'I'm pleased to welcome you to my show.' At which June Whitfield pushed him aside to say: 'His show? It's not his show at all.'

Hancock, fascinated by the new coffee bars springing up all over London with the mysterious espresso machinery and profusion of plant life, conceived the idea of a place where the vegetation attacked and slowly strangled the customers, while the espresso machine sank through the floor.

The idea was good.

'You wouldn't believe,' said Hancock later, 'how difficult it was to persuade potted plants to garotte people at a given moment.

'Ours waited until an actor had a line to speak and then they strangulated his voice. The fact is that we should have had six months' preparation and we only had a few days. The results were weird and hilarious but in the wrong sort of way.'

He and Cicely became members of the boat-owning classes by acquiring for £100 a converted pontoon on the River Wey. *Shemara II* frequently sank, being, Hancock maintained, built entirely of rusty metal and blotting paper.

Freddie arranged for the boat to be launched by Noel Whitcomb, the Fleet Street columnist. He used a bottle of Coca-Cola. Hancock christened the pontoon *Shemara II*, the original *Shemara* being the costly yacht owned by Sir Bernard and Lady Docker who constantly decorated the gossip columns of the day with their trivial adventures.

One evening while they were on the boat, Cicely persuaded him to take her to a local 'do'. He dressed up in his midnight blue dinner jacket and suède shoes of a make called 'Playboy'. They were just about to leave when two men came alongside in a leaky canoe and shouted for assistance. Hancock instantly became the mariner, ready to uphold the loftiest traditions of those in peril on the sea.

'Leave it to me,' he shouted, as he helped them aboard the pontoon. Then he stepped into the canoe to tie it up and it sank.

He found himself walking along the bottom of the River Wey in his midnight blue suit and his Playboy shoes.

Cicely said, 'What did you want to do that for?'

'It wasn't for the sake of a cheap laugh,' replied Hancock with dignity.

Ultimately the pontoon sank again and was left to rot. Their next boat was in the South of France.

He loved France. If he had only a few days he would go to Paris; any longer and he would rush to Antibes.

Once, in Paris, he sat in the sun outside the Café des Beaux Arts on the Left Bank and found himself surrounded by a complete brass band, drinking aperitifs. He caught the eye of the trombonist and winked.

The trombonist started to play some jazz. The rest of the band joined in.

'I was in paradise,' Hancock said later. 'I went crazy and ordered drinks all round and they responded by playing away like mad.'

He once told Freddie that he would end up as a derelict but did not mind as long as he could get a good spot over one of the warm air outlets of the Metro with a copy of *Le Figaro* as a blanket and an empty wine bottle by his side.

Chapter Five

Back home, *Hancock's Half Hour* was steadily increasing its grip on the affections of the public. Not all the laughs were shared by the listeners. In November 1955, the strain of twice nightly purgatory at the Adelphi was lifted. Certainly there had been a routine, but it was not without its exemptions. There had been two periods away through illness and a week spent in Coventry fulfilling a previous engagement on which Freddie accompanied him. It was, she says, purely platonic and professional. She served him eagerly. As usual, he had no underwear with him so she went shopping for underpants. She selected chorus girls and helped him to drill them for 'The Crooner' which by now she knew backwards. He learned to lean heavily on her talent for organisation.

Once he was free of *Talk of the Town* Hancock became happier and more relaxed, taking strength from a constant flow of acclamation and admiration.

One of the extraordinary things about him – extraordinary, that is, for a comedian – was his ability to listen intently to any story he was told. He was always eager to laugh. If he thought a script was funny he could fall over with laughing and roll about gasping, 'Oh dear! Oh dear! Oh dear!' – a White Rabbit afflicted by the uncontrollable giggles.

As he grew in confidence and it was still all new and fresh and lovely, he became remarkably generous with his lines. 'Oh give that one to Sid,' he would say – or Hattie Jacques or Bill Kerr or Kenneth Williams – 'He will be able to do it better than I can.'

When he was feeling happy he was ready to dispense benefits to everyone.

After the show would come the unwinding session in a nearby pub. The cast, the production staff and the technicians would meet and the tension would gradually flow out of them. Cicely was usually in high spirits on these occasions, responding to the temporary relief from strain. Hancock would convivially burble away to everyone and usually end up in a corner talking to Freddie.

Freddie occasionally found herself mentioned in the script as 'Madame Freda' the clairvoyant, or some stray character called Fred.

'If you hear recordings of the shows, mine is the loudest laugh whenever this happens,' she says. 'The fact that my name was used like that was a kind of mating call. After a while anyone would respond to it. Tony was obviously unhappy and unsure of himself. He needed confidence poured into him non-stop. I found him amenable and manageable – and, every so often, completely and absolutely belligerent.'

Inevitably, she found herself in absurd and embarrassing situations. Even though she was not yet Hancock's mistress there had been intimate moments between them that imposed a strain on the most ordinary activities.

Once when the Hancocks had been holidaying in the South of France, Freddie received a telephone call from them in which they asked her to fly to Paris with some extra money. It was her first visit to the city and Cicely drove her round to see the sights. Then she caught a plane back to London. When Hancock followed a few days afterwards he telephoned her and said he wanted to see her urgently. He arrived at her office and said he wanted to apologise.

'It was terrible to be in Paris with you and her,' he said. 'I can't take that sort of stuff. You must never do it again.'

Freddie said, 'But you asked me to come.'

He did not consider this was a valid objection.

Some of the funniest things in *Hancock's Half Hour* were only heard by the studio audience. In one show Bill Kerr, after boasting that he had been to Eton and Harrow, Oxford and Cambridge, was saying how good he was with the girls. The line was: 'Many's the time I've been punting down the Cam with a bird in a boat.'

It came out wrong. The audience at the Playhouse Theatre, where the show was being taped, gasped. There was silence save for the sound of Hancock's choking. Then he said, 'William, I think you ought to read that line again.'

William read it again. This time it came out worse. By the time he had made his fourth attempt Hancock was sitting on the stage holding his stomach and incapable of going on.

Another time the situation was that Sid James had talked Hancock into lending him the money to hire a boat in order to do some smuggling. Hancock agrees, providing he can be the one who steers the boat and has all the egg and custard round his cap.

They put to sea, seagulls come up from the effects man and they eventually meet a French trawler – Sid shouts, 'Allo Jacques, ici Sid 'ere' and his next line was, 'Bring the boat alongside and get the stuff aboard.'

It came out as 'Bring the boat alongside and stuff the broad I'll read that again.'

Hancock could not proceed for ten minutes.

Once the whole recording system broke down during the middle of a show. The producer apologised to the audience and said they would have to start again when the repairs were made. The cast stood about in the wings and the audience sat there quietly and Hancock said, 'We can't just leave 'em sitting there. Let's do some quickies. Anyone know any crossovers?'

A crossover is where a comedian stands in the centre of the stage saying things like 'It's a funny old world we live in' while another comes on and interrupts. Bill Kerr did the Smithfield Market crossover.

'I say, I say, I say, I've been to Smithfield Market.'

'You've been to Smithfield Market?'

'Yes I've been to Smithfield Market.'

'What for?'

'What for? I got a pound of meat for one and two.'

'You got a pound of meat for one and two?'

'Yes I got a pound of meat for one and two.'

'Was it mutton?'

'No, it was rotten.'

Then it was the turn of Kenneth Williams who had been given the woofle dust crossover.

Kenneth Williams: 'I had to come on like a ballet dancer and throw myself about the stage making these sprinkling gestures. Then I'm asked, "What are you doing," and I say, "I'm sprinkling woofle dust to kill the lions." And the comic in the middle is supposed to say, "But there aren't any lions around here," and I say, "It's just as well, this isn't real woofle dust."

'Well, I came on and threw myself about like some mad ballet dancer and Tony didn't say anything and eventually I had to say out loud in front of the audience, "Go on ask me what I'm doing," and he said, "We all know about you, dear."

'It got a big laugh because there I was cavorting about like some outrageous poof and the house fell about and afterwards I said, "That was outrageous," and he said, "It wasn't deliberate. I just forgot what I had to say."'

But the really important comedy was coming out over the air.

Anthony Aloysius St John Hancock of 23 Railway Cuttings,

East Cheam, was taking shape. In fact many people thought the Aloysius St John was Hancock's real name and, for a time, he encouraged this by assuring interviewers that it was. It was only later, when he realised with some alarm the deep identification he had created with the character, that he shrugged it off as just part of the comic creation.

Anthony Aloysius St John was, to use Galton and Simpson's description, 'a shrewd, cunning, high-powered mug,' and they surrounded him with hostile friends. There was Sid James, crooked as the elbow-joints he was always hacking off neighbours' drainpipes to sell for scrap; Bill Kerr, the inarticulate Australian, a cousin only in a colonial sense; the mountainous Hattie Jacques as Miss Pugh, the defiant secretary, susceptible to dreams of romance; and Kenneth Williams who had the capacity to make 'good-evening' sound snide and frequently did.

In the centre sat Hancock, pictured in a Homburg hat and the astrakhan-collared coat of the seedy comedian with grandiose ideas. He was belligerent, pompous, frequently childish and petulant, suspicious yet so easily taken in that Sid had only to hint at some shady scheme for betterment and he would rush headlong to disaster.

At a time when the citizens of Britain were being assured that they had never had it so good, he was the inadequate one who was missing out and wanted to know why. He was the puritan who always suspected that someone somewhere was having a good time. He was the man doomed to be forever out who desperately wanted to be in.

Hancock was Galton and Simpson and Hancock.

Galton and Simpson are artists and Hancock was the raw material from which they hewed the finished masterpiece. They followed the natural tensions of the original as good sculptors follow the inherent flaws and grain of marble. But the sculptural analogy can be taken too far. There was a strong community of interests and attitudes between the three of them. Their coming together was as happy as Gilbert's meeting with Sullivan, as inevitable as bacon and eggs.

Galton and Simpson have reached the kind of understanding where, when one talks, the other nods in agreement. Both are bearded, Simpson looking like some eminent Victorian cricketer, Galton hairy like a respectable and successful artist.

'There was a lot of Tony in the character and a great deal of us,' they said. 'Aspects of him we picked up in private talk crept in. There were phrases and little idiosyncrasies of his that we used.

But sometimes the attitude we gave the character was completely opposite to Tony's.

'Take his attitude towards food and France, for instance. One week we'd give him "Bloody French food, don't stick that foreign muck in front of me," when Tony himself loved both food and France. We'd make the character very chauvinistic and if there was one thing Tony really hated it was patriotism in the nationalistic sense of the word. At other times we'd go the other way. He'd have an argument with Sid about culture and he'd praise French culture and literature and French food. It worked because the radio Hancock was a man whose attitudes would change depending upon the kind of person he was talking to. If he met an intellectual he would either try to keep up with him or he would say, "What a load of old rubbish!" If he was talking to a clod like Sid or Bill he would go the other way.'

Galton and Simpson put Hancock in Railway Cuttings, East Cheam, in order to place him firmly in the worst area of a very genteel neighbourhood.

'It could have been St John's Wood or Maida Vale,' they said, 'but as we lived out that way our idea of a genteel area was Sutton and Cheam. Cheam, in fact, was a nicer area than Sutton. It was *East* Cheam because he couldn't quite manage Cheam itself. Anthony Aloysius came from a family that once had money but it was a long time ago. He clung to his heritage.'

Occasionally, though he rarely if ever threw temperaments, Hancock would want changes made in a script or refuse to do it at all. Once he did get a little ratty. He was overweight and went into the London Clinic for three weeks to try to lose two stone. He was let out every Sunday to do the recording. His diet was a bleak apple and pear and bits of dry toast and he suddenly got cross because there had been two or three episodes which he thought had sleazy settings – in a doss-house, down at the labour, in gaol.

He called Main Wilson to the Clinic. 'Tony trying to get angry was quite a giggle,' says Main Wilson, 'because he didn't do it very well.'

Hancock threatened, 'You'd better tell the boys that if they don't get me out of the doss-house I know other writers.'

Galton and Simpson remember two or three scripts being turned down because there was too much accent on Sid's criminal aspect. It was not from a moral, but an artistic point of view. Hancock thought they were too corny.

Towards the end, Hancock got worried about the possibility of someone seeing a homosexual relationship between him and Sid.

One script started with Hancock doing the housework and saying, 'I work my fingers to the bone and you don't appreciate a thing I do.'

Hancock said no. 'It's too poofy,' he said, 'and we can't do it.' The script was rewritten with Tony doing the work just because someone had to do it.

Later there were to be many analyses of the strands that made up Hancock's kind of comedy and Hancock himself struggled to define it, never with much success.

Worth far more than any of them is a close look at a typical *Hancock's Half Hour* script as heard on radio. Like the one where he stood for Parliament.

It opens with Hancock, Miss Pugh (Hattie Jacques) and Bill Kerr sitting down for breakfast and Hancock demanding that he should be the one to open the new packet of cornflakes as he wants first chance at the little plastic soldier. It is a month in which the manufacturers are urging cornflake eaters to make up their own guards' band and Hancock needs a trumpet player to complete his set. He has already got six trombone players. Miss Pugh protests. She bought forty-three packets for him last month just to find the flute player.

'They'll never get eaten,' she complains.

'Yes they will,' says Hancock. 'The next party we have, put some salt on them and tell everybody they're crisps.'

Miss Pugh is scornful. When she buys cornflakes she buys them for the cornflakes not little plastic guardsmen.

A typical woman's attitude, says Hancock. No imagination. 'It's the thrill of the hunt,' he says. 'Getting your set together. Look at them up there on the mantelpiece. Marching along there. What a stirring sight. A complete band . . . minus a trumpet player.'

Then emotionally: 'I've been waiting three weeks for that trumpet player. Breakfast is making me a nervous wreck I don't mind telling you . . .'

Bill asks him for the trombone player and offers a drummer. Hancock refuses. Miss Pugh tells them to stop squabbling. 'Next week they'll probably finish with the guardsmen and start an entirely different set.'

Hancock is indignant. 'Oh will they. Miss Pugh, take a letter to the makers. Dear Sir, I hereby warn you that if you discontinue putting guardsmen in your cornflakes before I've got my set, I shall in future eat porridge. Yours sincerely, A. Hancock. Age seven and a half. There. That'll frighten them.'

Now he is ready for his bacon and pease pudding. Miss Pugh is already tucking into hers. 'Look at her plate piled up there. You can't see her, just her arms coming round the sides. Are you there?'

Bill Kerr is reading the paper and Hancock snatches it from him. 'By the time you've stumbled through it, it'll be yesterday's. Give us it here.'

He reads out bits. 'Hallo, I see he's got three years. I knew he was guilty when I saw his photo last week. He had a moustache. That was enough for me.'

There are long, audacious pauses between each item.

'Butter's going up in China . . . snow in the North of Scotland . . . Man denies weekend in caravan.'

He turns the page. 'Oh, she's nice . . . seventeen-year-old model from Gateshead . . . record crop of rice in Tibet this year . . . vicar punches driving instructor . . . she doesn't look seventeen, does she?'

The question about whether the beauty from Gateshead is seventeen or older becomes a running gag for the rest of the half hour. But there is another item – an election in East Cheam.

Hancock hasn't any time for politicians – they're all the same. 'I have nothing but the utmost dislike for politicians.'

Kerr's been thinking: 'If you break the end of the trombone, it'll look like a trumpet,' he says.

Hancock tells him to shut up.

Sid enters on his way after working all night. He puts down his sack in the corner. It clanks. Hancock looks into it. It's full of stolen metal. Sid offers to pay for his breakfast with two foot of waste pipe. Hancock orders him to take it off his table.

Sid assures him that it's worth seven and a tanner. Hancock is offended, stands on principle. 'You come in here trying to barter with your night's pickings, two foot of pipe for some cornflakes and pease pudding. Whatever next? It's worth two curly bits and a section of guttering any time, that is.'

The deal is on.

Sid gets his cornflakes and asks where the little plastic guardsman is. He too needs a trumpet player. He knows a bloke in Epsom who's got six trumpet players and is after a trombone player.

'Stone me!' says Hancock. 'I've got a boxful of trombone players. It's the distribution that's all wrong.' He didn't have this trouble with his fag cards.

Sid is resigned. 'That's the way it goes. Anything in the papers?'

'No, nice bird from Gateshead on page two. Seventeen it says.'

Sid doesn't think she's seventeen either, reads about the price of Chinese butter, comments on a man sent to gaol for three years and says: 'I reckon this bird's nearer twenty-one, you know.'

They get back to politics via the paper's cartoon which they both admire, though they confess that they don't know what it means.

Hancock's profession is established. Saying the girl was seventeen might have been a printer's error.

'It does happen,' says Hancock. 'They called me Tommy Hitchcock the other week.'

He had written in demanding an apology. 'Look!' Sid reads: 'We apologise for any embarrassment caused last week when we wrote about Mr Tommy Hitchcock. We were of course referring to that celebrated comedian Mr Terry Hancick.'

'Well it's near enough,' said Hancock. 'You can't keep writing can you?'

They talk about the local MP's application for the Chiltern Hundreds.

Hancock knows what it means. 'The Chiltern Hundreds,' he explains, 'is an ancient custom. They apply for it when they want promotion. They get a hundred pounds, a new suit, and a badge allowing them to use the House of Lords canteen without being accompanied by Black Rod. I think you'll find that's right.'

There is a knock at the door. Kenneth Williams is there with his 'good morning'. He asks Miss Pugh if she's Mrs Hancock. 'Do you want a punch on the nose?' she replies.

He comes in and Hancock is identified as 'the fat one in the red nightshirt'. He thinks it is another seeker after food. 'I'm sorry, mush,' he says, 'there's no breakfast left.'

But the caller doesn't want breakfast. He is from the East Cheam Independents and they want Hancock to stand as their candidate in the forthcoming election. It doesn't matter that he knows nothing about politics. He has been on television, hasn't he? Well, that's all they demand of any candidate. Hancock's final shred of reluctance is swept away when he is told that he could even become Prime Minister.

'That'd be good. I could step out of an aeroplane waving me hat, couldn't I?'

Yes, he is told, and go straight through customs. This has an immediate appeal for Sid. 'Think of all those watches we could get through.'

Hancock agrees to stand.

As he is leaving, the caller spies the cornflake packet. 'You don't happen to have . . .' he begins when Hancock interrupts: 'No, only four trombone players.'

To Hancock, the election is a mere formality. He feels very important. He quotes: 'This is a far, far better thing I do now than I have ever done. Rembrandt.'

Questions at an election meeting introduce the only 'joke' in the script.

'Does the continual watching of television affect the eyes?'

'Only if it's switched on. Next.'

He is asked: 'What do you intend to do about England entering into the European Common Market, thus bringing about a more sound economic structure of Europe without endangering our interest in Commonwealth trade and Imperial Preference?'

'Come now, sir,' he replies with dignity, 'this is no time for frivolous questions.'

Polling day finds him with a House of Commons badge already on his bike. He declines Sid's offer to beat up the other candidates. 'I careth not for what they say but I will defend with my life their right to say it. Beethoven.'

The results come through. Hancock has polled one.

He demands a recount.

Not even his friends voted for him.

'Oh well, if at first you don't succeed try, try, again. Rimsky-Korsakov.'

As consolation, the local independent party send him 50 packets of cornflakes. He thinks he will have some. He takes a spoonful. He chokes. He has swallowed something. The doctor says that the X-ray shows that it appears to be a little plastic guardsman. And what's more, the doctor's afraid it is wedged and they cannot get it out.

Hancock must know how bad it is. 'You can tell me,' he says heroically, 'I can take it. I don't want you to lie to me. I want you to give it to me straight. What instrument is he playing?'

The answer is of course a trumpet.

'Stone me,' says Hancock, 'isn't it marvellous?'

It is worth noting what aspects of Hancock were crammed into that half an hour:

Childishness, obstinacy, indignation, rudeness, prejudice, lechery, the abandonment of principles for profit or status, ignorance, arrogance, smugness, ambition, pomposity, stupidity and cunning. Atoning for all are three kinds of resignation, deep vulnerability and an unquenchable resilience.

Other comedians sketch in one or two characteristics or draw attention to a physical oddity as an aid to instant identity. Bob Hope has a ski-run nose and affects devout cowardice; Les

Dawson 'gargoyles' his face and slanders his loved ones; Ronnie Corbett is small and cocky and John Cleese has a funny walk and a manic disposition. None of these things lessen their qualities as comedians but they look thin beside the complexities of the Hancock character.

Denis Norden says: 'Galton and Simpson didn't write a series, they wrote a novel. They created a most marvellous person and Tony filled it out like no other person in the world could, capturing every tiny nuance. But he didn't exist before Galton and Simpson and he didn't exist after they left.'

To the public Tony Hancock *was* Anthony Aloysius St John Hancock. The affection mounted until it could quite literally stop the traffic.

He was threading his way across Kensington Gore one day for a walk in Hyde Park with Kenneth Williams when a bus suddenly pulled up in his path and the driver leaned out of his cab and shouted, 'Tony, oy, Tony.' Hancock looked up and smiled and the bus driver said, 'You're great, mate, you're great.' Hancock muttered, 'Thank you, but hadn't you better get the bus moving?'

The driver jumped out of the cab and said: 'I don't care about that, I'm going to shake your hand; you've given me more laughs than anybody else.'

Hancock, now embarrassed, said, 'For God's sake get the bus moving or I'll drive it myself.' The bus driver, a big man, got hold of him and hoisted him up into the cab. Angry drivers got out of their cars and came towards them. But their attitude changed as soon as they saw who it was. 'What the hell . . . oh it's you, Tony, let me shake you by the hand.'

Eventually Hancock scrambled clear and they got into the park. Kenneth Williams was deeply impressed. 'It's fantastic,' he said, 'the way they do adore you.'

'Yes,' said Hancock. 'But it's the money that worries me. Look at the vast sums they're paying me for this series and think what that bus driver gets.'

Hancock grew more and more worried about the Meaning Of It All. In his search for answers to the questions that perplexed him he saw analysts and began a course of reading that was to carry him awestruck through years of philosophy, history, anthropology and sociology to emerge at the end more muddled than ever.

'When you start reading the history of the world,' he said, 'it certainly kills your ego. You soon realise what an insignificant speck you are. It puts things into perspective.'

Would that it had. He was reading Kant's *Critique of Pure*

Reason at the same time as he was refusing to wear green socks on the grounds that it was unlucky.

He read Leibnitz, Spinoza, Schopenhauer and Wells' *Outline of History*.

Above all, he read Bertrand Russell's *History of Western Philosophy* and carried it around with him everywhere, even on holiday. He bought a set of encyclopaedias which were also as necessary a part of his luggage as his toothbrush.

He had no faith himself and he acted as if he were the first man to discover doubt. He talked long into the night with anyone who would listen about the need for faith. He said things like, 'What if there's no one up there; what if it's all a joke?' and thought he was making a revolutionary suggestion.

In his autobiography, *Just Williams*, Kenneth Williams recalls visiting Hancock in the London Clinic 'during one of his slimming bouts' and finding Wells' *Outline of History* on the bed.

'We talked at length about theories of historical inevitability, the Malthusian doctrine and the decline of great civilisations,' Williams writes. 'Tony always returned to the same themes – "What is the purpose of human existence?" and "Is there a discernible pattern in human progress?" Again and again he held that such imponderables were unanswerable and when I ventured to suggest that only faith would explain apparent meaninglessness, he rejected that on the grounds that it was unprovable. "Our reasoning must be answered by reason," he would say. "Men want a rational answer, not mystery and magic." He was married to Cicely then and I remember the nights at their flat in Hyde Park Gate where she would wearily announce that she was going to bed, leaving the two of us arguing into the early hours with the wreckage of empty wine bottles and overflowing ash trays all around us.'

As Priestley puts it, he 'overdrew on his intellectual bank balance'.

Kenneth Williams suggested that he should study privately with a Professor of Philosophy and put some order into his thoughts, but he did not take to the idea. The yearning to understand was accompanied by a total rejection of intellectual discipline. Of all discipline, for that matter, except that immediately connected with the business of comedy.

He worked at that, striving all the time for greater reality but with a growing consciousness of what, to him, was a dangerous identification of the clown with his mask. And an even greater danger of finding himself part of a double act.

81

A clown is essentially a solitary man. He may work as part of a team for a time but his destiny and his need is to stand in front of an audience alone and say, in effect, 'Look at me. I am absurd. I am you. Laugh.'

Hancock was always conscious of this absurdity. 'Underneath the hand-made crocodile shoes,' he would say, 'there are still toes.' Or, 'Man's shape is ridiculous. When I think of bicycle clips I die with laughter.'

He must have read in the glowing Audience Research reports that he and Sid James and Kenneth Williams were being classed as a great comedy team.

When, in July 1956, *Hancock's Half Hour* made its inevitable move to television, there was a partial attempt to break the bonds.

Sid James was to stay longest, Hattie Jacques would be used occasionally. The door was shut on Bill Kerr. Kenneth Williams would stay for the first series of six programmes only.

'I think,' says Williams, 'that if you have a vision in your head – as Tony did – of the way comedy should be played then inevitably you move towards being a solo performer. It is too simple and too glib to reduce a man like that to being jealous of someone else getting laughs.'

Hancock kept saying to Galton and Simpson, 'I don't want this to develop into a double act.'

It was Williams' decision to leave the radio series. He told the producer that he felt all the character was being left out of the scripts and he was getting fewer and fewer lines. Once or twice his special kind of voice came up – whenever they wanted it Galton and Simpson used to write 'snide' in brackets.

One day at rehearsal, Hancock erupted. In front of Williams he rounded on Galton and Simpson and said: 'Look, I've asked you to cut this out. I don't want this double act, I don't want this voice.'

'But Tony,' they said, 'it's quite funny, it gives it a lift.'

Hancock said: 'I don't care about that. I don't want it. It's a gimmick and I will not start relying on gimmicks. I want real characters, not funny voices.'

Kenneth Williams describes the incident in his book and goes on to say: 'Hancock was at great pains to say that it was nothing personal, that it wasn't me he was getting at, which was supposed to placate me, but I didn't see then and I don't see now that you can divorce the actor from his work. Tony's endless analysis of the scripts and the characters was becoming destructive, but I stuck it out and ostensibly everything continued amicably to the end of the series in June.'

In 1962 Williams was a great success in the double bill *The Private Ear and the Public Eye* at the Globe Theatre. One night he was told that Hancock was in the audience. After the show he thought it strange that there had been no dressing-room visit. But calling in on Maggie Smith, his co-star, he found Hancock sitting there telling her how wonderful she had been.

'I came in,' said Williams, 'and he said, "Hallo, nice to see you again." It was just like meeting an acquaintance. He said he was very busy – he was making the film *The Punch and Judy Man* – and he said, "I don't know what you thought about all those things we used to do on sound but to me they were cardboard, the characters were cardboard. I want to get to grips with the real thing, just keep a camera on a man's face for ten minutes if necessary, because that's what life is." '

What was past was of no importance: the door was shut. There was to be a desperate knocking on it a few years later.

Freddie was with Hancock in Maggie Smith's dressing room and says that he was quite unconscious of offending Williams.

All the same Williams was offended.

Chapter Six

The first television show on 6 July 1956 was received as coolly as the first radio show had been. Galton and Simpson, obeying their own inclinations and Hancock's insistence on reality, decided that as they were doing a first show on television they should write a script about doing a first show on television.

Oddly enough, this was not a very televisual subject and would probably have been more suited to radio. Sid James was the one who knew the most about working to cameras as he had played crooks and cab drivers in scores of films.

The viewing figures were respectable – 16 per cent of the adult population of the United Kingdom, the equivalent to 36 per cent of the TV-owning public. The fact that a lot of them did not like what they saw was unfortunate. A number of sound radio fans said they had been disappointed and a grocer wrote: 'Adult mentality is surely above this sort of rubbish. Senseless bilge from beginning to end.'

It is amazing how *angry* people get merely through not finding half an hour on television to their liking. It is equally amazing how possessive and protective they get when they enjoy something. A kind of electronic love affair develops in which the passions are as human and as undulled as in any personal relationship.

Hancock on television pioneered two things – money and technique. He was the first man to be paid £1000 for half an hour – though, of course, it involved a week's work. It also involved repeats and sales to Australia, New Zealand and other places which more or less doubled his fees. From then on until his death, throughout the years of disappointment and dejection, his earning potential never dropped below £2000–£3000 a week. At the same time Galton and Simpson raised the status of television writer from comedian's labourer to parity by also getting £1000 a week.

The second and to the viewer the most important advance was an insistence on perfection that, along with opportune technical developments, set entirely new standards of production and performance.

The first shows went out live or were on tape that could not be edited in any way. Any mistakes that were made remained in the transmitted programme. Any changes of scene required filler shots. *Whacko!*, the Jimmy Edwards comedy series written by Muir and Norden about the same time, was full of shots of the school clock. Whatever else was uncertain, the viewers always knew what time it was.

The crunch came for Hancock with the incident of the shaking house.

The script required him and Sid James to sell a house situated at the end of the main runway at London Airport. The house was due to start shaking and the furniture to disintegrate at the end and, at rehearsals, everything went according to the script.

The day for recording arrived. Five minutes before destruction was due, Hancock advanced, as rehearsed, to a table in the middle of the room and placed his hand on it. He felt it give. Dick Emery, playing a surveyor, walked into position and expected Hancock to join him. Hancock was rooted to the table. Emery looked at Hancock glassy-eyed and Hancock looked at Emery. Then Emery realised what the trouble was. He and Hancock nearly burst themselves trying not to explode with laughter.

Up in the gallery producer Duncan Wood suddenly found all his carefully planned camera angles useless. They played the rest of the scene and he shot it, completely off the cuff. When the right moment came, Hancock let go of the table and it collapsed with the rest of the furniture as planned.

Many comedians would have exploited the situation, turning it from one kind of joke into another. Hancock couldn't do that. In one sense he enjoyed it because it was funny; in another he hated it because it was imperfect. But in recounting the story later, he was unable to resist the temptation to cap the joke by adding, 'As I stood there, my braces broke.'

Hancock insisted that some way must be found that would permit discontinuous recording; some method by which the half-hour could be broken up into segments.

Wood and his technicians got hold of an old show by another comic and experimented by chopping it up and then joining it in different ways. They proved that this way they could move from one full-scale production number to another, simply by cutting out the intervening sketch.

The recording sessions for *Hancock's Half Hour* suddenly

became more like a film studio. The thirty minutes were split into several sessions. After every scene the recording could be stopped while the cameras were moved and make-up and lighting altered. The breaks were 'natural' like interval curtains in a theatre. In this way the audience's attention was not destroyed. If a mistake occurred it merely meant another five-minute 'take' at the most.

A new kind of television writing became possible from the fall-out of the new technique. Bridging dialogue was no longer necessary. More cameras could be used in any one particular scene which meant more close-ups, more facial opportunities for Hancock to exploit. Actors did not have to wear two sets of costume, tearing the outer one off under cover of some ill-motivated distraction.

There is no doubting Hancock's influence in this break-through. Bluntly, he told Tom Sloan, head of Light Entertainment, that he was simply not interested in doing a third series unless the stop-start system was introduced. It put hours on the time taken in the studio and vastly increased production costs. But he and Duncan Wood insisted and they won the day.

With the increased freedom *Hancock's Half Hour* – while still continuing on radio – gathered strength on television. In April 1957 it attracted 23 per cent of the adult population of the United Kingdom. By November 1959 it was reaching 27 per cent, in March 1960, 28 per cent and in May 1961, 30 per cent.

These are phenomenal figures. Light entertainment shows in 1957, for example, had an average viewing figure of 11 per cent.

Viewers were ecstatic in their praise. 'Tony Hancock is fabulous. He is a genius as a comedian – no one in Britain can touch him,' one wrote.

'I am at a loss for words to describe my liking for Hancock, *the* comedian of TV today,' said a bank clerk.

But phrases also crept in like, 'Tony Hancock would not be the same without Sidney James.' 'Sid James is the perfect partner for Hancock.' 'A *Hancock's Half Hour* without Sid is as unthinkable as one without Hancock.'

No one was going to play Ernie Wise to Hancock's Eric Morecambe. Much as he admired them, he was not interested in producing that kind of comedy.

As early as 1957 he had long discussions with Duncan Wood on how a greater reality could be injected into the half hour. One way was to stop using comedians or comic actors and get straight actors to play the supporting roles.

If a police constable entered 23 Railway Cuttings, East Cheam, and he was played by, say, Kenneth Williams, the audience did not believe in the policeman at all – it was Kenneth Williams being funny. And if there was no reality in the policeman, there could be no reality in the subsequent situation.

With some hesitation and the sacrifice, at first, of a few laughs, they started using ordinary actors.

Supporting roles were cast purely on the demands of the character.

One of the difficulties was in finding the right actors. The insecurities of the legitimate actor – as the quaint term goes – are as formidable as any comic's and the general feeling then was that if a 'serious' actor appeared in television situation comedy, somebody would set fire to him or pull his trousers down or he would be expected to slip on a banana skin.

But they came along. Raymond Huntley appeared in one episode and he was followed by Jack Hawkins.

Hancock had set himself up as an elocution teacher, and the first shot was of a house with a notice in the window reading: *Anthony Hancock, Elocution Lessons, 2s. 6d. an hour, The Method, 1s. 9d.*

Jack Hawkins knocks on the door saying that he has been recommended by Trevor Howard as they are both up for the same part. Mr Howard's motive is very quickly apparent, particularly in the scene where Hancock rephrases 'To be or not to be' for Hawkins.

Hancock asks his new client for his name: 'Jack Hawkins.' He says, 'Jack Hawkins? Never get anywhere in the theatre with a name like that. Sounds like a scrap metal merchant. We'll have to think of a more theatrical name for you.'

The two of them pore over an AA book and come up with Studholme Berkeley. Re-equipped, Hawkins goes off to an Old Vic audition.

The better the actor, the better Hancock worked. He was – and he was frequently told that he was – a very good actor. He found it hard to believe. 'Me?' he laughed. 'I'm just a buffoon.'

But he had got over the terrible humility that afflicted him when he played a straight acting role on radio for Dennis Main Wilson.

Main Wilson produced a dramatised version of H. G. Wells' short story *The Man Who Could Work Miracles* for the BBC Home Service on New Year's Eve, 1956. He cast Hancock in the leading role as the miracle worker, George McWhirter Fotheringay.

There is a scene at the end where Fotheringay, an ordinary chap, who has been made omnipotent by the gods, orders the heads of state, the prime ministers, the dictators, all the powerful of the world, to appear before him.

Playing them were a number who were powerful in the world of acting, highly-respected actors who had passed a lifetime in the service of the drama.

They included André Morell, Dennis Price, Robert Eddison, Howard Marion-Crawford, Miriam Karlin, Warren Mitchell and many others.

There were forty of them and to achieve a distancing effect Main Wilson placed them all on one side of the microphone with Hancock facing them on the other. On the second day of rehearsal, Hancock shuffled up to him uneasily and said: 'Look, don't think I'm being awkward but I find this terribly embarrassing – all these marvellous actors facing me and there's me, rubbish, looking at them and making an ass of meself.'

The only way Main Wilson could satisfy him was by placing all the actors *behind* Hancock so that they could not see his face and he could not see them at all while he was trying to act.

There was one purely technical aspect of acting that Hancock could never acquire – he could not learn his lines without enormous labour. His method was to tape everyone else's lines in the show, leaving blanks for his own. Then he would play the recording over and over again. It was strange that, of all mechanical objects, the early cumbersome and complicated tape recorders presented no problem to him.

Necessity is also the mother of competence.

Even with this technique there were sometimes odd gaps in his memory and it was just as well the show was, by now, using the stop-start system.

In one episode the opening shot was of the back garden of 23 Railway Cuttings wrecked by vandals. Hancock and James come out of the back door and survey the scene.

Hancock's first line should have been, 'Cor blimey, who's been mucking about with me concrete toadstools?' It came out as, 'Cor blimey, who's been mucking about with me cardboard nutmegs?'

There was another time when Hancock was in an aircraft and looking out of the window was to say something about the earth being laid out below like a patchwork quilt. It came out as the 'earth below laid out like a porcelain chart'.

They were the kind of slips of the tongue that delight psychiatrists – and no doubt they did. Hancock, by now, was seeing analysts regularly and was reading books like Freud's *Interpretation of Dreams* and *Totem and Taboo*.

88

In December 1957 Hancock won the title of Comedian of the Year from the Guild of Television Producers and Directors. Shortly afterwards he and Cicely left London and bought a house in Lingfield, Surrey.

It had stood empty for a while because if you went down to the bottom of the garden and looked over the fence, you could see council houses.

It had a large garden, five bedrooms and a big entrance hall with a fireplace. The house was originally called Val Fleury which was not to the Hancocks' liking. They rechristened it MacConkeys because MacConkey was the name of the original owner. There was a stone unicorn on the roof and a portrait of the Marquis of Worcester – though some people said it was a saint – built by some whim of the builder into the stonework over the door. Hancock maintained that in fact it was Spike Milligan.

The entrance hall was very big and they put down a huge white carpet. There was a bar, some bar stools, a large table, a television set and a couple of armchairs. One of the rooms leading off the hall contained a grand piano and a settee. There was a big kitchen with every mod. con.

The main bedroom was furnished. The others were not. One of them served as a clutter room for Cicely and another as a study for Tony. In it he had a desk, a couple of chairs, a telephone, a portable typewriter, a tape machine and books which included the *Kinsey Report*, dictionaries and a glossy magazine about how the BBC Television Centre would look when it was finished. There was a white wall and shortly after he moved in he began writing on it in black crayon. His object was to chart the whole history of evolution.

Eventually, he would announce that he would write a comedy which embraced all life 'from the first plip to the final plop'.

When the local people first heard that Hancock was moving in it caused quite a sensation. Then they settled down and accepted them as ordinary neighbours. Hancock's eccentricity of never carrying any money around with him – already known and vaguely resented by members of the cast he would borrow from – became in time a burden local shopkeepers and publicans learned to cope with by referring bills to his accountant.

A few yards from MacConkeys was the Red Barn, a country club and restaurant, where much of the local social life took place. The Hancocks were frequent visitors there from the beginning and became very friendly with its owner, Mrs Eileen Fryer, a firm motherly lady of steady religious convictions.

When they went to Lingfield, the Hancocks were judged to be a decent married couple, very fond of each other, who had occasional rows and ups-and-downs just as everyone else.

Cicely enjoyed her rose and kitchen gardens and their two large poodles, Mr Brown and Charlie, were in heaven. Mr Brown had had a bad time with his previous owner and used to jump at shadows. Hancock was immensely sympathetic about this and felt that he should be able to do something about it, but couldn't quite think what.

He had a soft spot for animals though he turned down the offer of a basset hound because he felt its feet were similar to his. 'I'd look a right bloody fool, taking it out for a walk,' he said.

He was looking out of the window one day when he spotted a rabbit in the garden. 'Look, look,' said Hancock excitedly to a friend who was with him. He started to twitch his nose and do all sorts of rabbity things. He was delighted. They went out into the garden to have a closer look and found that the rabbit was suffering from myxomatosis. Hancock ran back into the house. It was Cicely who had to get a gun and shoot it.

Some of his favourite books were the Winnie-the-Pooh stories by A. A. Milne. He and Cicely used to sit up in bed reading them aloud to each other. Hancock hated Christopher Robin and though quite fond of Pooh himself preferred Eeyore. He particularly liked the story of Tigger's arrival. Tigger eats Eeyore's thistles, the ones he has been saving for a special birthday treat.

Piglet has introduced Tigger to Eeyore saying, 'He's just come.' Eeyore thinks for a long time, then says, 'When's he going?'

He and Cicely had a lot of stuffed animals about the house. They frequently held conversations with and about them. It could be a little unnerving for a visitor to walk into a room and find one or the other gravely addressing a stuffed penguin or engaged in conversation about the health of a teddy bear.

Sometimes Cicely would surprise everyone by suddenly coming out with a piece of idiomatically perfect Hancock. They were sitting in the garden one summer's day, Tony in shorts, when a bee buzzed about him and, finally settling on his bare knee, advanced onwards and upwards. Hancock, nervous about bees, sat there like a stone. Cicely leaned over and addressed the bee, 'I wouldn't if I were you, mate,' she said, 'it's horrible up there.'

Sid James and his wife Valerie, Galton and Simpson and a lot of other friends visited the house frequently. They observed, if they did not already know, that the Hancocks were drinking a lot. It had been happening for so long that it caused no surprise and little comment.

Between series, Hancock played in Gogol's *The Government Inspector* on BBC TV and it was commented that the part of the poor Russian clerk who takes advantage when the citizens of a provincial town mistake him for an official could have been written for him.

The Rank Organisation started talking about a film but Hancock backed out when, he said, 'they wanted to cut the money and put in a love interest.'

In 1958 he was again in the Royal Variety Show, this time held at the Coliseum. It is a vast theatre but the day before the show, a Sunday, nearly all the stalls were filled with agents, impresarios, newspapermen, friends of the cast and those in the cast who were not required on stage. The producer, Robert Nesbitt, sat about fifteen rows back, a small table set up in front of him with a telephone, papers and a half bottle of champagne. When Mr Nesbitt is working he discourages laughter, his attitude being that no one is at rehearsals to enjoy himself. This is understandable as he has only one day to create a spectacular and smooth-running show out of a huge company grossly overstocked with egos.

Laughter holds things up.

When the curtain went up on Hancock, Mr Nesbitt, who had been known to make a John Tiller girl feel small, was as powerless as Canute before the rising tide of laughter.

Hancock was in a cage dressed as a budgerigar. He strutted up and down, his head bobbing, admiring himself in the mirror, giving the bell a jab with his beak. He was hilarious and totally irresistible. The audience rocked backwards and forwards and howled with glee. Mr Nesbitt himself was observed to smile. There was no doubt who the hit of the 1958 Royal Variety Show would be.

At the actual performance itself Hancock's budgerigar never got off the ground. The performance was limp and bedraggled and the words were muttered into the feathers. 'It was,' wrote one critic, 'the brightest new idea in humour, but the cold audience froze it off the stage.'

It was not that at all. The audience did not freeze Eartha Kitt or Bruce Forsyth off the stage and they warmed so much to the then unknown Roy Castle that he made headlines the following day. The only thing wrong with Hancock was that he had given one good performance and that was enough.

On television he was still providing comedy in a crystal-clear stream. Off it, he became very cerebral and kept hazarding new definitions. 'Comedy,' he said, 'is frustration, misery, boredom, worry – all the things people suffer from.' They were all the things he was suffering from.

Not all the time, though. There were frequent visits to the South of France and generous invitations to friends to join him there.

One such holiday is remembered by Beryl Vertue, the former secretary at Associated London Scripts who became so efficient that the board of directors – Frankie Howerd, Milligan, Sykes, Galton and Simpson – put her in charge.

The Hancocks drove down in their spanking new pale blue Mercedes and were joined by Tony's mother, Galton and Simpson and Mrs Vertue.

'His mother,' says Mrs Vertue, 'is quite an extraordinary woman with a very dominant personality and Tony was like her in a lot of ways. She was something of a little actress, full of funny anecdotes and with a kind of feigned vagueness about how to tackle any particular problem. She would come on the beach with all her clobber and almost hold court.

'I remember one evening we had a super French dinner at a very ordinary place – Tony was not one for dashing off to the Negresco – and he knew the people who ran it intimately. It was very casual and he relaxed there. It was a second home to him. We had a lot of wine and then we played poker for matchsticks.

'The matchsticks were worth a fortune and the card game went on for hours. It was one of those rare occasions I remember being hysterical with laughter, he was so funny. Ray was doing particularly well and had a lot of matches. Tony didn't have any. He would look at Ray and in a very posh voice would say, "Mr Galton, I wonder if you could see your way clear to financing a little project." It was a happy time.'

There were other occasions when there was more strain. Once he took Spike Milligan and his first wife out to dinner in Antibes and recommended a fish dish. The fish was served whole and Mrs Milligan found the stare from the cold dead eyes a little unnerving.

'Oh, I couldn't eat that,' she said. Hancock was vastly irritated. 'That's that, then,' he grunted. 'Garçon! Some beans on toast and a cup o' tea.'

Mrs Milligan was very upset and Spike himself was not too happy. 'The meal fell apart from there on,' he says.

In many ways 1959 was a crucial year for Hancock. He finished his television series in November with a regular thirteen and a half million viewers, a record for any comedy programme, and signed a contract for ten more shows the following March.

He was again pronounced Comedian of the Year by the Guild of Television Producers and Directors and, this time, Galton and Simpson were named television writers of the year.

In the same year, Hancock's stepfather Robert Walker committed suicide. Hancock dashed to Bournemouth to be with his mother. The suicide upset him a great deal. He could not understand it as there seemed to be no reason behind it. As he left the inquest with his agent, Stanley Dale, Hancock said: 'That will happen to me one day.'

In his worst moments, Hancock was inclined to doom-laden apocalyptic pronouncements but, discussing the suicide with Freddie a couple of days later, he could say with equal conviction, 'It's a coward's way out. The only thing to do when life gets difficult is to take it on the chin.'

Nineteen fifty-nine was also the year that the inevitable finally happened and Freddie became his mistress. There would be times in the future when they would part but they always returned to each other. It took marriage to bring about the final, irrevocable rift.

'I ran away after each of the first two occasions we slept together,' says Freddie. 'Once I spent three months in America. I was scared of what I was getting into. But all the time we were parted I knew I could lift up the phone and get him back and he knew the same about me. I didn't know what would happen but I knew we would end up with each other.'

It would be another three years before they were actually to live with each other on any permanent basis, but it soon became clear that Hancock could not be confined to a peripheral role in anyone's life. He demanded total devotion and dedication even if he was not prepared to give it himself.

On one occasion, Freddie was about to hold a dinner party at her flat in Dorset Square when Hancock, who had not been invited, telephoned her and asked her to meet him at a pub in Hendon Way. She said she couldn't as she had friends coming to dinner. He insisted, became belligerent. 'It was easier to go there than to start arguing,' says Freddie.

She waited for him for two hours. When he came in he briefly apologised, explaining that he had met someone he just had to talk to, and offered her a drink.

She gave him a sharp no and they both climbed into her car. She backed into a post and drove angrily to Dorset Square. He followed her up the stairs.

She had ordered Chinese food from a restaurant. 'I don't like Chinese food,' Hancock complained. 'You're not invited,' Freddie said. 'You can go.'

Hancock said he would just sit there for a little while. The guests arrived and he sat hunched up in the corner while they ate.

'He was extremely unpleasant to everyone,' says Freddie, 'but was the last to go. I had to put up with this kind of ridiculous possessiveness. Of course I was annoyed but equally I was flattered. What woman isn't flattered by that kind of public attention? It was like a public declaration. I'd be inhuman if I said I wasn't flattered by it.'

Professionally, Hancock's main preoccupation was with thoughts of international status.

He had already been to America in an effort to achieve recognition. With Stanley Dale and Ronnie Waldman of the BBC Hancock visited New York in the early days of his television series, armed with half a dozen recordings of the show. The television executive they saw was very powerful and very courteous. In their presence he picked up his telephone and ordered a subordinate to make all the necessary arrangements for viewing facilities for the well-known British comedian Mr Tommy Hancock.[3]

Hancock saw Coney Island, Skid Row, Zero Mostel and a few other famous New York landmarks and came home.

Pondering the problem of becoming international, he decided upon three things. First of all he had to make a film; secondly, he had to prove once and for all that, much as he loved Sid James as a friend, he did not need him as a foil. Thirdly, he had to get out of East Cheam and drop such slang phrases as 'Stone me!' and 'bonkers' which he felt sure were preventing him from being understood by the Americans.

He was, in addition, mortally tired of 23 Railway Cuttings. He told Freddie: 'I've done everything in that bloody room except be indecent in it. I've stood all over it. I've touched all parts of it. I can tell you where every knot is in the wood. Where I burped. It's like a bloody death cell with an execution once a week.'

In May 1960 he made his last programme with Sid James and in July started work on *The Rebel*, his first starring film.

But before that happened the country was given its first glimpse of the troubled complex mind that lay behind the comic certainties of the Hancock they knew.

John Freeman – the British Ambassador to the United States of America from 1969 to 1971, formerly editor of the *New Statesman*, a past junior minister in the first post-war Labour Government, soon to be appointed High Commissioner for India – was the most successful, apparently self-effacing interviewer ever to imprint himself on television.

His manner was as gentle as his questions were probing. The title of his series was *Face to Face* and it was something of a misnomer. The viewer rarely saw Freeman's face; the camera kept on the subject, exploring *his* face, leaving it only to cut to the tensions expressed by the hands.

It could be a merciless ordeal.

Freeman had spent some time with Hancock before the interview took place and they had become friendly enough for Hancock to watch the transmission of the programme from Freeman's house in Hampstead.

Freeman's first question was, 'Are you in a mood to come clean and tell the truth?'

Hancock said he was. He said he had always wanted to do comedy and, looking like he did, perhaps it was the only thing to do.

(He genuinely felt that he was an unattractive man though he had frequent evidence to the contrary.)

Freeman pressed him about how much money he earned, putting it at £35,000 a year. Hancock denied this. Freeman refused to accept that he was getting less than £30,000 a year from the BBC and Hancock, embarrassed, shuffled out of it by saying, 'Just about,' possibly assuaging his conscience by the thought that a lot of it came from overseas. He added that there were long periods when he did not work.[4]

Comedy, Hancock said, was part of the business of finding the truth about life. 'It isn't a character I play,' he said. 'It's a part of me and part of everybody else I see!' There was no message; if you thought of it that way you would lose the intuition. He had, he said, often found in the scripts something that he had said in all seriousness and had been rather pompous about. But in the script it had been funny. He didn't dislike pomposity or affectation; he accepted them. 'There are certain things,' he said, 'I'd like to get away from now. They are impossible to talk about.'

Freeman asked him if he wanted to reform the world and he hastily answered that he was not capable of doing it.

Hancock said he had no religion though he was deeply interested in it and was trying to find faith. 'But I have had to throw away the initial faith – Anglican – and I am starting again from scratch,' he said.

Freeman found it hard to believe that Hancock had left his public school because he did not like the idea of being forced into a mould and pressed him about his opinion on his place in the class structure. 'Lower-middle-class?' hazarded Hancock and Freeman said, 'Yes, that's right.'

Hancock talked about his need to educate himself by reading. 'It seems as if for the first thirty years my eyes were closed,' he said.

Asked why he had no children he said he did not want any. He didn't know why and had nothing against children.

He was asked: 'Did you have a happy childhood?' and replied: 'Perhaps the earlier part, yes.'

Freeman questioned him about his breakdowns and Hancock said they were due to long-running stage shows and doing the same thing each night.

'Are you happy or not?' – 'I have been very fortunate. I have had everything anybody could want to make them happy. But the only happiness I could achieve is to perfect the talent I have, however small it may be.'

'Something appears to me to be eating you,' said Freeman.

'I wouldn't expect happiness,' said Hancock. 'I don't think that's possible. I am very fortunate in being able to work in something that I like. It's all anybody can ask.'

And he added: 'If the time came when I found that I had come to the end of what I could develop out of my own ability I wouldn't want to do it any more.'

Freeman summed up: 'You've got cars that you don't drive, health which you tell me is a bit ropey because you find it so difficult to learn your lines, money you can't really spend. You worry about your weight . . .'

Hancock: 'I didn't say my health was ropey. I spend the money. I do. I enjoy it.'

It was an interview that pressed hard and when the recording was seen by a number of BBC executives before transmission there were considerable doubts about whether it should be shown or not. Didn't Hancock come out looking a little shallow, a bit of a solemn ass? How would viewers take the disclosure that their lovable little man did not want children? Didn't he twitch rather a lot and wasn't there something a bit pathetic – in the wrong sort of way – about his craving for knowledge, about his pretensions towards the intellectual? Would it not harm their biggest human investment?

But when the interview was shown any abuse that was around was

Hancock as the incompetent recipient of an SOS call in 'The Radio Ham'

Above: Hancock, Frank Thornton and June Whitfield in Hancock's most famous television show, 'The Blood Donor', 1961. At this time, during the peak period of his career, Hancock was watched by 30 per cent of the adult population of the United Kingdom

*Above: In 'The Bedsitter',
1961, an astonishing and
unique monologue, Hancock
grapples with the mysteries
of philosophy. Far left: A
sequence from 'The Bedsitter',
showing the range and control
of Hancock's facial
expressions, and (left), also
from 'The Bedsitter', Hancock
receives a disappointing phone
call*

John Freeman interrogates Hancock in Face to Face. *Although Hancock liked and admired Freeman the interview had a disturbing effect on him*

Top: Hancock in the film The Rebel *as the London clerk who abandons his job to become an artist in Paris, where he meets a connoisseur, played by George Sanders (above left). In spite of the appalling quality of his work he is hailed as a genius (above right)*

Above: From left to right, the co-author David Nathan with Trevor Howard, Leslie Mallory and Hancock at the Cannes film festival in 1960

Right: The photograph of Freddie which Hancock carried with him on all his travels

Left: Hancock encouraged close-ups which gave access to his swift and subtle changes of mood

Hancock with impresario Bernard Delfont. The commercial television series, set up by Delfont, was not a success

heaped on Freeman. So much so that he was constrained to write to the *Daily Telegraph* to say:

> I judged, I believe correctly, that more of Hancock's complex and fascinating personality would appear on the screen if he was kept at pretty full stretch. I hope viewers generally did not equate that with hostility. I am sure Hancock didn't.
>
> May I, however, put it beyond doubt that I not only regard him, in public, as one of the half-dozen great comics of the age, but that I have a warm admiration and affection for his private integrity and intelligence.

'There are certain things I'd like to get away from now. They are impossible to talk about.'

Not in public certainly. In private he was talking more and more to Galton and Simpson and Duncan Wood about the need for change. They agreed with him. He told Duncan Wood that he was utterly frustrated with the limitations of the room in Railway Cuttings and the character in the Homburg hat and the coat with the astrakhan collar. He said that he would do no more *Hancock's Half Hours*. There were long meetings at Lingfield where they all sat round with miserable faces. Eventually, Hancock said he would carry on if they got rid of Sid James and the East Cheam setting.

Galton and Simpson understood. 'We went along with him,' they say, 'because we realised that Tony's success – or the show's success – could be maintained without Sid. He was a marvellous foil but he could work separately.'

As far as the change in setting was concerned, 'all we did was to move him from East Cheam to a bedsitting room in Earl's Court which is exactly where he would have lived if he'd had to move from East Cheam. The character didn't really change. It just wore a different hat and got a bit trendy.

'The basic thinking behind it was to go international. He thought the East Cheam set-up and Sid's cockney were much too parochial and that moving the character into more of a limbo land would make it more internationally acceptable.

Nor did Galton and Simpson have any objection to agreeing to Hancock's request to cut out the slang.

'We didn't take much notice of it really,' they say. 'All the slang we used would be understandable to anyone in context. In the six he did on his own we didn't change a bit. All we did was to take away the regular props and the regular cast.'

The BBC made substantial offers to induce Hancock and

James to stay together but, once he had made up his mind, Hancock could never be deflected by money – or very much else, for that matter.

The two men remained close friends, and sometimes holidayed together in the South of France.

Hancock and James only ever had one blazing row. They were playing pontoon and James stuck on twelve. Hancock said this was illegal; James said it was allowed. There was no point in arguing about the bigger issue of whether to stick or bust as a comedy team.

James would have liked to have continued with Hancock professionally, not for the money – he was getting plenty of lucrative film offers – but because he liked him so much.

Hancock shut the door on James firmly, if not brutally, as far as their professional life was concerned. Some years later James attempted to open it and for a few hours it looked as if he might succeed. He had been sent a film script written for them both. It looked good to him and he took it to show Hancock who was then appearing at the theatre-restaurant Talk of the Town. They spent most of the night discussing it and Hancock was enthusiastic. The following afternoon they met the producer and Hancock was still keen.

But the next day James got a letter from Hancock saying that he had had second thoughts and felt that it would be a backward step for him to work with James.

Recalling the incident later, James said: 'It was unbelievable. He just didn't want to know when the real chance for us to get back together came up.'

But James should have known.

He should have remembered that when Galton and Simpson wrote him into the film *The Rebel* with a couple of seconds' appearance just for a quick joke, Hancock made them take him out.

The Rebel cast Hancock as a bowler-hatted London clerk who abandons his job to paint pictures in Paris. His method is to slosh paint on a canvas and ride a bicycle over it. When someone else's work gets mistakenly attributed to him he is hailed as a genius. There were some easy gags at the expense of modern art but there was also some vintage Hancock.

'So anyway, I said to Dali, "Salvador, I said . . .”'

For one splendidly elaborate joke he reverted to the bird disguise he first tried at the 1958 Royal Variety Show. This time he was dressed as a canary for a fancy-dress ball held on a yacht. The yacht blows up and Hancock gets away in a speedboat still in his costume. He goes straight to the airport. 'I want to fly to London,' he says.

The day of the press show, Tony and Cicely, Galton and Simpson and Philip Oakes, poet, novelist and journalist, who had become friendly with Hancock after interviewing him for a literary magazine, spent most of the afternoon in a drinking club in Jermyn Street.

That night the Hancocks and Oakes continued the party by taking a suite at the Ritz. Dinner was served in the suite and there was a large decanter of port. Eventually they went off to bed.

In the morning Hancock saw that half the port was still left. He considered the problem for a while, then said, 'We'll have to take it away or those waiters will nick it all.'

If there is such a word, he 'undecanted' the remainder of the port by pouring it into an empty wine bottle. There was about 15s. worth. He then cheerfully paid his 45 guineas bill for the suite.

The Rebel was not well received by the film critics though *The Times* thought it a 'gratifying success'.

But the film made money and the distributors, the Associated British Picture Corporation, were happy about the three more films he had contracted to do for them.

More important, it was considered to be the best film début ever made by a British comic. The truth is that, Sellers apart, and Wisdom on a slapstick level, virtually no British comic has ever made a good start in films. Later, Hancock was to say about *The Rebel*: 'There were ideas I wanted to use but other people said no. When I saw it again six months afterwards I knew I'd been right. Next time I'm going to have more control over my own ideas.'

In the spring of 1961 Hancock went out on tour proving his immense pulling power by filling 3000-seater cinemas, the coachloads coming from miles around. He did 'The Crooner' and impersonated Robert Newton (then dead for six years) and Sir Laurence Olivier as Henry IV (Part II), and Richard III. John Vyvyan, the 4ft 11in. crumple-faced feed who was a constant guest at MacConkeys, was his stooge and would bustle on to say, 'Sir Laurence doesn't do it like that.'

'I know,' was the reply, 'but we can't all make a fortune out of fags.' (There was an Olivier cigarette on the market.)

He also had an act as a hapless juggler in which he was bombarded with hoops and balls and battled valiantly and hopelessly against his own incompetence and the malignancy of other people and things.

When he returned to London he began his last series of *Hancock's Half Hour*. He was out of East Cheam and without Sid James. And he created some of the most marvellous comedy ever seen.

Chapter Seven

On Friday, 26 May 1961, from 8 p.m. until 8.25 p.m. Hancock was truly alone. It was as if Galton and Simpson had challenged him to accept the full logic of his actions. They gave him a script which had no supporting cast whatsoever. He met the ordeal unflinchingly and overcame it superbly.

The opening shot was of the Earl's Court area, the heart of bedsitter land. All the houses have rows of nameplates and bell pushes. The camera focuses on one which says, 'Anthony Hancock No. 16.'

There is a dissolve into Hancock's room. The kitchen is in one corner, hidden by a curtain. A single bed is against one wall. A table stands in the middle of the room and there is a gas fire with a meter. In one corner is a television set and record player and a small radio.

There are some books open, face downwards on the table – *Das Kapital, The Outsider, Look Back in Anger, The History of Western Philosophy, The Intellectual in a Decadent Society* and *Glam* with a pin-up on the cover. Against the wall is a pole with a nuclear disarmament sign on it.

Hancock is lying on the bed, fully dressed, smoking a cigarette. He tries to blow smoke rings. He keeps trying until the cigarette burns his lips. He stubs it out, reaches for another, but the packet is empty. He tosses it away with irritation.

He lies there for a few moments then yawns.

He looks at his feet and wiggles them.

How much was Galton and Simpson? How much was Hancock? Look at the detailed instructions in the script:

'He then puts one foot vertically with the heel resting on the bed. Then he puts the other foot on top of it with the heel resting on the toes. He takes the bottom foot out and places it on top of the other one with the heel again resting on the toes. Now his two feet are a couple of feet off the bed. One on top of the other, thus causing a strain on his stomach muscles. These give way and his feet collapse on the bed. He rubs his stomach and winces.

'TONY:"Getting old."

'He relaxes again. Suddenly he realises his lips still hurt. He touches them delicately. He sticks the bottom one out as far as it will go and cocks his head to try and see the burn on it. He gets up with his lip still sticking out and goes to the sink. There is a cabinet above the sink. He opens it and looks at various bottles of medicine, ointments, pills, etc. All the bottles are old. The white stuff resting on the bottom and the brown stuff on the top. He takes an old bottle. Looks at the label.'

He reads the inscription on the bottle: *Master A. Hancock. To be taken as directed.* He can't remember what the directions were.

He rummages through the cabinet and finds all sorts of revolting objects – sticking plaster impregnated with lung syrup, a nose-dropper, ancient pills.

He decides to put some butter on his lip – 'a touch of the old New Zealand.'

His lip is still sticking out. So he does an impersonation of Maurice Chevalier. He consoles himself with the thought that he could have burnt his tongue and would have had to go round with his tongue sticking out. 'Very dangerous that. Meet a couple of Irish decorators and I'd be in dead trouble.'

He wonders if the milkman has been. He'd like a cup of tea. He looks at his teeth in the mirror. 'Is that loose or is it my fingers going in and out?'

He reminisces about the girls who have told him what a good set of teeth he has got. He wonders which one is the bicuspid. He tries out the word, savours it. Bi-cus-pid. He analyses it. 'Bi . . . meaning two. One each side. Cus . . . meaning to swear, I expect . . . pid . . . pid. I should think that's Greek. Greek for teeth. I should think. That's it then. Bicuspid. Two swearing teeth.'

He flops on the bed again. Starts reading. He can't remember who the characters are or what the book is about. All he recalls is that she'd met him and they'd gone up into the hayloft.

He attributes his lack of concentration to the fact that there is so much going on in his mind – nuclear disarmament, the future of mankind, China, learning Russian. It's hard to be an intellectual these days. It was easier in the Middle Ages – 'Read, write and know the Corn Laws and you were away.'

He perseveres. 'The intellect is the only thing worth having,' he tells himself. 'Let's have a go at old Bertie Russell.'

He reads a couple of sentences, looks puzzled, finds a dictionary. He has to consult the dictionary frequently. Then comments, 'Well, why don't they say so if that's what they mean.'

He doesn't know what Russell is talking about. But he presses on. 'It's in English,' he tells himself. 'I should know what he's talking about. He's only a human being same as me, using words, English words, available to us all.'

He very nearly comprehends something but it eludes him again. This time he blames Russell – a rotten writer. He tosses the book away and picks up a gaudy detective novel. He reads a few sentences and then has to consult the dictionary again.[5]

He tosses the detective story away, sighs, scratches himself, yawns, sings 'The Star-Spangled Banner' then lies there 'doing things with his mouth'.

He gets up, stretches, looks round, aimlessly picks up things, finds a chocolate box, shakes it. There is one left in it. He compares it with the plan on the box. Throws it back.

'Marzipan. Oh dear, oh dear.'

He paces aimlessly about the room again studying the way he walks, practising jumping to attention like a guardsman. He pretends to be a bandmaster and is numbering off in different voices when the telephone rings. He dashes to it eagerly but there is no one there. He goes on about telephones and people who get wrong numbers. He discovers there is no Q or Z on the dial and feels sorry for the people who have telephone numbers starting with Z and who are sitting at home wondering why nobody rings them.

He speculates what the telephone exchange would be – Zetland, Zebra, Zephyr, Zodiac, Zylophone.

The telephone rings again. He picks it up in a panic – the wrong way round. A girl is asking for Fred. He was the chap who lived there before. He starts a flirtation. He guesses her age. She guesses his. 'What do you mean, fifty?' They exchange names – Joyce and Anthony. He describes himself. 'You know . . . sort of well built . . . No, no not fat. Well built I said. Tallish. No, not quite six foot. Taller than average though . . .'

He tells her he does not work because he doesn't agree with the social system and has contracted out. He sits and contemplates. And he has his books. Bored? How could he be with his books?

Then to his delight she invites him to a party in place of the absent Fred. He will know her, she says, by her leopard tights and green sweater.

He starts singing with happiness at the prospect of getting in with all the spare birds who live in Earl's Court. He thinks he'll have another go at Bertie Russell. After two and a half hours it is time to get ready for the party and he is still on page one.

He dances round the room singing to himself as he chooses the right clothes – jeans, an open-neck shirt and a medallion round his neck. He lathers for shaving, sees himself with a soap moustache and does a quick impersonation of Harold Macmillan.

After the shave he takes some astringent, knows it will burn and hesitates. He applies it and yelps. Takes two tins of talcum powder from the cabinet. 'What shall we hit her with? The attar of roses or – in a deep voice – Prince William . . . for men.'

He has trouble in combing his hair so that it goes with the gear he's wearing. He tries a variety of styles. He sees a grey hair and goes ashen. He finds a lot more. Suddenly he is deflated. He is growing old. He is thirty-five and has achieved nothing. What is he doing going to parties at his age. He gets cocky again. He thinks he would look a sensation with grey hair. Look at Stewart Grainger, David Niven, Cary Grant. He has seen the world, knows what it's all about. He's got *savoir faire*. He is better looking now than when he was twenty. He is the type that improves with age.

'You're like old cheese,' he tells himself, hastily correcting it to old wine.

He is ready for anything. He wonders what is on television and looks at the programme guide in the paper. It is a gangster series. He mimes the opening, making a gun from his hand. It is either the gangster or Professor Bronowski. He feels it should be Bron-owski, but he had not been able to understand him last week when he was talking about time space. 'He's all right on theories but when it comes to adding up sums, he's right out of his depth.'

He switches on the television. The set only shows horizontal lines. He fiddles with it, bangs it, manipulates the indoor aerial, moves about the room with it. He stands on a chair in front of the set and holds the aerial above his head. A faint picture appears. When he gets down the picture goes away. He backs to the window, opens it and holds the aerial outside. He climbs out of the window and sits on the sill with his legs inside. The picture gets a little better. He shuts the window on to his knees. The picture gets quite good. He watches it through the window. It starts to rain. He comes back into the room and the picture immediately reverts to horizontal lines. He moves to the door with the aerial and goes outside. The picture comes on. He watches it through the crack in the door. He fiddles with the aerial and the picture becomes perfect. He puts the aerial down and tiptoes back into the room.

The picture goes back to horizontal lines as he is halfway

across. He steps back and the picture returns. He hovers on the spot, his eyes on the set. He sways and the picture comes and goes. He gets the picture right and stands rooted. He feels for a chair. As he sits, the picture goes into lines again. Hancock's face registers his reactions. (Galton and Simpson knew when to leave it to him.)

Then announcer Michael Aspel appears on the scene and proclaims regret for interference due to circumstances beyond their control.

He decides to get rid of his television set and invest the rental of 8s. 6d. on the football pools. The additional 408 lines will bring his total to 1500 lines. That should do the trick. He fantasises about the rich life. He is holding a party and excuses himself from Charles Clore and the Archbishop of Canterbury because he has just caught sight of the Duchess of Liechtenstein on her tod. He waltzes with her, gets dizzy and sits on the bed. Then he recalls that the first dividend last week was 15s. 9d. He covers himself with a blanket and tries to read the Bertrand Russell book again and goes to sleep. Dozing, he hears the sound of high heels pass the door. It is the girl upstairs going out. She is probably just waiting for him to make the first move. Without doubt, she fancies him. Tonight he'll have an early night. He has been overdoing things. The telephone rings. Sleepily, he says, 'Oh, it's you. Now what? No, I would not like to go out with you and Fred.'

As the camera pulls away he is saying, 'No, I'm not lonely, I'm quite all right by myself. Tell Fred thank you, it's nice of him to think of me, but I'm all right. Yes, what do you mean you feel sorry for me, what do you mean? I am not a poor little man. Now you listen to me, madam . . . pardon? I don't want you to come round and sit with me. Poky little bedsitter? How dare you, this is my home . . .'

Hancock prepared for this solo performance by getting another actor, Alec Bregonzi, to stand in for him during part of the rehearsals while he sat in the producer's gallery with Duncan Wood and studied the situations. He made suggestions to Wood about where and when the camera could move in closer, saying things like, 'I think I can do something with my face there . . . we can exploit that a bit more.'

There are few actors who can sustain a one-man performance. And those that can usually do it under the protective mask of some powerful personality out of life or literature.

Hancock did it in the knowledge that a large amount of his own personality was being exposed, even mocked at, and that the producer had no alternative but to keep the camera pointed at him for all but a few seconds of the 25-minute show.

But it certainly proved his point that he could work alone. And it also proved his dictum that great comedy could spring from 'frustration, misery, boredom, worry and insomnia'.

Of course, he had not been really alone. Galton and Simpson were with him.

It had been a good start but there was better to come. It was the time of 'The Radio Ham' and 'The Blood Donor' and if the series as a whole was the peak of his achievement, with a viewing figure that averaged 15½ million people, 'The Blood Donor' was the summit of the series. It was Hancock at his most pompous, most belligerent and most cowardly. It was gloriously, humanly funny.

It opens with Hancock self-importantly presenting himself at a hospital to give some of his blood. He has come in answer to their poster, 'the one on the wall next to the Eagle Laundry in Pelham Road. You must have seen it,' he tells the receptionist. 'There's a nurse pointing at you, a Red Cross lady actually, I believe, with a moustache and a beard, pencilled in of course. You must know it, it's one of yours next to Hands off Cuba, just above the cricket stumps. It says your blood can save a life.'

Hancock's blood is a precious liquid but he is in the mood to be a good citizen. He has been considering for a long time what form of social service this should take. It was, after all, the duty of every human being to do one unselfish act with no thought of profit or gain, something that was to the benefit of the country as a whole. It was a toss-up between becoming a blood donor or joining the Young Conservatives – 'but as I'm not looking for a wife and I can't play table tennis, here I am, a bodyful of good British blood and raring to go.'

Filling in the form presents the opportunity to fill in some of the background of the new, ex-East Cheam Hancock. He is only asked for his name but he gives her the lot – twice candidate for the county council elections, defeated, hon. sec. British Legion Earl's Court branch, treasurer of the darts team and the outings committee . . .

He is devious about his age. Reluctantly admitting to thirty-five. Nationality? 'You've got nothing to worry about there. It's the blood you're thinking about isn't it. British. Undiluted for twelve generations. One hundred per cent Anglo-Saxon with perhaps just a dash of Viking, but nothing else has crept in.'

This Hancock is so racialist and class conscious that he thinks his blood should not be given to anybody under a baronet. And no life peers.

The receptionist tells him that blood is the same the world over, classified by groups, not accidents of birth.

He tells her that he is not there for a lecture on Communism, young lady.

He is asked if he has ever given blood before. 'Given, no. Spilt, yes. There's a good few drops lying about on the battlefields of Europe.' And he starts reminiscing about von Rundstedt's last push in the Ardennes when he and Tiger Harrison were cut off . . .

Eventually, he joins the other waiting donors and immediately resumes his thoughts on the need for good citizenship. 'Some people all they do is take, take, take out of life, never put anything back. Well, that's not my way of living, never has been.'

Did they give them a badge for doing this? No? Pity. There should be something whereby other people could pick them out. Nothing grand, a little enamelled thing with a motto, nothing pretentious, he gaveth for others so that others may live, that kind of thing.

He irritates beyond measure his neighbours on the bench by his observations on how much he has given to charity. Left alone, he crosses his legs and bangs his knee with the side of his hand to make his leg jump up. It doesn't. He bangs harder. He still doesn't get a reflex action. He stops. The knee jerks up. He takes his pulse and can't find it, puts his hand over his heart and smiles in relief as he feels the beat.

The nurse returns and he goes on at her about her vocation and how hard it must be humping great trolley-loads of mince about all day long and with those bossy sisters . . .

The nurse is a sister.

He wonders if everything is all right, after all, he had seen poor devils pass out at the sight of a needle, men built like oak trees. No, needles didn't bother him. He is interrupted by being told that Dr McTaggart is ready for him. Hancock marches in nervously and greets him with:

'Ah, guid morning, it's a braw bricht moonlicht nicht the morning mista, it's a bonny wee lassie ye got there, helping you hoots . . .the noo.'

The doctor asks him to sit down in an educated English accent.

The doctor takes a smear for testing and Hancock believes he can now go off for his tea and biscuits. He is horrified when he is told that a pint is needed. He can't believe it. A pint! 'Why that's nearly an armful.' And he's not walking around with an empty arm for anybody.

It has all been a mistake; he's been misinformed. He'll do some other useful thing like becoming a traffic warden. The doctor says it is a great shame because he has a very rare blood group. Hancock is pleased. 'Rare eh? It's funny. I've always felt instinctively that I was somehow different from the rest of the herd. Something apart. I never fitted into society. I've never belonged . . . one of nature's aristocrats.'

He gives his blood.

Lying on a bed recovering, he has a long talk full of health clichés with his neighbour. 'The main thing is . . . look after yourself.' His neighbour says, 'You look after your body and your body will look after you.'

It is a chance for Hancock to air his knowledge.

'That's very wise. Of course, the Greeks they knew all this years ago.'

His neighbour is impressed. Hancock goes on about the Greeks and then applies his mind to the Common Market. The neighbour is more impressed. 'No man is an island,' he observes. Hancock is delighted. He agrees, adding, 'Necessity is the mother of invention.'

The platitudes stream out ending, as the man leaves, with Hancock enjoining him, 'Don't do anything I wouldn't do.'

Then, to himself: 'A nice man, that, a very nice man. Very intelligent. Good conversationalist. A cut above the type you meet down the pub.'

Then he discovers that the man has walked off with his wine gums.

Back home he keeps ringing Dr McTaggart. He wants to know if they have used his blood yet. He wants to make sure it goes to the right person. The doctor is extremely rude. Hancock puts the phone down and goes into the kitchen muttering that he will report him to the Hospital Management Committee. He cuts a slice of bread. Ambulance. Casualty ward.

Hancock has cut himself, and fainting, has lost a lot of blood. They have just one pint of the right blood in stock. He gets it. Dr McTaggart comes in and groans at the sight of him. 'He only gave it yesterday,' he tells the doctor treating Hancock.

'At least,' says Hancock, 'I know it's going to the right sort of person.'

Hancock works it all out:

'These blood banks are just like ordinary banks really. Put it in when you're flush, draw it out when you need it. Come on bang it in, I'm getting dizzy. I'll let you have it back later on. (To nurse) Do you get tea and biscuits after getting blood as well? What's on the menu tonight? Got any mince?'

That script is a work of art. Hancock did it hardly knowing one line.

The previous week, driving home with Cicely after the broadcast there had been a slight accident and Hancock had gone through the windscreen suffering minor concussion.

Rehearsals for 'The Blood Donor' were due to start on Monday and carry through until Saturday for recording on Sunday. Hancock could not rehearse until Thursday when he arrived at the studio looking like a panda with his two black eyes. He did not know one line of the script as he was having trouble seeing properly and even if he had been able to read, the minor concussion, on top of his usual difficulty in learning, would have prevented him from remembering.

It was proposed that the show should be cancelled but Hancock insisted that it should go on. By Sunday he had learned about four of the forty-three pages and the rest were on teleprompters and what, in the studio, are called idiot boards.

When it came to transmission, experts could spot that his eyes were always looking a little to the side of the camera but the public reaction was so good that Hancock gratefully relinquished his terrible burden of learning lines. He did the remaining three in the series with the aid of idiot boards and teleprompters and believed that he could always get away with it.

He was wrong. But there were other things bothering him.

The most important was to find the right subject for his second film. If there is one thing more difficult than making a successful début it is making a successful follow-up.

Hancock could now control his films absolutely. He could choose his director, his supporting actors and his writers. He was almost at the stage achieved by his twin film idols – Jacques Tati and Charlie Chaplin. It was not the pathetic Chaplin he admired. He despised pathos and when he used it he invariably ended by puncturing it.

'The idea of the "little man" in comedy is mostly mistaken,' he told journalist Philip Purser in an interview for the *Sunday Telegraph*. 'Chaplin is always referred to as a little man. Sometimes he is extremely aggressive. Remember the scene in *City Lights* when he is in a Rolls-Royce and he gets out of the car, kicks a tramp in the stomach, picks up a cigar butt and drives off. Nowadays you would probably be advised not to do it. Only the great could get away with it.'

In the same interview he said: 'It is difficult to avoid sounding pompous, but I do believe comedy is terribly important in the world today and can really help. When people say that you really have made them laugh and they say it honestly, it is not a thing to throw away and say it doesn't matter. It is a compliment. It is the real thing.'

The consultations with Galton and Simpson about the next film were long and arduous. Hancock was very worried and wanted it to be absolutely right. Galton and Simpson virtually moved in to MacConkeys during the preliminary discussions. They came up with an idea that all three were enthusiastic about. Tony would be the black sheep of four brothers. The other three were very successful and when their father died, Hancock would return from abroad and work for each of his brothers in turn, a destructive, anarchic force.

Galton and Simpson left him at Lingfield and had written about a third of the film when Hancock telephoned them to say that he had thought about the idea and it wasn't international enough.

Galton and Simpson said, 'Fine, we'll try again,' and returned to Lingfield. This time they decided to send Hancock on a cruise. There would be no plot, just incidents that happened day by day. It would, of course, be very international. Hancock was pleased with the idea and they went away again to write.

Hancock telephoned them before they had finished and said it was so much like *Monsieur Hulot's Holiday* that people would make comparisons.

They tried again. This time Hancock, to quote Galton and Simpson, 'really went overboard for the idea'. The working title was *The Day Off* and it was just about a man's day off from work and what he does with it. Galton and Simpson spent two months writing it and then Hancock decided that he did not want to do it.

By this time they had worked six months without earning any money and they told him they could not spare any more time.

Hancock told them: 'You do some television. I've got an idea I'd like to work on a bit and when you've finished the television perhaps we can get back together and do it.'

His idea, he told them, was about a Punch and Judy man. They had already discussed it earlier but could not see any development.

It is untrue to say that there was no bitterness in the subsequent break-up of the Galton and Simpson-Hancock partnership. Hancock insulted them in a way which would be wounding to any writer – he did not bother to read their work. To do it to two men with whom he had travelled so far was even more hurtful.

'We were terribly annoyed and upset,' they say. 'We put in a hell of a lot of work and then he just turned round, without even reading the first two scripts, and said, "It's just not right. We can do better; we can get something to really knock their eyes out."'

He had changed his mind about the ideas; there was no reasoned and detailed rejection.

While all this was going on Hancock spent a lot of time in the offices of Associated London Scripts, now in Orme Court, Bayswater, talking to his agent Mrs Vertue.

'It was almost as though he was willing Ray and Alan not to write a script he would like,' says Mrs Vertue. 'He kept saying things to me like, "I'm sure I'm not going to like it." He seemed to have conditioned himself not to like it.'

Hancock had taken a flat in the White House, a large block of anonymity near Regent's Park with a bar, restaurant and swimming pool. It was there that he called Galton and Simpson and Mrs Vertue to a meeting on Sunday afternoon in the autumn of 1961.

Within a few minutes of their arrival Hancock said bluntly, 'I have decided that I don't want to do any more programmes with you.' Then he turned to Mrs Vertue and said with equal bluntness: 'Because of your involvement with Alan and Ray it would be too embarrassing for you to look after me so I don't want you to do that either.'

Says Mrs Vertue: 'We were all staggered. It was the first time I personally had seen his ruthless quality. He had given no warning and made no apology. The boys had gone up there expecting him to criticise the film: I'd gone simply because he had asked me.

'I felt desperately near to tears and the terrible shock of it made me ill for a week afterwards. He had already abandoned Sid James and the way he did that was unhappy, but to abandon Alan and Ray . . . He could afford to abandon me because there are other good agents in London who could have looked after him. But I couldn't understand about Alan and Ray. They wrote for him so marvellously that when you heard the three of them talking together it was like a script in itself. They were him and he was them. They created this character between them. They observed him so closely and he gave so much that something marvellous came out of it. But it was more than that. We were devoted to him and he dismissed the friendship of years in an effort to attain a height in his career which we could all have helped him to achieve out of friendship and regard.'

Hancock's brother Roger was a key man in the agency by this time. Tony insisted that his brother should leave with him and look after him. It caused some disruption. And the arrangement lasted only a few years.

Hancock's decision to part company with Galton and Simpson came as a shock to the BBC.

Tom Sloan pleaded with Hancock to change his mind, using the usual arguments that you don't give up a winning streak, that there was room for development. Hancock would not budge. He said he felt the character and the setting had been exhausted. More money was offered.[6]

Even Sid James generously tried to persuade Hancock that he had made a grave error. It was no use.

Sloan tried to salvage what he could from the wreckage. He told Galton and Simpson: 'How would you like to write ten comedy programmes, all different? We will cast them as required and call it *Comedy Playhouse.*'

Galton and Simpson agreed. Number five in the series was 'Steptoe and Son'. Its eventual shattering success when turned into a series with Harry H. Corbett and Wilfrid Brambell did much to soothe the wounds Hancock had inflicted.

Hancock never worked for the BBC again except obliquely when BBC2 televised his Festival Hall performance against Tom Sloan's judgement.

There was a meeting a few years later between Hancock, Sloan and Donald Baverstock. They had dinner together.

Sloan says: 'He came up with some idea. I can't remember what it was but it was rotten. Donald and I were quite sure at the end of the dinner that Tony was totally unrepentant about his mistakes. We could see no future whatever in what he was proposing.'

The stress and strain that Hancock was undergoing was reflected in a deeper attachment to the bottle and, as usual, in a rougher, tougher time for Freddie.

In this way, after 101 radio scripts and 51 television shows, one film and an assortment of stage material, Hancock shut the door on Galton and Simpson.

Chapter Eight

When Hancock moved to Lingfield, Oakes was living about ten miles away. They had become good friends and there was frequent, but vague talk about them writing something together. Hancock spent part of the summer travelling. He went to film festivals in Beirut in Lebanon and Karlovy Vary in Czechoslovakia.

By the time he went to New York in October 1961 for the American première of *The Rebel* he had broken with Galton and Simpson and had arranged with Oakes that they would write *The Punch and Judy Man* together on his return.

Hancock went off to the US with high hopes and a dream that *The Rebel* would introduce him to the star-spangled stages of Las Vegas where he would take his place alongside Frank Sinatra and Noël Coward and all the other high-ranking performers labelled with that most potent of words – international.

He also wanted to see Las Vegas because he had the idea by then of creating a vast entertainment complex in London comprising a theatre, cinema, restaurants and bars where the very best would be available at popular prices. The gambling city, though not exactly designed to cater for the proletariat, was nevertheless practising multifarious entertainment and he could hope to pick up a few pointers.

The New York critics loathed *The Rebel*, retitled *Call Me Genius* for the American market. Hancock fled America but could not face a direct return to England. Instead he went to Paris from where he called Oakes and asked him to join him, ostensibly to start work on *The Punch and Judy Man*.

Oakes arrived at Hancock's hotel near the Arc de Triomphe. It was in the Rue des Acacias. 'It is,' Hancock was fond of observing ruefully, 'a long way to go to get to Acacia Avenue.' He and Oakes conscientiously bought paper and carbons and arranged for a room equipped with a table to be set aside for them to work in.

They sat there for three days, then Hancock proposed that he should take Oakes on a *tour gastronomique* of Paris. It turned out to be a tour *alcoholique*. After three days Hancock had to take to his bed, ill. Hancock insisted that it was due to bad oysters.

Hancock decided to return to England. He was convinced that the press would be waiting for him at the airport to question him about the bad notices *The Rebel* had got in New York so he planned elaborate avoiding action. They cashed in their air tickets, travelled to Calais, and took a boat to Dover where Oakes's wife, already briefed, was waiting for them in a car.

Oakes, who was now living in Kent, moved into MacConkeys with the Hancocks to work on the new film.

Hancock had dug deep into boyhood memories of Bourne-mouth and saw the Punch and Judy man, the sand sculptor and the beach photographer as anarchic artists at odds with the stifling respectability of the seaside burghers.

He had a theory, possibly based on his own experience and certainly not very original or profound, that if a man played a certain role for long enough and often enough it would affect his real life. He did not think, for instance, that it was possible for someone who manipulated the ferocious marital disputes of Punch and Judy to have a happy domestic life.

Oakes would urge sleepy, bedraggled Hancock to rise at 8.30 every morning and get down to work. Oakes would write and Hancock would suggest and develop. Oakes would create a situation and ask Hancock how he would react in it. Hancock would sometimes come up with good lines and sometimes his reactions would suggest a wholly new development.

The opening scene of the film shows Hancock as the Punch and Judy man and his wife, played by Sylvia Syms, coming down to breakfast and eating without saying a word to each other. The sequence, a quarter of an hour long, is punctuated by the sound of rattling crockery, crunching toast, rustling paper and shifting chairs. It firmly establishes a marriage that is held together only by habit.

Hancock told Oakes: 'It's an atmosphere of mutual hatred – that's what it's about.'

And Oakes says: 'He knew, without any equivocation at all, that the film was about him and Cicely.'

Hancock and Oakes moved to Hancock's *pied-à-terre* at the White House and continued working on the script there, 'in order to be removed from domestic pressures'.

Opposite, a terrace of houses was being demolished and throughout the day they were battered by the noise of a huge steel ball as it swung against the brickwork.

One of the White House services is the provision of milk machines in the corridors and Hancock and Oakes would regularly stock up with milk whenever they felt they should be taking some nourishment. When they left there were 144 cartons of milk in the refrigerator.

Freddie was by now firmly established as mistress, mother-substitute and publicist, her main function in the latter job being to shield her client from publicity. She had grown so adept at putting down Hancock's increasingly frequent dashes into nursing homes and clinics of all kinds to 'strain' and 'virus pneumonia' and other euphemisms that he told her, 'One day you'll run out of diseases.'

She helped to sustain life in the two captives in the White House by supplying them with pies and by cooking the occasional meal for them. 'Trust me,' he used to say with mock resignation, 'to get a girl-friend called Fred.'

Some afternoons when the script was proving more than usually obdurate, Oakes, Freddie and Hancock went to the zoo. Hancock was greatly bothered by Guy the gorilla, and was both fascinated and saddened by the chimpanzees.

One evening they went off to see *Stop the World, I Want to Get Off*, the Tony Newley-Leslie Bricusse musical which was all about the sadness of being a clown. Hancock saw it five times in all and wept. He identified strongly with one of the songs, 'What kind of Fool am I?' There was at the time a tendency to wallow in self-pity. He also wept when he played – as he did frequently – Siobhan McKenna's record of the Molly Bloom soliloquy from *Ulysses*. Often he just sat and watched television, roundly cursing, whenever he got the chance, one particular comic he claimed had pinched all his mannerisms.

By this time he had made up his mind that *The Rebel* had been, he told Oakes, 'an excruciatingly vulgar' picture and that he hated it passionately. *The Punch and Judy Man* was going to be different.

The script was eventually finished and the studio bosses liked it though they suggested that the ending could be broadened a little. Hancock and Oakes both thought they might be right and tried all sorts of slapstick. But eventually the ending was left pretty much as they had written it – a kind of dying fall and a gritting of the teeth with life going on despite everything. The finished product was perhaps a slightly coarsened version of the original.

'Christ,' Hancock told Oakes, 'if this doesn't work I'm completely finished and I'll never work again.'

He wrote to Sir Arthur Bliss, then Master of the Queen's

Musick, asking him if he would write the score for the film. Bliss replied that while he tremendously admired Hancock, he was too old. Hancock carried the letter around with him until it fell to pieces.

Shooting on *The Punch and Judy Man* started on 2 April 1962, at ABPC studios, Elstree, with locations at Bognor Regis.

An announcement was also made that there would be a new television series, this time for the commercial channel, ATV, made by Hancock and London impresario Bernard Delfont.

Back at Lingfield, things were deteriorating rapidly. The drinking was on a phenomenal scale and Cicely told her mother: 'What goes down my throat does not go down his.'

The awful irony was that Hancock, like many men, found the sight of drunken women repellent.

In an effort to patch things up Hancock first bought Cicely a string of pearls, his first major present to her, and then, overcoming his superstition about things green – and as a gesture to Cicely who was part Irish – a diamond and emerald ring which cost more than £1000.

Things got worse. The ring was several times thrown at him or thrown away and – as many of the scenes took place in the Red Barn, by now no longer a country club but a guest house and therefore more private – Mrs Fryer frequently rescued it. Hancock, the disciple of Bertrand Russell, apostle of the power of reason, blamed the ring.

He often went away saying he was leaving Cicely but usually returned after a few days. After one big row he left home once again but later telephoned Mrs Fryer and asked her to make arrangements to get rid of the ring. It was changed to a single stone diamond. Nothing else changed.

The violence started. He occasionally hit Cicely but he did not always have it his own way.

'My dear,' says her mother, Mrs Romanis, who like her husband remembers Hancock with deep and abiding affection, 'she hit back. She was frightfully strong and she knew a certain amount of ju-jitsu. She knocked Tony down one night. But I don't know how it ever got to that pitch.'

Despite the scenes and the terrible bloodiness and bitterness of a marriage foundering on a sea of drink, Hancock was still capable of extraordinary acts of kindness and thoughtfulness.

Mrs Fryer remembers how, at a time when he had every reason to avoid journalists, an old flintlock pistol was found in the Red Barn's pond and Hancock insisted that he should pose for some pictures with it in order to give the place maximum publicity.

Once Philip Oakes casually mentioned that his parents-in-law were going to France via Dover. Immediately Hancock telephoned all the officials he knew there and, to their gratified astonishment, the couple were whisked aboard the boat with full VIP treatment.

And he frequently descended on old people's homes in the Lingfield area with enormous parcels of goodies. Once, when he found the press waiting for him, having been called by the superintendent, he warned that if it ever happened again there would be a swift end to the visits.

He had taken to Mrs Fryer, marvelling at her broadly based, immovable, undoubting faith, and there were long conversations, sometimes lasting until 7 a.m., in which he questioned her about her certainties and discussed his doubts.

Priestley, in his book *London End*, describes the comedian he calls Lon Bracton – who he now says is a portrait of Hancock in every way except physically – as follows, firstly through the eyes of his American agent:

> Tried nearly everything, Lon has. Been analysed twice the lot. Look – half the time – no, say a third – he's a wonderful hardworking comic. For two years they worshipped him on the box – television I mean. They rolled over soon as they heard his name. Then suddenly he couldn't do it – broke his contract – doctor's orders of course. Same with pictures. Same with live shows.
>
> The money's been enormous, but even so I've had more trouble with him than any other three clients put together. 'Cos the other two-thirds of the time Lon's beany, foofoo, nutty as a fruit-cake. It's not the sauce, the hard stuff, though he can lap it up. It isn't even the women though there's always one around, sometimes married to him, sometimes not. It's Lon himself. He's several people. He goes to the can a good sweet guy and comes back a lousy bastard. You help yourself to a drink, turn round, and it isn't the same fella. He'll keep you up and you'll be falling about laughing, and the very next day he'll tell you he can't work. For weeks on end he can be more dippy-batty than half the people put away in mental homes. Yet when he's really working and it's all coming through, I tell you, this is a great comic – the best we've got.

Later, after the agent and Professor Tuby, the man he is consulting about Bracton's 'image', have been turned away from the comedian's door by his 'bodyguard', an ex-pugilist (Hancock about this time became friendly with an ex-wrestler, Stan Gibbons, who used to describe himself as Hancock's 'bodyguard'), the agent says:

> You'd think he was lushing it up – or had three girls in there – wouldn't you? Or a poker game, maybe. No, sir! My bet – and one gets you five – all he's doing up there is reading a book. Some days you can't stop him. He just has to read books. Can you beat it?

And he adds: 'I don't think he knows what the hell he's reading.'

Tuby concludes that Bracton 'would have been a happier man if he'd stayed at the end of a pier pulling faces'. Bracton's chief trouble, he says, 'is that he has far too much money for the sense he's got. It's as if a child were given a full-sized locomotive to play with. On twenty pounds a week Bracton would probably be a sensible fellow. With hundreds and hundreds of pounds a week he's insufferable.'

Eventually, he diagnoses Bracton's basic trouble and suggests the remedy. He tells him:

> You're a neurotic man who plays an even more neurotic man. Instead of trying to fight it, you go right along with it. Any audience you have will always have its share of neurotic people, but you, Lon Bracton, will never fail to seem a damn sight worse than they are.
>
> And they'll tell one another – not just the neurotic types but the whole of them – that Lon Bracton's just as barmy off stage as he is on it – crackers – bonkers! And as long as you watch your timing – and you know all about that, Lon – you can go on and do almost anything you like – and they'll love it. You could eat your supper and read the evening paper on the stage – and they'd still love it.

Tuby proposes:

> From now on you don't suppress your neurotic condition, you exploit it. You don't try to behave normally and rationally and then do something enormously silly . . . you indulge your whims and fancies all the time. And if you do that, you'll probably be quite sensible about important things.

Tuby has been to see one of Bracton's films. 'Bracton had his funny moments,' Priestley writes,

> but all too often he just missed the mark . . . Unequal as Lon Bracton might be, when he was absent from the screen the film was trifling and tedious.

Certainly, Hancock had a puritan guilt about money but it is by no means likely that he would have been happier pulling faces at the end of a pier for £20 a week. The man was driven by ambition and prepared to sacrifice anything and anyone to it.

It was not necessarily ignoble; in fact, there was something almost impersonal about it. He had a vocation to entertain and make people laugh as strong as any felt by priest or doctor. And vocation is only another more sensitive word for compulsion. The more he drank the less he was able to meet the demands his comic genius made upon his talent.

It was in this way that he started on *The Punch and Judy Man*.

He had been dissuaded, not without some effort, from directing it himself.

Instead, he chose Jeremy Summers, a competent young director. It would have needed someone with the combined authority of John Huston, Sir Carol Reed and David Lean to manage Hancock at this stage.

Sylvia Syms recalls: 'He would discuss an idea with you which was so funny he'd have you rolling on the floor and you'd think "Gosh, that's marvellous", and the first time he did it it would be marvellous. But he'd never leave it at that and would do it again and again until he killed it. He'd make the director do it over and over again and you would see it die in front of you. It was almost as though Tony didn't want it to be good.'

Hancock was what is called a reaction comic. A tremendous amount of his comedy came from close-ups of his face over which the expressions could chase each other like Keystone Cops on the heels of a fugitive, only infinitely more subtle.

His face was his fortune and his face was stiffening with drink. His reactions were slow; his timing was going . . . 'And as long as you watch your timing – and you know all about that, Lon . . . you can go on and do almost anything you like.'

It is when the timing goes that things stop being funny for no apparent reason.

There was a sequence in a milk bar when Hancock and a small boy – actually Sylvia Syms' nephew Nicholas Webb – faced each other eating huge ice-creams. Hancock hated ice-cream but kept insisting that the scene should be reshot. Between each take he washed out his mouth with vodka. The scene lasted seven minutes on film which was far too long. When it was suggested that it should be cut to five minutes Hancock threw a temperament and insisted that it should all be kept in.

Nicholas, eight years old at the time, got on well with Hancock.

The comedian spent hours playing snap and other games with him. Nicholas not only learned his own lines but everyone else's. If Hancock paused he would prompt him: Hancock remained tolerant.

He had long discussions with Miss Syms about children. She was pregnant at the time and having already had two miscarriages, had adopted a little boy.

Hancock kept asking her why she was having another child when she knew it was dangerous and she told him that it was not so dangerous that she could die and thought it worth the risk.

He told her: 'I don't ever want children. I don't want the responsibility.'

'Yet,' she says, 'he seemed obsessed with talking about them, and I couldn't understand his attitude.'

Once she got angry with him and said: 'You are moaning because you are lonely yet you won't take the step that will change your life and give you responsibility.'

It was, perhaps, goaded by this that one day he suddenly announced that he and Cicely were having a baby.

Philip Oakes and Miss Syms were delighted at the news and congratulated him and Oakes made some comment like, 'Oh, Cicely's pregnant, is she?'

Hancock said: 'No. We've just decided we are going to have a baby.'

It was clearly fantasy.

When Hancock married Freddie she wanted to have children but his psychiatrist told her not to have one until Hancock had kept off the drink for at least eighteen months. 'I wanted to have one to give him some kind of stability and to prove to him that I cared about him,' says Freddie. 'He was strange with children. He said he didn't understand them or get on with them but my little niece, for instance, adored him and worshipped him. And he adored her. Tony always said that Cicely did not want to have children; that she was frightened of the actual birth. I don't know whether this was true or not.

'At the end I don't think Tony was capable of having children; the drink must have destroyed his capability. I think if they had had a child it would have made a great difference to Cicely. But when people used to ask me if I had any children I would say, "Yes, one." When they asked boy or girl and how old, I would say, "Boy, aged forty-four."'

Cicely frequently visited the studio while *The Punch and Judy Man* was being made and whenever she did there were more rows, more drinking. Her appearances grew to be resented by the actors and technicians because of the disruptions they heralded.

Gradually a pall descended upon everyone concerned with the film. About halfway through, Hancock himself lost heart, looked around for someone to blame and decided that the culprit was Punch.

Pat Williams is a writer who got to know Hancock shortly before shooting started on *The Punch and Judy Man*. She was writing a book on the supernatural at the time and at MacConkeys for 'one of those long, endless drinking days' she started fooling about with fortune-telling. She took Tony's hand and he withdrew it rapidly with an, 'Oh no you don't.' She asked: 'Why?' and he said: 'I don't want to know. All this is much closer to me than you realise and I'm scared; I hate it.'

'I got the feeling,' says Miss Williams, 'that he was immensely sensitive to all kinds of things. He knew he was destroying himself and didn't want to know; he knew that he was being stupid about his friends and he didn't want to know. He knew that all this information about himself was just behind a thin partition in his mind and he didn't want to know.'

Once at a dinner party the subject of drugs like LSD and marijuana came up. Hancock was almost hysterically against the idea of using them. But not on moral grounds. 'I simply don't want to know what's inside me,' he said. 'There's so much there it would destroy me if I knew. It would destroy anyone if they knew what was inside them. It's very wrong.'

Hancock told her that he was sensitive to people's feelings and could feel warmth or cold in them, almost immediately he met them.

'He was almost mediumistic,' Miss Williams said. 'He didn't like it.'

He did not talk in terms of faith healing but he said he could tell just by touching people how they were feeling and he felt he was able to influence them.

She was visiting the *Punch and Judy* set when Hancock took her aside. They sat on a couple of boxes in a darkened corner and there was a long silence.

Then he said: 'It's very important, this.' Pat waited. Hancock just said one word – 'Doomed'. She asked him what he meant. 'It's Punch,' he said, 'he won't let it happen.'

Hancock had tried to master the 'swozzle', the little gadget that, stuck in the roof of the mouth, produces the Punch voice. He was terrified of swallowing it. A real Punch and Judy man did all the voices. Shortly after he finished the film the Punch and Judy man died. So did Mario Fabrizi, a support comedian of whom Hancock was extremely fond.

The unit went on location at Bognor Regis. Hancock had written to George Fairweather in Bournemouth asking him to dig up some memories about sand sculptors.

As a reward he promised Fairweather a small part in the film. When the call came, Fairweather was cutting hair in his barber's shop but he set off on his motor-bike for Bognor. It was cold and wet and filming did not finish until 11 o'clock. He shared a room with Hancock that night and they talked until 5 a.m. about the old concert-party days. Hancock plundered George's memories and recollections of his father. George, a very practical man whether cutting hair, playing golf or performing comedy, said: 'Where are the funnies in this film? Where are the laughs?'

Hancock said: 'It's not supposed to be funny.' George told him, 'It will die; it will fall on its ear.'

'I don't care whether it does,' said Hancock. 'I'm going to prove to them that I'm all right.'

'You know what's the matter with you,' said George. 'You're trying to do a Chaplin.'

Hancock grinned and admitted that his ambition was to write, produce, direct and act in a film. He would have wanted to turn the camera and get the tea as well if it were possible.

In fact, he did operate the camera a couple of times on *The Punch and Judy Man* but the results were so obviously disastrous that he gave it up.

While at Bognor, Pat Williams gave him a slinky, one of those toys made of fine coiled steel that seems to move, snake-like, with a life of its own.

It frightened Hancock. He did not just throw it away, he tried to destroy it. He hit it and stamped on it and then, because coiled, sprung steel is very difficult to destroy, he took it down to the beach at night and buried it.

The panic mounted in Hancock.

It spread inside him making insatiable demands for reassurance. Work and vodka and love were temporary alleviations, analgesics that dulled for a short while the sharp edges of despair.

He and Freddie were going through one of their temporary separations and he fancied himself in love with Sylvia Syms and, both nervous for different reasons, they joked their way around and out of this fantasy.

They were sitting talking in her dressing room when 'he just looked at me with a terribly sweet expression, a sort of quizzical smile and said, "Do you fancy me?" '

She laughed and said, 'I love you, you're gorgeous – a lovely feller.'

'I don't half fancy you,' said Hancock, keeping the mood light and jokey, waiting warily for the rebuff. 'What about it?'

Sylvia laughed, shattering the highly-charged moment into fragments.

'There was just a minute of seriousness in it,' she said later. 'He was looking so much for somebody, not for me – really not for me. He wasn't an Adonis, he wasn't attractive in that way but he had this dangerous thing – you wanted to help him and you wanted to mother him. You wanted to say, "Go on, love, it's going to be all right," and put your arms round him. But when he said this I suddenly realised that he wanted more. But I would have been no use to him at all because he frightened me as well. He was never violent when I was there. But I'm afraid of people when they're drunk. Once or twice I would get this set expression on my face. I suppose, a look of rather puritan disapproval, and he'd look at me black with thunder and I knew he wanted to say, "Oh, turn off that crappy face," but he wouldn't. He'd turn it into a kind of joke and say, "Oh gawd, there's old fiddle face again." '

As the film dragged on Hancock became more and more difficult.

Back at the studios, his dressing room was always thronged with people and he began complaining about 'the buggers all sitting round and drinking my drink'. Oakes got so fed up that he gave him a cheque for £20. Hancock carried it around with him for three weeks but eventually cashed it.

He was appallingly rude to interviewers who can be a nuisance but who are generally considered as inherent a part of film-making as, putting it at its lowest, the third assistant director. He as good as told one television interviewer that he thought him a homosexual because he had long fingernails. Needless to say, he had selected a well-known heterosexual and the man stormed off in a fury.

The publicity man on the film resigned and Oakes took over his duties. He had to make sure that all applicants were sympathetic and unlikely to ask awkward or silly questions; a difficult, virtually impossible, task.

Eventually work on the film was completed and everyone slunk away. The atmosphere was bitter. All the same, Hancock remembered to give young Nicholas a handsome chess-set as a parting present. When the film was ready it was not even given a West End première, a sure vote of no confidence by the distributors.

The general critical reaction was mirrored by the *Daily Mail* with its headline, 'This Just Isn't Your Kind of Film, Tony,' but *The Times* again found some merit in it, saying that it was 'Mr Hancock's Best Film' – it was only his second, after all – and detecting a kinship in it with W. C. Fields.

The film lost a lot of money. The other three films due under Hancock's contract with ABPC were never made.

After shooting finished Oakes was retained by Hancock as script adviser on his new ITV series. Hancock started commissioning scripts himself and Oakes did not like them. There were arguments. Hancock told him, 'What the bloody hell do you know about it? I'm paying the money.' Oakes resigned.

As Hancock himself had not shut the door this time, the breach was not irreparable. When the BBC wanted him to do a regular hour-long record programme called *Listen with Hancock* Oakes evolved a formula in which every record was linked by a personal reminiscence, chatter about people Hancock had known or some of his ideas. Hancock turned it down. After all, how could he natter on jokily about the good old days with Galton and Simpson or Sid James and all the others? He thought by now that most of the people from his past hated him because of the way he had treated them. He reasoned that they had every right to. In fact, no one who knew him ever hated Hancock.

Occasionally he and Oakes ran into each other. The last time they met, Hancock was eager for Oakes to do another film with him. 'I've got this idea and we must go into it,' he said.

But it was the same old stuff he had been talking about for years, his film about the evolution of man 'from the first plip to the final plop'.

Oakes wanted to do a subject called *The Courier* in which Hancock would play a guide for a broken-down travel agency specialising in mystery trips round Britain – finding himself in Scunthorpe, say, in November with a mixed coachload of Irish priests and Italian commercial travellers. It would have let Hancock loose on an exploration of Britain. He was not interested. 'That,' he said, 'would be going back to my old self.'

Oakes told him that it would not be going back, it would be going deeper. But Hancock wouldn't hear of it.

Chapter Nine

The fun had stopped at MacConkeys. Cicely, superb cook, splendid seamstress, good pianist, had never been much of a housekeeper. Now even the food supplies ran low.

One evening, Cicely was walking in the garden with the dogs when she fell, breaking her leg. She was taken to hospital in Redhill. Tony was staying in London at the time, officially at John Freeman's flat. He spent the nights, however, at Freddie's. When news came of Cicely's accident, he told Freddie: 'She's done it on purpose to get me back.'

'I had to nag him before he would go and see her,' says Freddie.

Mrs Fryer's daughter, Lynn, now married to Barry Took, one of television's best comedy writers, was doing part-time secretarial work for Hancock. She visited Cicely in hospital. When Hancock came home she urged him to see his wife. He kept putting it off until one Saturday she told him: 'I'm going to the hospital and I'm taking you.'

Hancock took his wife a Bertrand Russell book and, as she lay there, read out passages from it. Then he went off to sign autographs in another ward. When he returned he told Cicely, 'I think I'm going to get a psychiatrist to see you.'

Cicely broke down and sobbed, 'I don't think I need the psychiatrist – you need one.'

Hancock had once before tried to force psychiatric treatment on Cicely. He had taken an eminent practitioner to MacConkeys but Cicely very firmly refused to co-operate.

When they got back to MacConkeys, Hancock said he was hungry and Lynn got some lettuce from the garden, found a steak in the deep freeze and cooked him a meal. While she was preparing it he started drinking and lost his appetite.

'I asked Tony about Cicely,' says Mrs Took, 'and he said that he didn't love her and hadn't loved her for some time but felt sorry for her.

'I asked him what he was going to do about it and he said he didn't know. He started talking about Freddie. He didn't know about her either. I said, "You know how cruel it was to take Cicely the Bertrand Russell book when you hadn't seen her for so long? Can't you imagine how she was feeling?" But it didn't mean a thing to him.'

Cicely came home from hospital and at the Red Barn Mrs Fryer and her husband became weary of constant scenes. Hancock, who at one time would never tell a smutty joke and rarely used bad language, started to use obscenities before Mrs Fryer.

Hancock stopped drinking: there was work to do. He was going out on tour again, playing the theatres, meeting the people. He needed a writer to help him with his act and it was suggested that Terry Nation could well be the right man. Nation was later to invent *Dr Who*, the space series, but nothing that ever happened in that was quite as out of this world as the next few months with Hancock.

Nation went to MacConkeys and the two men walked about the garden and talked about the nature of the universe for a while. As soon as Hancock was satisfied that Nation's appreciation of the cosmic was sufficiently high, they got down to the comic.

Hancock wanted to start the following Friday but Nation had a dinner engagement. Hancock suggested they should meet afterwards at John Freeman's flat in Hampstead which he was using during Freeman's absence.

They met at midnight. The following Monday Nation went home to get a clean shirt. Neither he nor Hancock had been to bed. Most of the time was spent in talking and drinking, getting to know each other. Hancock supplied wake-up pills and they wrote some stuff between them. They thought it was hilarious all the way to the audience and then they found it was disastrous.

He and Hancock assembled the act together in rehearsal rooms in London, putting in new material, remembering old gags. Hancock decided he wanted to do an impersonation of Nat King Cole with whom, years previously, he had shared a variety tour. For hours he listened to Cole's recording of 'Let There Be Love'.

Hancock always gave immense encouragement to his writers by his wholehearted laughter whenever he thought something was funny. It was only when he had to deliver the joke to an audience that he suddenly became wary and hesitant about it.

They opened at Southsea and travelled there on a Sunday morning in September 1962 in a huge, hired, chauffeur-driven American car. On Sunday evening he called at the theatre and went through a kind of sniffing-out process. He stood on the stage and smelt the place. He looked at the rows of empty seats and saw where the nearest and furthest members of the audience would be sitting. He touched walls and paced the stage. He stretched himself and flexed his muscles like a boxer about to enter a ring. He went through this routine in every theatre he played.

All day Monday the show rehearsed but Hancock sat numbly in a corner muttering lines. As the day progressed he would cut more and more of the new material he and Nation had put in the act, replacing it with older, safer stuff.

He ordered Nation to stay in the wings with the 'book' during this and all subsequent performances, though in fact he never had to call on him for a prompt.

Hancock like most comics was frightened of new material. Arthur Koestler says that making a joke is a jump into space and comedians have a constant fear that the parachute, though packed and folded by the expert hands of writers, producers and directors, will never open in time. They yearn for the security of the dead cert laugh and Hancock was an exception to the general rule only in that his fears were greater.

So he fell back on the stag's head on the wall joke – 'My God, he must have been going at speed when he hit the other side of that wall.' And when it failed to get the laughs it used to get – as it inevitably did – he still kept it in, blaming the audiences.

He also returned to the Shakespearian mélange, originally written for him by Galton and Simpson but subsequently added to and changed. He relished its mockingly grandiose buffoonery – another of his favourite words.

'Once more unto the breach, dear friends, once more, or close the wall up with our English dead! In peace [and here he did a kind of hop, skip and jump to the microphone] there's nothing so becomes a man as modest stillness and humility. Stillness and humility or not to be. *That* is the question. Whether 'tis nobler in the mind to suffer the slings [mimes slings] and arrows [mimes bow] of outrageous fortune oooooorrrrr, to take arms [spreads arms] against a sea [hornpipe] of troubles.'

He would stop there and giggle. 'It's a game, innit?'

And then go on, mangling Shakespeare in a demonstration of cultural pretension robbed of real affectation by massive ignorance. The hop, skip and jump he did in that speech always drew a laugh until one performance when it was greeted by silence. Afterwards he said: 'It was the timing: I timed the foot all wrong.' For the rest of the tour, no matter how well things were going elsewhere in the act, he fought to get that one, small laugh back. It had started off almost as an unconscious bit of business. Once it became important he tried too hard and he never quite succeeded in retrieving the lost laugh.

First house, Monday in Southsea – or anywhere else – is thin and cold and as inspiring as a wet sock. To top it, many of the London critics were there for the much-heralded 'new' Hancock. He gave them Charles Laughton as Captain Bligh and George Arliss and his gems from Shakespeare. He got himself entangled with the microphone lead and the curtains and he did the opening montage of Gaumont British News. The critics were not impressed.

This, they pointed out with some truth, was not a new Hancock. To do him justice he had never said it would be; the story had been put out by a friend's daughter he had permitted to take some photographs of him.

The tour progressed and got better. New material was tried out and found workable. Audiences were more and more responsive and, some nights, were ecstatic. Hancock drank a little at lunchtimes but then remained dry until after his performance. But he would not sleep alone and insisted that Nation shared a room with him.

'I had finished the writing,' said Nation, 'and he could have got rid of me at any time. But he was paying me £100 a week virtually to baby-sit with him.'

They lay in their twin beds and talked until five in the morning. The subjects, of course, were religion and What Life is All About, and the nature of man and the nature of death. One of Hancock's favourite quotations was something that Arthur Miller said when asked if he were going to Marilyn Monroe's funeral – 'Why? Will she be there?'

At work Hancock was still a superb technician. He used a number of stooges in his Crooner act – he was still doing a version of 'The Crooner' though crooners of that type had long ceased to exist – and at one point the feed had to stamp on Hancock's foot. Usually he pulled back or missed, not wanting to hurt him.

'Stamp on it properly,' he would insist. 'Hurt me. The pain stops when they laugh and they don't laugh unless you really stamp on it.'

Once he thought his toe had been broken and went to a local hospital. It was, in fact, badly bruised. 'How did this happen?' asked the nurse as she attended to it. The reply, to her astonishment, was, 'A feller stamps on it twice a night.'

At Nottingham the man on the lights had the bright idea of

putting a green on him while he was doing the Quasimodo 'I'm so ugly, I'm so ugly' bit. The laughter died instantly. For once in his life Hancock ad-libbed and said, 'Hello, somebody must have put a mouldy penny in the meter.' The light went white again and the laughter resumed but nowhere near its previous intensity. Afterwards, Hancock told Nation: 'Comedy has to be played in a white light. There's no other way. If green comes on they lose your face. It's all with the face. They've got to see these bleeding eyes.'

On the Saturday night in Liverpool, Hancock was hitting his peak, and was, as they say, hot. First house had been good and the second house shrieked with laughter the moment he stepped into view. He said 'hello' and they shrieked again.

It was an enlargement of what comics call a billing laugh which is when passers-by see the name of a comic on the bill outside the theatre and, pointing at it, laugh.

Suddenly there was a scuffle in the dress circle and the audience's attention wavered. Those who saw what was happening gasped and Hancock was stopped for a second. Then he worked faster and faster, running through the laughs.

A keen fan of Hancock's, who had travelled from Wales to see him, had sat through the first house and then hidden himself in a lavatory. As soon as the second house audience started coming in he had gone to the bar and put down a lot of drink. He drank all though the supporting acts until Hancock came on. Then he walked down the centre aisle of the circle, climbed on to the balcony and sat there with his feet dangling, about to launch himself into space, when he was grabbed by an usher. The police were called and he was taken away.

Audiences become frightened when incidents like this happen. Everything is cosy and warm, safe and enclosed, when suddenly a threat appears among them. Anarchy can only be viewed on the stage, a safe distance away. Even the presence of actors in the auditorium – as the more *avant-garde* directors know – has a disturbing effect, partly nullified only by the knowledge that they are there for a specific purpose and are unlikely to do any real damage.

It takes enormous skill to relieve their fears and bring them back to security. Hancock did it consummately and his triumph was accidentally capped in his curtain speech. It was one of those speeches that are really part of the act, beginning, in fact, halfway through it. He would pretend to finish and then say, 'I just want to thank you all for coming tonight. I want to thank Abdullah for the fags, and Kayser Bondor for the socks, Frank Sinatra for the boots which are killing me and are going back and I want to thank the police for controlling the crowds . . . inside the theatre.'

It was a standard line but that night it had a special relevance. The audience laughed and cheered in their delight at this apparent display of an authority equal to any emergency.

That night, Hancock and friends travelled back to London on the night sleeper in a highly euphoric state. Matt Monro had been on the same bill and first there had been a party in his room. On the train they unpacked the hamper the hotel had prepared for the journey. Hancock, Nation, Monro and Glyn Jones, Hancock's road manager who worked for the Delfont Agency, rode to London enveloped in the kind of protective warmth a platoon of soldiers feel after surviving a particularly bloody battle. There was also a lot of wine.

Finally, they went to their respective compartments and slept. In the morning the train was in the station and Nation went to call on Hancock. The clown was lying stark naked on the bed and Glyn Jones was pulling the shade down over the window. Hancock woke to find Jones trying to get his socks on. He studied the situation and then announced: 'Glyn is trying to give me a fitting for a sock.'

As they walked down the platform Hancock kept asking anxiously, 'Did I offend anybody last night?' They assured him that he had not. 'Are you sure?' he asked. 'I sometimes wander out into the corridors stark naked. Are you sure I didn't offend anyone?' They kept saying that everything had been perfectly proper and all right.

Some time later Nation wrote a television script for Hancock in which he made him wake up in a hotel room and anxiously demand over and over again, 'Did I offend anybody last night?'

When Hancock first read it he turned on Nation, grinned and said, 'You bastard.'

Both Cicely and Freddie had appeared from time to time on the tour, but separately. Hancock had rows with both of them. Basically he did not want any women around him when he was working. They were dismissed as irrelevant distractions and even Nation's wife, Kate, when she visited them one week, found that there was no place for her. He was not discourteous; he just politely ignored her.

The tour finished in Brighton the week of the October 1962 Cuba crisis. Hancock thought that this might be the moment of man's ultimate destiny and, of course, he could have been right. He thought it funny that he should be playing Brighton the week the world ended.

But the world did not end and there was the ATV television series to do.

For this all slang was out. The Americans, he felt, would not understand phrases like 'stone me'. On one of his visits to America, Hancock had been to see Stan Laurel and had asked him how to become an international star.

Laurel was old and, looking back on his great days with Hardy, saw things from the viewpoint of a 1930s' film comedian. He told Hancock to cut out the slang. It was altogether too simplistic an answer but it was the only one Hancock could find to explain his failure to conquer the American market. And it put the blame squarely on his writer. What he could never appreciate was that the Bob Hopes and Jack Bennys are joke-tellers and he wasn't; that American comics who, like himself, relied on being extravagant projections of their society, were acceptable in American films because their points of reference were familiar to foreign audiences long saturated with the basic facts of the American way of life through exposure to the American cinema. Too many of the factors which made Hancock funny to British audiences were oblique reflections of a mysterious social order totally incomprehensible in Oshkosh or Kenosha.

It is a fact of life, too, that the language differences are a one-way handicap even when free of slang. British audiences know what elevators and apartments are; American audiences still think lifts and flats are quaint, if they gather the meaning at all.

'I am tired of being common,' said Hancock. 'It is about time I got a bit of class. I am aiming at a universal comedy that will transcend class and state barriers. Like Chaplin, all I can do is entertain and do it simply and sympathetically showing our common weaknesses and vices.'

In three weeks the series, called *Hancock*, which started by being looked at in more than seven and three-quarter million homes, slid to five and a half million. By the end of January 1963 it had dropped out of the Top Twenty programme listings. On BBC television Galton and Simpson's *Steptoe and Son*[7] was in third place.

Hancock blamed power cuts for his fall from favour. 'There are 365 reasons why people don't watch you,' he said, 'but in this case I really believe the viewers hadn't the chance. All they could see was a postage-sized Hancock and so they switched off. There is nothing, absolutely nothing wrong with my new series. Within a few weeks everything will be all right.

'They will love me and laugh at me. The series will be a winner on the American market.'

But they had not switched off; they had switched over. And the series never stood a chance of being sold to American television.

About the same time as he was saying there was nothing, absolutely nothing wrong with the series in public, he was calling on Nation for help. Nation became script editor and produced some quickly written material. The best of it, he says, was a poor imitation of Galton and Simpson.

Hancock had, in fact, asked Galton and Simpson to write for him again for the series. 'We couldn't,' they said, 'because we were heavily involved in Steptoe.'

But if they had had the time? 'We probably wouldn't because from our point of view we had, for the first time in our career, become identified as ourselves. Before that we had been known as Hancock's scriptwriters. The success of Steptoe convinced us that we didn't want to write for comics as such any more; that it was much better to write for actors. You don't have to worry so much. So we probably wouldn't have done it even if we could. I think by that time it was a relief on both sides that we weren't working together.'

'The series was doomed, anyway,' Nation said. 'Tony wouldn't rehearse and for the first time he was boozing while he was working.'

And, of course, he was not making much effort to learn his lines, relying almost entirely on teleprompters. Hancock was more and more bewildered. It was one thing for the critics to attack him but he could not believe that the audience were deserting him, that he had lost their love. In a sense he hadn't. Millions of admirers gave him unstinted support right to the very end. But certainly a couple of million fringe adherents became bored and turned away and they were enough to make a significant change in the all-important ratings.

As soon as the series finished Hancock flew to Paris. A week later he was in a nursing home with 'pneumonia'. It meant cancelling a trip to Australia where he was due to present some television awards. Freddie had to do a lot of covering up.

That spring, the Hancocks invited Terry and Kate Nation to spend a few weeks with them on their yacht in the South of France. The Nations accepted eagerly and set off for Antibes and the world of graceful white hulls and scrubbed decks, of white sails billowing against the blues of a Mediterranean sky and sea.

The *Wokki* was a disreputable old converted Breton fishing boat, thirty-five foot long, which could putter out to sea on a calm day at a good one and a half knots. Originally she had been called the *Fredericka* but Wokki was Tony's pet name for Cicely, and on acquiring the boat he immediately renamed her.

It had two cabins but one was used as a sail locker. 'You don't mind if we all sleep in the same cabin do you?' Hancock asked the Nations as they went aboard. 'It's not worth clearing the sail locker out, is it?'

It was, the Nations recall, a strange three weeks. The Hancocks were at permanent battle stations, totally undeterred by the proximity of the Nations.

Arguments would develop about the most trivial matters.

'Let's take the dinghy around the harbour,' Hancock would propose by way of passing the time.

'No,' said Cicely.

It would become a point of principle.

It would become essential to Hancock to take the dinghy round the harbour; it would become important to Cicely that the dinghy remained where it was.

The result would be a blazing row ending with Hancock taking the dinghy round the harbour though it was the last thing he wanted to do.

One night they all got back late after a good dinner and fell on to their bunks. During the night the boat must have rocked a little and a book fell off a shelf landing on Cicely's stomach. She woke up thinking that Hancock had hit her so she hit him. He woke and hit her. The Nations lay cowering in their corner pretending to be asleep while the Hancocks lay in theirs hitting each other until they were exhausted.

In the morning they woke and the Nations wondered if the fight would go on. Cicely said: 'It's a lovely day. What shall we do today?' The book was still lying on the bunk. It was called *The Dawn of Civilisation*. Hancock was fond of sitting on deck quoting huge chunks from it.

Hancock dished out tranquillisers which helped to keep tempers tolerably below losing point. Once Kate saw Cicely take a drink from Tony's glass and she asked her why she drank so much. Cicely gave her the same answer she had given her mother – 'Every one I drink is one less for him to drink.'

One night they drove to a three-star restaurant and as it grew late, Cicely became tired and slumped on the table. Hancock told her to wake up or go and sit in the car and wait. She went out to the car.

When the other three joined her she was leaning over the wheel, asleep.

She was the only driver. Hancock shook her and said, 'Do your job. I do mine. It doesn't matter how I feel – I've got to go on. Now do your job – drive the bloody car and get me home.'

And he propped her up and held her head and somehow she drove them back to the boat.

While they were at Antibes, Hancock celebrated his fortieth birthday. The four of them dressed up as well as they could and went off to the Hotel Provençal, Hancock in his big, scuffed suède boots.

The Hotel Provençal usually has more English staying in it than Claridge's and appears to be inhabited mainly by retired admirals and their ladies. In fact, Hancock heard someone say, 'Evenin', admiral' as they walked in and this put him in high humour for the rest of the evening. He sent a note to the bandleader requesting him to play 'Holiday for Strings', but the bandleader just smiled and ignored it. He knew when his leg was being pulled. Hancock had done the same thing once before in Liverpool to the three ladies who constituted a palm court orchestra and they had complied. Hancock had sat there, listening gravely to the awful noises they made.

They had a parrot on board *Wokki* which they had brought from MacConkeys and there was an attempt to teach it to sing 'Brown Boots'.

Nation pictures the scene: 'Hancock in rags crouched with a bottle of booze and a glass and me crouched beside him looking just as bad and the girls looking pretty terrible crouched nearby and all of us singing "Brown Boots" to the parrot.'

Hancock thought this was terribly funny and, ignoring the fact that 50 per cent of the company were women, insisted on calling them the Cap d'Antibes Male Voice Choir. When they returned to London there were reporters at the airport. The only thing he would say was, ''Ave you heard the Cap d'Antibes Male Voice Choir? Because if you 'aven't you soon will.'

The flight from Nice had not been uneventful. As soon as they were on board a loudspeaker announcement by the captain informed them that a mistral was blowing up and it would be a good idea if they kept their seat belts fastened. Hancock, who hated flying, sat down and pulled his coat over his head. As soon as they were airborne he ordered champagne and they drank it all the way to London.

Hancock had a theory that tall, square-jawed, cool-eyed

aircraft captains just did not exist. True, a man who looked like that usually walked through the aircraft just before take-off and disappeared inside the cockpit. Shortly afterwards a deep, calm, reassuring voice would come over the loudspeaker to say, 'This is your captain speaking . . .'

Hancock believed that as the hero-figure in captain's uniform walked along the aisle, a red-eyed, unshaven, fat and perspiring creature in crumpled dungarees was being hoisted, struggling, into the pilot's seat, and that when square-jaw disappeared into the crew quarters he immediately left the plane by another door and went on to the next aircraft where he went through the same motions.

Once he was flying from New York when the captain announced: 'We are turning back to Idlewild with mechanical trouble . . .'

'*Idlewild*,' muttered Hancock to his next-door neighbour. 'What sort of bloody captain's this if he doesn't know it's been Kennedy Airport for years?'

Hancock swallowed a few sustaining drinks and then sweated until the plane landed safely at Kennedy Airport. Then he marched to the Pan-American reception desk and demanded that his luggage be taken off and that he be re-booked on a British aircraft. There was some resistance by the Pan-Am official and Hancock found himself angrily explaining to the man standing next to him at the airline desk that he had recently sustained a badly sprained ankle. 'It's a Pott's fracture,' he said. 'Named after Sir Percival Pott, 1780. I was in plaster for weeks . . . very painful.'

How could they expect him to fly about in shaky planes with captains who didn't even know the name of the airfield? And with a leg in that condition? He wanted to fly British and he wasn't going to stand any nonsense about not being able to transfer luggage.

'Leave it to me, old chap,' said the man and Hancock suddenly realised he was talking to Douglas Bader, the legless wartime air ace.

While waiting for the next plane, Hancock telephoned Freddie and talked to her for about an hour. He often spent more money on telephones than it cost to get where he was telephoning from. They even had rows by telephone when one would bang the receiver down and the other would call back 7000 miles or so to ask angrily, 'How dare you put the receiver down on me?' and then hang up without waiting for a reply.

After talking to Freddie for some time he suddenly remembered a message he had been given. 'Will you ring a Mr Snodgrass in Walton-on-Thames,' he said, 'and tell him that Douglas Bader will be late.'

It took him a long time to convince Freddie that he was not out of his mind with booze.

Arriving in London from Antibes, the Hancocks and the Nations decided to stay the night in one of the airport hotels. The whole holiday had been virtually at the Hancocks' expense, air tickets included. There had been vastly expensive meals and rivers of vintage wine. There couldn't have been a more generous host.

Hancock sent for a bottle of vodka and was asked to sign a bill for £3. He nearly walked out of the hotel in his rage at what he considered to be an exorbitant charge.

It was in 1963 that Freddie and Hancock started to live with each other openly. Over the years he had frequently told Freddie that he had left Cicely, a claim he insisted could be proved by the presence of his set of encyclopaedias in the boot of the car. He was buying the volumes at intervals and every time he left Cicely he insisted on taking the set with him or, to show how seriously he meant it, would send for them a day or two later. As time passed, the number of volumes increased and the load grew heavier. But home was where his encyclopaedias were. This time it did look permanent. Not only were there more encyclopaedias than ever but he even consulted a solicitor about a divorce from Cicely. After a few weeks, however, he dropped the idea and it was a year before he took it up again.

The intermittent and, on the whole, secret affair became more permanent and more open after Hancock returned from one of his visits to the South of France, leaving Cicely there.

Freddie had been out all evening at the opening of a new restaurant for which she was handling the publicity.

Hancock telephoned several times during the evening and Freddie thought that he sounded very ill. She asked her secretary, Sally Knight, and her husband John if they would drive to Lingfield with her.

Sally Knight recalls that the first she knew about the relationship between Freddie and Hancock was when she heard Freddie spend thirty minutes trying to persuade someone at the other end of a telephone to go back to his wife. She only discovered at the end of the conversation who it was.

The three of them arrived at MacConkeys about 1 a.m. and found the front door open and the house in darkness. It was not known if Cicely had returned or not so Freddie and Sally sat in the car while John explored. He found Hancock lying stark naked on a bed breathing heavily. It took thirty minutes to wake him.

John Knight says: 'Eventually, he woke up, smiled and said something which I suppose was meant as an endearment to Freddie. We persuaded him to put on his underpants and got him downstairs. Freddie looked round for some food and found eggs and a couple of tins of red beans. She made a red bean omelette topped with anchovies.'

Hancock would not eat it until Freddie pretended it was a children's game and spoon-fed him. He swallowed a few mouthfuls.

'He always made a gesture to eat something of any meal Freddie cooked,' says Sally Knight.

'He managed to burn Freddie's dress which caused something of a diversion,' says John Knight. 'He still appeared to be very drunk.'

'He insisted on playing a Carmen McRae record over and over again and kept saying, "Listen to that, innit great?" At last he seemed to sober up, assured us that he was all right and thanked us for coming. We drove Freddie back to London.'

'I think,' says Freddie, 'that was the night I decided for good or ill that I was going to look after him. For a time he lived in an hotel near my flat but then he moved in and I paid all the expenses. I was a funny kind of mistress. I paid the rent and didn't get any expensive gifts. In fact, I was always buying him things. He paid the drink bills, though.'

And Hancock was an unusual lover. Sometimes he would sit in his chair and watch television with a well-worn slipper perched on his head. 'It gave him a sense of comfort,' says Freddie, who found such eccentricities both funny and endearing.

Freddie's solicitor brother, Leonard Ross, had his office on the floor below the flat and was inevitably involved in their frequent dramas.

While her parents opposed the liaison on the grounds that he was a married man *and* a non-Jew, Leonard got on very well with Hancock.

'My sister,' he says, 'was very naive. I couldn't believe – before she told me – that she could have an affair at all. She had a very naive approach to sex and to men in general. It was a violent relationship she had with Tony – either fantastically good or disastrous. There was no normality in it. I was involved much more than I wanted to be. Freddie felt very badly about this, but she couldn't help herself.'

Leonard not only intervened in arguments but in suicide attempts as well.

'Tony rang me at home on Saturday afternoon. He was very drunk. He said, "Come over, there's been an argument and some violence. She's taken pills, I don't know what to do."

'I found him in the square in carpet slippers looking very distressed. Freddie was lying on a couch upstairs. The rooms looked as if a typhoon had hit them. God knows what had been going on. I thought she was shamming. She had obviously been crying. I said, "Come on, Freddie, I'm here; it's going to be all right." I gave her a little push and she fell off the couch striking her head on an enamel-topped table. She was a dead weight. I called the doctor and he ordered her to hospital. Tony and I followed in a taxi. He was in a terrible state, very upset.'

Despite scenes like this Ross can still say, 'Overall, the balance of his character was in his favour. When he was sober there was no one like him. He was generous and kind and we had a lot of interests in common – boxing, cricket, art and cinema. He was very intelligent and we got on well. I can speak nothing but good of him. I know he treated Freddie very badly but I felt this was an enormous clash of temperament rather than cruelty on his side or misunderstanding on hers. Over the years she had succeeded in bringing him round from time to time and I think she felt she could do more for him by living with him. I always doubted whether this would be the case.'

Ross sees their eventual marriage as something of no great significance. As far as he was concerned they had lived a marriage long before the ceremony took place.

'I didn't try to dissuade her from it,' he said. 'At those times, any attempt to influence her frequently ended in argument.'

Freddie was trying to save Hancock and the way she saw it his struggles with her were like a drowning man's fight to free himself from his rescuer. It was certainly no reason to abandon the attempt.

One of Freddie's assistants in the publicity business was Sally Mordant. She observed the effect of the new situation on her boss.

'She became a totally different person in Tony's presence,' she said. 'The fighting personality, the push and the drive was softened and mellowed. She became more feminine. She tried to give him the kind of home she felt he had never had with Cicely. Of course, he said it was like living in Emergency Ward 10 because as he flicked ash into an ashtray she would remove it and clean it. She thought that if she gave him the security of a well-run home, that if she organised him like an office, it would give him an anchorage. But it was too late; he didn't want it.

'Tony was jealous and possessive. If she wore the most simple thing he would say it was provocative and designed to attract men. She once wore a suit with an anchor on the breast pocket. Tony told her that it was to draw attention to her bosom and stopped her wearing it.

'If they went to the Savoy, where she had organised press receptions in the past, the waiters and staff who knew her would naturally greet her. Hancock accused her of having slept with them, and would insist on walking out. Freddie would bite her tongue and say quietly, "All right, Tony." Under other conditions she would have created merry hell.

'I used to dread going to Dorset Square' – Freddie's flat was also her office – 'for I never knew what to expect – whether Freddie had a migraine or had been hit on the head by a bottle.

'Her suicide bids made me feel sick because there could be a time when she might do it and no one would be around to pick her up. Freddie could not do anything less than the big gesture. Everything was for an Oscar.

'She guarded her love for Tony and it was a very genuine thing. Even after all the beatings she had from him you would never hear her criticise him. She thought all along that she might be the one who could change him. But it was too late. She was a great fighter though. She did a tremendous amount for him professionally, not only in getting him appearances and arranging television things, but also as a moral support. She always had unshakeable faith in his talent. He would lean on her judgement a great deal.

'And he could often be most endearing and tender to Freddie. Inside he wanted affection. He could be extremely kind and amusing.

'But even at the best times she could not relax; she was always on the lookout for danger signals, always petrified that when he went back to Cicely she might encourage him to drink again.

'But he was always the man she wanted to marry and though they had some terrible times together I don't think she would rather have not had them for all the good times they had.'

Freddie says: 'He didn't have many clothes until we started living together. Then he became more clothes-conscious, possibly due to my influence. He was a tremendous influence on me, too. I tended to overdress and wear too many bangles and baubles. He stopped me doing that. It was a sign of insecurity that many women get when they work in a masculine world.

'And he loved the place being tidy.'

She and Tony spent a lot of time socially with the Knights. Once they were all listening to a record of the Hancock *Face to Face* with John Freeman when Hancock observed rather smugly, 'I wasn't bad there, was I? Pour me a drink, Fred.'

Fred had been watching him drink steadily all evening and was desperately anxious for him to stop.

'A large one?' she asked, trying to fight him with sarcasm.

'A *very* large one,' he said.

Freddie rose, picked up a bottle of brandy and walked towards him. When she reached him she lifted the bottle and poured the contents over his head. It was done with great deliberation. He sat there quietly until the last drop was dripped.

It was funny in a breath-taking sort of way. It was quite on the cards that Hancock would take a swipe at her there and then. Instead, he said, very quietly, 'Usually I take a spot of soda with it.'

And they all collapsed helpless with laughter.

One weekend Freddie had to go to Yorkshire to see Max Jaffa, the violinist, who was one of her clients. The Knights were going with her and, at the last minute, Hancock decided to join them.

'This,' he announced, 'is a weekend to be dedicated to the girls. We will make an overnight stop in Stratford.'

That evening the four of them booked in at the Leofric Hotel, Coventry. 'Coventry,' said Hancock, 'is not far from Stratford. It is not a bad miss.'

About 7 p.m. John Knight got a call from Hancock. 'I've been given a forty-eight-hour pass,' he announced gleefully. 'Freddie suggests I meet you in the bar for a drink.'

In the bar he ordered half a bitter.

'It was clear,' reports Knight, 'that he was trying to do the right thing.'

After half an hour they were about to rejoin their partners when a man approached them. 'Excuse me,' he said politely, 'but aren't you Tony Hancock?'

'Yes.'

'I wonder if you would allow me to buy you and your friend a drink?'

'That's very kind of you; I'll have half a bitter.'

The fan bought two halves of bitter and after about twenty minutes' chat, Knight said, 'I really think we must go.'

The fan said, 'So that's how it is, is it? It's a bit rough if you can't drink with a fan.'

'I tell you what,' said Hancock. 'I'll buy you one.'

An hour later, the stranger said, 'If you dare get up from this table while I'm drinking with you I'll make a big scene.'

The situation looked extremely nasty; the man was either drunk or mad, possibly both.

Knight made signs to the barman. As the barman persuaded the man to leave, Hancock was paged to the bar telephone. It was Freddie. 'You'll never believe this,' he began.

He was right. 'You're telling me,' she said, and put down the telephone.

Hancock turned gloomily to Knight. 'John,' he announced, 'we're in the shit.'

They went upstairs. As he opened the bedroom door, Hancock said: 'The funniest thing has happened . . .' and between them, he and Knight went through the whole story. Neither Freddie nor Sally believed a word of it; they flounced out and went off to the cinema, leaving the men alone.

Said Tony: 'That's just my bleeding luck. Everyone says I'm a bloody boozer and I try and do the right thing on one occasion and what happens – a nutcase waylays me in a bar.'

The weekend never quite recovered. The hotel they stayed in in Yorkshire was awful.

There was no one to carry their luggage and when Hancock whispered to Knight, 'Tell the porter to park the car,' and Knight said, 'Park the car, please,' the porter said, 'Park it your bloody self.'

Freddie then had a migraine and they had to take her to hospital for treatment and Hancock and Max Jaffa, when they met, did not seem to hit it off too well.

On the way back to London it was obvious that Hancock was badly in need of a drink. They had little money left but between them they managed to collect enough to buy half a bottle of vodka.

That summer Hancock agreed to appear at the Talk of the Town in Leicester Square for six weeks. It was a place that exposed an artist mercilessly. The audience was not safely in front of the performer but encircled him like the arms of a huge, two-tiered horseshoe. The structure of a normal theatre places the performer in a superior position to the audience. He is in light; they are in darkness; he is alone, in command; they are in ranks, subject to the discipline of a convention that requires silence save for licensed moments of laughter or applause. Cabaret gives the audience a dangerous equality. The light is more evenly distributed and, minutes before they too have been performers, have eaten and drunk and tried to amuse their friends. In the strictest military sense they must be brought to attention, an authority must be established. It is something that requires a great deal of skill.

Bernard Delfont, who had booked him into Talk of the Town, went to see him in Manchester where he was working up his act at the Palace Theatre.

'When I went to his dressing room,' Delfont said, 'he had gone down well with the audience and seemed happy.'

Joan Littlewood, former director of Theatre Workshop, was another visitor and Hancock told her he had always fancied himself as an actor more than a comic. They had similar ideas about the need for a multi-purpose entertainment centre where the best would be available at reasonable prices.

A few days later Delfont, now back in London, had a call from Hancock. Hancock was worried about letting him down but he felt he was not right for Talk of the Town at that moment.

Joan Turner went on in his place. Hancock was in the audience one evening and later went backstage to see her. He told her, 'At least, you've got some new impressions in your act; my lot are all dead.'

They talked until about 2 a.m. and as they left he suddenly excused himself. Miss Turner watched him walk on stage in the semi-darkness, feeling it with his feet as if to make sure it was secure and would not collapse underneath him. She said, 'What are you doing, Tony?' And he replied: 'I am just getting the feel of the stage because I shall come here.'

He walked around a bit and sniffed a bit and looked up at where the gods used to be when the place was the Hippodrome and said: 'Yes, I think I'm going to be all right.'

In July 1963 he picked up some £10,000 from British Railways for a series of advertisements and in August he played the Palladium for the first time.

Arthur Haynes, the starring comic, was taken ill. The moment he heard about it, Hancock telephoned Billy Marsh who ran the agency side of the Delfont organisation.

'You in trouble?' he asked Marsh. Marsh, who later became his agent but had already arranged his variety tours for some years, confessed that he was. 'All right,' said Hancock, 'if you want me I'll go in.'

Money was not mentioned and Hancock had no idea how long the substitution would last. He was there, in fact, for six weeks. This time he did not have to pretend to himself or anyone else that there was a 'new' Hancock. He had ridden in to the rescue at the last minute and nobody could expect him to be on a fresh horse.

After the Palladium came a wretched time. Hancock's search for the ultimate perfection in comedy was getting more and more desperate; Cicely sat at home in Lingfield nursing a bottle and the fragments of her broken marriage and Freddie tried to run her publicity business and spend twenty-four hours a day with Hancock in an effort to keep him away from drink.

Hancock's search led him back to Denis Norden whose great skill as a writer of comedy had helped him in the distant and now almost dear old Adelphi days.

'He rang me up to have lunch and talk about doing a show with him,' recalls Norden. 'It was impossible right from the outset. He started off with three triple brandies and at lunch he talked nonsense. But suddenly he got to reminiscing about forgotten acts in the variety theatres and we remembered a conjuror who did the egg in a black bag trick which anyone can buy at any magic shop. You pull the black bag inside out, show there's nothing in it and then produce an egg. The conjuror used to cap his trick by turning to the audience and saying in a marvelling tone, "The man must be in league with the devil."

'Tony recognised his kind of humour instantly and was delighted. He said, "That's it!" But he couldn't make it on his own. Only Galton and Simpson could do it for him.'

There was always pressure on Galton and Simpson and Hancock to get back together again but neither side was willing.

Spike Milligan even mapped out in some detail the way they should do it. 'It starts,' he told Galton and Simpson, 'with Tony in the Labour Exchange and behind him is Sid and all the other people he put out of work. Then you see him get off a bus a few doors from the Galton and Simpson office. He takes a taxi so that he can draw up in style. He shouts up at the window. "Hello lads. I want to give you another chance." And then he starts telling you where you went wrong. "It was when you decided not to write for me any more," he said. "All this Steptoe and Son stuff – there's nothing in it." Then, when it comes to re-employing Sid, he wants more money and a contract.'

But Galton and Simpson were not interested.

Nor, for that matter, was Hancock. It would have meant going back. His idea of going forward then was to play the Fool to Wilfrid Lawson's King Lear.

Lawson was a marvellous actor with a strange distant quality in his acting that made it appear at times almost as if his voice – a high, slurred voice with eccentric vowel sounds – issued from his mouth through the agency of some special ventriloquist. He was an actor's actor, beloved by other actors like Trevor Howard, Nicol Williamson – and Hancock.

Lawson was also frequently drunk.

He and Hancock discussed their Lear project over countless brandies. There was something in Lear's definition of a man as a 'forked animal' that appealed strongly to Hancock's cosmic perspective. It was a proposal that could never have got off the ground. No one would have risked a penny on a production which depended upon two such notoriously unreliable men. But if it had happened it would have been a great experience – one night in fifty. The rest of the time it would have been an unutterable shambles.

Christmas 1963 – like all festive occasions – saw Hancock morose and melancholy. Holidays and the thought of family life and other people enjoying themselves always brought on great doom-laden crises which blew themselves out in a storm of drink and fury.

But 1964 dawned with the promise of some interesting work and a major artistic breakthrough.

First, there was a proposal that Hancock should play the lead in the film of *Harvey*, Sid Field's old vehicle. Then he was given a substantial role in *Those Magnificent Men in Their Flying Machines*, a multi-starred spectacular in which Hancock played an eccentric and clumsy pilot taking part in the 1910 London–Paris air race.

It was shortly before this that he sustained his 'Pott's fracture' and feared for a time that it would prevent him from making the picture. But, plaster-encased as he was, they still wanted him and the pain and the awkwardness added a deeper conviction to his portrayal of the dedicated, fanatical flyer. Of course, his fellow-actors accused him of putting it on to impress.

Most gratifying of all, he was asked to make the film of *Rhinoceros*, the Ionesco play in which Sir Laurence Olivier had appeared on the London stage.

There's glory for you; there's recognition. The clown was at last there among the acknowledged artists linked with Woodfall Films and, therefore, with John Osborne, another non-conforming hero. But the real triumph was in the thought of those peculiar feet stepping into shoes once worn by Olivier.

'Next thing you know,' said Hancock, 'it'll be a touch o' burnt cork and Othello.'

'Hancock . . . a comedian with a touch of genius who had no enemy but himself'
J. B. Priestley

Above: Hancock felt persecuted by the power of his name. He tried to draw a distinction between the public Hancock and his true personality

Below: John Le Mesurier as the Sandman, and Hancock as Wally, are oblivious of their neighbour, played by Gerald Harper, in The Punch and Judy Man, *1962, a film which, though it has moments of brilliance, is overshadowed by a sense of decline*

Filming of The Punch and Judy Man *was beset with problems, which included Hancock's drinking bouts and his rows with Cicely and Freddie. Hancock was convinced that the project was doomed because of Punch's malign influence*

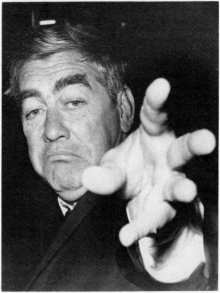

Above: Freddie and Hancock after their marriage. It was a volatile relationship, in which Freddie tried, in vain, to rescue Hancock's talent
Right: Hancock became increasingly belligerent as his dependence on alcohol deepened

Above left: Hancock checks the time on his wedding day
Left: Hancock and Freddie are married on 2 December 1965

Hancock in 1965. Impending tragedy was sensed by his friends, all of whom retained their affection for Hancock, even when his problems overwhelmed him

Above: Simpson (centre) and Galton (right) reluctantly discussing a musical, Noah, *with Hancock in 1965. The project came to nothing*
Below: 'The Croupier' sketch, from Hancock's. *In spite of brief periods of abstinence, Hancock had lost his mobility of expression as the result of drink. After viewing the playback of this show Hancock began to drink heavily again*

Hancock rehearsing for one of the Australian Channel 7 episodes. After a disastrous start at the beginning of the series, Hancock made a tremendous effort and sobered up. But Hancock's psychiatrist held out no hope for a permanent cure

Did Hancock yearn to play Hamlet? He always denied it strenuously but there is equally no doubt that he always seized any opportunity to grapple with a real acting role. 'Could Olivier do twelve minutes at the Palladium?' he would ask, asserting his authority in his own sphere. As a matter of fact, Olivier could – and did. He has appeared at the Palladium and larked about in sketches with considerable success on such charitable occasions as 'The Night of 100 Stars'.

The postponement and eventual cancellation of the *Harvey* project was insignificant beside this new challenge.

Bérenger, the hero of *Rhinoceros*, lives with his friend, Jean, in a small town. One day a couple of rhinos are observed charging down the main street. Gradually more and more rhinos appear. They are, in fact, the town's citizens who are gradually being transformed into rhinos. They suffer from a compulsion that makes them actually desire this metamorphosis. The allegory is easy enough – rhinos are strong, sturdy and insensitive beasts who live limited conformist and contented lives. All of humanity is changing into rhinos. Even Jean and Daisy, Bérenger's girl-friend, eventually put forward sound arguments why they should do as everyone else is doing.

Only Bérenger himself retains his humanity, becoming the last surviving member of the human race.

'Hancock,' says Oscar Lewenstein, the producer of the film, 'was enthusiastic but impatient. He did not seem able to grasp that it takes a long time to get the right script and to build a dummy rhino that would really work.'

The director was to be Alexander Mackendrick, a precise, painstaking man who likes to have everything prepared down to the last detail before he begins shooting. His and Hancock's temperaments were utterly at odds. There was also some trouble in getting insurance cover for Hancock for the film. Eventually this was sorted out though there was a clause in the policy which said:

> In the event of any insurance claims arising through the Artiste having met with an accident or suffering from an illness attributable directly or indirectly to alcoholism, such claims will be subject to a deduction in excess of $10,000.

Negotiations and discussions about *Rhinoceros* dragged on throughout most of 1964 and finally petered out in the summer of the following year. Quite early on in the proceedings it was clear that both parties were having second thoughts. Lewenstein wrote to Hancock:

I think I ought to say that I don't feel that you should sign the contract for any other reason than that you want to do the film because if you do it for any other reason I don't see how the film can be a pleasure for any of us. May I suggest, therefore, that you should think carefully about the matter and if you feel happy to work on the film with Sandy Mackendrick directing it and with our company [Woodfall] producing it, then I would like to exchange contracts with you. If you don't want to do this then please let us know through Billy Marsh. If we have not exchanged contracts within the next three days then we will take it that the whole thing is off.

Both Sandy and I feel it would be a tremendous pity if you were not to do the film in which we feel you are absolutely ideally cast, but if you do it we want you to do it of your own free will and not for any reasons of obligations.

Billy Marsh was by then Hancock's agent, the arrangement with his brother Roger having come to an end.

Evidently Hancock telephoned Lewenstein after receiving this letter, doubts were settled on both sides and the contracts were signed. It made no difference – the film was never made.

'It would have been quite marvellous if we had been able to do it,' Oscar Lewenstein says. 'Olivier had to *play* the part but Hancock was Bérenger to the life – an aggressive man but nonetheless more human than any of the others. Hancock would have been the right survivor for the human race.'

One thing came out of *Rhinoceros* that delighted Hancock – a meeting with John Osborne who, in the radio *Half Hour* days, was parodied as John Eastbourne, The Hungry Young Man.

He telephoned Osborne to ask him to lunch at a point where he was becoming worried about the film and they met at the Mirabelle restaurant.

'He was very suspicious at first,' says Osborne who was a warm admirer of Hancock. 'I'm not socially adroit myself but we soon got on pretty well. We had so much to drink before lunch it was ridiculous – more than I usually have in the whole day. Then he made a big thing about the wine and it was 3.30 p.m. before we finished.'

After lunch he and Hancock poured themselves into a cab and went to the Wig and Pen Club in the Strand where they drank two or three bottles of champagne.

'I remember,' says Osborne, 'we both had a schoolboy enthusiasm for limericks, and we exchanged these for at least an hour and a half.'

Osborne felt that Hancock was very isolated and lonely and wanted someone to talk to. He got the feeling that he hated writers or at least bitterly resented them.

'The mere act of writing implied to him an assault on any spontaneity.

'He gave me the impression that he was rather like I am myself – one of those people who somehow conceal themselves from other people's work because they feel in some way it may intrude on what they are doing themselves. I think he rather didn't want to know what other people were doing.

'He had this extraordinary bruised smile. He had a melancholy presence.'

The two men ended the day walking arm-in-arm down the Strand. After he left Hancock Osborne took to his bed for three days. Hancock, he felt, was all right.

He was not all right, as a matter of fact. It was about that time that he went into a nursing-home for four days. Then he became a voluntary patient at the Charing Cross Hospital psychiatric unit. He did not stay long.

Chapter Ten

In November 1964, Hancock, having turned down offers for years, appeared as the star of *Sunday Night at the London Palladium* on television. His salary was £1000, average for top billing.

In November 1964 he also announced that he wanted a divorce from Cicely because he was going to marry Freddie.

Freddie, if she had not already had sufficient warning of the disaster course on which she was heading, got it almost immediately. And so, for that matter, did Hancock. Marriage between them took on the appearance of having been arranged by a demented computer. She thought she could reform him, bring him back to his former greatness, exert a steadying influence. It was all a monstrous illusion for which she – and he – paid dearly.

Hancock had left Cicely for what was going to be the last time and had moved into the Maharajah Suite of the Mayfair Hotel. The 'engagement' to Freddie was about to be announced and Hancock, his brother Roger and road manager Glyn Jones were drinking champagne when Freddie left them to attend a publicity event she had organised for one of her clients. She returned at lunchtime with her assistant, Sally Mordant.

'It was,' says Mrs Mordant, 'the first time I had met Tony. He rang for the waiter and when he came he ordered plum duff. The waiter said he was sorry but they did not have plum duff. "All right," Hancock said, "spotted dick, then."'

'The waiter said he was very sorry and could he suggest something from the trolley.

'Tony said: "How dare you suggest anything to me. I want plum duff."'

'Freddie was saying, "Tony, darling," all soft and gentle. With Hancock in that mood I couldn't get out of the suite fast enough.'

Mrs Mordant was wearing a sequin-covered hat. Hancock had taken a dislike to it.

Freddie says: 'When everyone had left I said, "Darling, what is it? Have you got the blue blues?" He said, "Yes." He suddenly looked at me and said, "I'm going back to Cicely." He said it was because of Sally's hat. I went a bit hysterical. After about two hours of hysterics Glyn Jones came back and he saw me, still sobbing, into a taxi. Tony didn't want to know. He just sat quietly and ignored the whole situation. It is much more aggravating than if you have a good shout back.

'He always walked away from anything like that. I checked into the Savoy Hotel and said I had a migraine and didn't want to be disturbed. I took some pills and telephoned my brother. I didn't want to leave a note that would involve anybody. I told my brother to make sure that Tony's name was kept right out of it. My brother asked where I was and I wouldn't tell him. I just said it is somewhere where Tony and I were once very happy. He got hold of Tony and they worked out there were two places where I could be. They traced me to the Savoy – at least, my brother did – Tony took no part in it at all.'

There were five occasions on which Freddie tried to take her own life. A psychiatrist told her that she was not the suicidal type. It needs no expert to conclude that these were screams for help, calls for attention. It was a call to which Hancock was constitutionally unable to respond.

As she says herself: 'He always walked away from anything like that.'

At the time though they walked towards each other again and a kind of life went on.

She was with him when they went to Bournemouth to see his mother when Hancock's second stepfather, Harry Sennett, was dying.

Mrs Sennett, a spiritualist since her eldest son was killed during the war, knew a medium called Bill – to be mentioned later in one of Hancock's suicide notes. There was to be a laying-on of hands and Freddie suggested that as it was such a personal thing it might be better if she should leave. Hancock said he wanted her to stay with him.

'His mother and Bill, the medium, persuaded Tony to put his hands on his stepfather's chest,' says Freddie. 'The perspiration was coming from Tony's brow. It was a dramatic and traumatic experience and his mother's blind faith in Tony was rather moving in a way. She wanted to believe that he had this gift of healing.'

The course of events remained unchanged and Mrs Hancock's third husband died shortly afterwards.

Hancock himself half-believed he had some slight healing power. He would touch Freddie's forehead when she had migraine and say he could feel the pain coming into his hands.

Her migraine once brought out a flash of the old Hancock. They were sitting in the pictures waiting for the war film *The Longest Day* to start when Freddie slipped a pill into her mouth.

'What is it?' said Hancock.

'Headache pill,' she said.

'Better give me one.'

'Why, have you got a headache?'

'No – shell-shock.'

Hancock's appearance on television in *Sunday Night at the London Palladium* was rehearsed late at night in a deserted Talk of the Town, a facility specially laid on at his request by the Delfont Organisation. He paced about and mumbled but did not connect very strongly with the other people involved.

Freddie, tidy-minded, and an organiser, kept at him to work properly. 'Occasionally I acted like a sergeant-major,' she says, 'and would make him do it. He hated me for it. But I knew that unless he knew that act backwards, forwards and sideways he would be no good at all.'

The transmission showed that Hancock's pulling power was virtually undiminished. It gained the highest viewing figures of the week. This was unfortunate because he did not distinguish himself.

'Funny and sympathetic,' wrote Adrian Mitchell in the *Sun*, 'but not a raving hit.' This was the general opinion.

One of the funnier things was Hancock's attempt to be swinging and with it.

'Course,' he said, 'I'm one of the clan, you know. There's me, Frank Sinatra, Shirley MacLaine, Elsie and Doris Waters, Peter Lawford, Sandy Macpherson . . . oh, we're all in it.'

At least, that's what he should have said. But he went blank on the last name and, after a momentary hesitation, substituted 'Dame May Whitty' – who had died in 1948 at the age of eighty-two. He was very pleased about that.

Halfway through his act he realised that he had already embarked on the closing sequence and it was something of a struggle to get back to his proper place without finishing some four minutes short.

A few miles away, at the BBC Television Centre at Wood Lane, Galton and Simpson, Duncan Wood and Graham Stark watched him in a viewing-room. They saw Hancock close on his old Gaumont British News montage which normally ended with four dives to the ground. Hancock managed two and then only got to his feet with difficulty.

Galton commented: 'To be a performer you've got to be like an athlete – you've got to keep in condition physically as well as mentally.'

It was bad that Christmas. Hancock had a flat in Grosvenor Street and Freddie was staying with him at night. He drank, she threatened to take another overdose. Somehow she could never bring herself to understand that her threats or attempts at suicide did not act as a deterrent to Hancock's drinking and could very likely have spurred him on to make greater efforts to blot out a hateful situation.

There was a scene which resulted in her being ejected from the flat in the middle of the night wearing nothing but a coat. She could not go to her own flat because she did not have her keys. She telephoned John and Sally Knight in Harrow and they drove to Grosvenor Street. While Freddie sat in the car, John went upstairs. Hancock greeted him warmly and invited him in to have a drink. He could not understand why he wouldn't stay and have a chat but made no attempt to stop him collecting Freddie's clothes.

She left him, too frightened to return because of the threat of more beatings.

A couple of days later, Hancock was found in a terrible state. Apparently he had fallen while drunk and banged his forehead on the corner of a glass and wrought-iron dressing-table.

He was taken to a sanatorium in Virginia Water. Freddie drove down to see him. She was warned by the doctor in charge that his hair had been cut away because of a head injury. The doctor also gave her another warning.

'He told me,' says Freddie, 'that Tony was a chronic alcoholic and asked me if I understood what that meant.

'I said I did, but I didn't. I thought it was curable. The important thing to know about alcoholics is that the smallest, mildest drink sets them off. During the periods when Tony was not drinking we even avoided food cooked with wine. The patient has to admit to himself that he is an alcoholic and face these facts if there is to be any chance at all of a cure. Tony would never do that. I asked the doctor if he thought I could help him rebuild his career and he said I had about three chances in a hundred. He said, "If you were my daughter I would turn you round, show you the door and beg you to keep walking. You're in for a lot of heartache." I said I'd remember that.'

Twenty-one years later, Freddie recalls that alcoholism in the mid-sixties was a shameful and humiliating condition. 'No one,' she says, 'came out of a clinic like Betty Ford or Elizabeth Taylor do today to tell the world about it. Most of the attempts I made on my own life were due to the pressures of keeping others from knowing about Tony's alcoholism. There was no one I could talk to about it.'

Hancock was a shaky mess. He held her hand and stroked her hair and was clearly embarrassed at his predicament.

'He was just like a little baby, really,' says Freddie. 'That's why you never had the hardness to turn your back on him.'

She stayed in a nearby hotel and visited him every day. She was, by then, so estranged from her parents that they communicated by letter.

She had made a second attempt on her own life and her parents begged her to make a clean break with Hancock.

She replied: 'He is making such a fantastic effort that I for one am not going to slam the door in his face and I think that you underestimate him when you think that having got over these next few months he would ever go back on the smallest provocation. Believe me, he has only been like it for three or four years and then under the kind of pressures from which most people would have crumbled.'

Early in the New Year Freddie went into hospital for an operation and the day afterwards Hancock flew to New York with eight recorded television shows and tried, once more, to break into the American market. He did not have to go and the arrangements were only made after he knew she was to have an operation. It was a cast-iron excuse for not visiting her.

However, he telephoned her frequently and wrote that he loved her very much. In another letter he had said that someone had told him he looked twenty years younger. He had said that it was because of the divorce but really, he told Freddie, it was because of her.

He was missing her badly, he said, and the self-discipline was going well. He promised to try and write to her every day.

Hancock went to Los Angeles and still telephoned and wrote. He told her to remove at least one worry from her mind – him. He had never drunk so much coffee.

After watching a lot of television there, he wrote in another letter that he was quite certain there was nothing to beat.

It is clear from another of his letters that he was seriously considering emigrating to America if he could obtain the necessary work permits. Having uprooted himself from his past, he said, it seemed the perfect time to re-establish fresh roots. He didn't know how she would take to the idea. He didn't want to take her away from her family and friends but he thought they could discuss it on his return.

He loved her more and more each day, he said, and missed her terribly.

He exhausted the stationery in his room and wrote one letter on drawer lining paper.

It could have been that short trip to Hollywood that brought him his next big offer – a part in a Disney film.

He had returned to London and Freddie was out of hospital. The divorce and the negotiations over *Rhinoceros* were both dragging on and the two of them decided that a week on a health farm drinking carrot juice would do them a world of good.

They decided on a place near Bexhill, Sussex, and set off to drive there. Still in London they passed one of Hancock's favourite restaurants and, by mutual consent, decided to stop for one last decent meal.

Hancock, as usual, chose the wines carefully and, replete, they eventually resumed their journey to Bexhill. Hancock knew a good place on the way down to stop for tea so they stopped for tea. Nearing Bexhill they thought they may as well have a glass of beer as it was 6.30 and this would be their last chance. So he had a beer and she had a tomato juice and they both ate crisps and played a game of darts. They arrived at Bexhill prepared for starvation.

As they checked in the receptionist said, 'Will you please call the international operator – America has been trying to reach you for two hours.'

Disney wanted him.

There were calls to Los Angeles and calls to London and eventually they both drove down to the beach. It was raining. 'If you think,' said Hancock, 'that I can cope with all this on a glass of hot water and a slice of lemon you must be joking.'

'We had an agreement,' says Freddie, 'that in moments of stress he could drink as long as we had something to eat. I'm no drinker but I do eat.'

So they had fish and chips and pickled onions sitting in the car in Bexhill in the rain talking about Hollywood. The following day he decided that he could not cope with this new situation at all while undergoing the reducing treatment and they returned to London.

Hancock passed his medical examination for insurance on the Disney film. It was called *The Adventures of Bullwhip Griffin* and he had third billing. He was to play an itinerant Shakespearian actor caught up in the Western gold rush. He would wear a Homburg hat and a coat with an astrakhan collar. International stardom, it seemed, beckoned him only on one condition – that he appeared in the same guise he had thrown away, along with his national stardom, ten years earlier. But Hancock was in no mood to worry about things like that. By now he was so eager to go that he would have cheerfully embraced his RAF Gang Show role.

Lost. Hancock in Hollywood was lost and unutterably lonely. Day after day he sat in a suit under the shade of an umbrella by the swimming pool of the Beverly Wilshire Hotel going over and over his lines. He drank champagne because he was trying to lose weight – he believed it was less fattening than vodka – and he sat there in the heat muttering his lines over and over again. He made the people around him feel uneasy. Hollywood is a place of many insecurities and the cardinal sin is to show them. Hancock's air of desperation was too savage a reminder to other actors in the vicinity of the impermanence of fame and fortune. In a place where masks are donned with the arrival of the breakfast orange juice he was the man with the exposed nerves.

But there was nothing wrong with his behaviour while Bernie Lang, one of his American representatives and a man he was particularly fond of, was with him. After a couple of weeks, however, Lang had to return to New York and Hancock was left alone. He had been telephoning Freddie in London regularly and, suddenly, she began to detect the sound of drinking in his voice and manner. He had, he told her, met some people. Everything was all right.

Staying in the same hotel was an American actor with an English wife who had met Hancock once or twice in London. Her marriage was breaking up and would shortly be dissolved. Her husband was also studying a role he was about to play but preferred to do it in the privacy of his suite. Hancock was a frequent visitor and would spend hours playing records there. Or he would telephone the wife and say, 'Come and talk to me. I'm lonely.'

Possibly he felt attracted to her, possibly she played him along a little as she was also bored and unhappy. She says, however, that there was no affair. When Freddie telephoned and Hancock could not be found in his own room or by the pool she was frequently told by the operator that he might be in the actor's suite.

'I spoke to this actor,' says Freddie, 'and he told me, "For God's sake, I don't want to take any more calls," and he put the phone down. So I called him back and told him I was calling from 7000 miles away and thought he might at least have the courtesy to tell me if my husband [they were not married then but Hancock said the calls were from his "wife"] was in his suite or if I could speak to him. He said, "I am trying to study my lines. I have some scenes to do tomorrow. Everybody in the hotel knows where your husband is. It's common knowledge. He seems to be in love with my wife. Now I have a job to do so please get off the line."'

Back in Los Angeles, the actor's wife says Hancock took to 'looming'. He did it once too often. 'We were listening to a record one evening and suddenly he was there standing in the doorway, swaying. My husband got quite ugly about it and said, "You've taken advantage once too often. Get out."'

Hancock got out. He must have felt disgusted with himself.

'We were also getting a bit bored,' the wife says, 'by these calls from England which were coming through indiscriminately. Hancock was figuring too largely in our lives and took up too much time and consideration. I was sad because I was very sorry for him. He was totally lost and he was the sort of man you can't help caring about.'

Yes, she says, he got very intense about her. 'But then, I think he would have got intense about the flowers in the foyer if they had waved at him.'

Freddie flew out to Los Angeles. 'Tony finally persuaded me that I must go there; that he needed me,' she says. 'He said he would have a surprise at the airport for me and had planned something marvellous.'

Her surprise was that there was no one to meet her. She waited for half an hour and just as she was about to leave Hancock drove up in a cab, unshaven, red-eyed and crumpled.

'I asked a few pertinent questions about what had been going on and he said that it was all nonsense, just a couple of drunken scenes that had come to nothing.'

When they got to the hotel, the assistant manager, an Englishman, kept assuring her that there was nothing to worry about. This did not make her feel any better.

There was still a week to go before shooting started on the film.

It is probable, especially in the light of future events, that 'the couple of drunken scenes' and everything else were reported back to the Disney studios. Abnormalities are tolerated, indiscretions are not. The CIA could pick up a lot of pointers from the Hollywood espionage system.

Freddie and Hancock moved out of the Beverly Wilshire Hotel away from the limelight and nearer the studios, to the Sportsman's Lodge. They decided that 'we would put the past behind us and I would make an effort to get everything organised and this I did.'

Suddenly everything was domesticated, almost suburban. Freddie had relations in Los Angeles and there were a couple of dinner parties, to which they and representatives (and their wives) of the William Morris Agency, which handled Hancock's affairs in America, were invited. One was to celebrate Hancock's forty-first birthday and there was a cake. In turn, they too were invited out.

'We did the full devoted happy couple act,' says Freddie, 'so that everything he had done would be, we hoped, completely whitewashed. It was for our benefit as well because we were enjoying ourselves. He was being lovely and I gave him a birthday present of a pair of cufflinks. Inscribed on them were the first words I ever said to him in Blackpool in 1954 – "If I had a talent like yours I'd be proud". He alway wore them whenever he went on stage after that.'

Hancock started rehearsals. He was on call at 7.30 every morning. He would get up at 5.30 and rehearse his lines with Freddie – he was having tremendous difficulty in retaining them after all the years of dependence on a teleprompter – eat a small breakfast and Freddie would drive him to the studios.

Hancock did not like her on the set when he was working but he wanted her in the neighbourhood so she sat in his windowless dressing room which had a fridge which she stocked with food.

She prepared cheese and salad and cold drinks for lunch and after work was over for the day they would drive back to Sportsman's Lodge where he would go over his lines in the drawing room while she watched cowboy films in the bedroom.

'Every time I come into the bedroom I expect to see cowboys and injuns riding through,' he told her.

It was a disciplined life.

On 27 May it was hot in Hollywood and Freddie was roasting in the tiny dressing room. At lunchtime Hancock had a beer and listened to her complaints about the heat. He told her to go back to the hotel and lie by the pool. She did. In the middle of the afternoon she was called by the studio and told to get back there quickly. 'Your husband has been taken ill,' she heard. 'We think he has had a fit.'

The studio was only a quarter of an hour's drive away and by the time she got there Hancock was in his dressing room. He assured her that he was fine. He said he had not had a fit though he did not know the cause of the collapse unless it was the heat. He was wearing thick tweeds. The Disney executives had already called in specialists and were insisting that tests were carried out on Hancock because of the insurance cover.

Hancock objected, saying it was the heat, the studio lighting and the strain and stress of the part. He was asked to go to a hospital in Burbank but, instead, returned to the hotel. Freddie and Hancock's Hollywood agent argued that a visit to the hospital and submission to the tests were the best way he could clear himself and prove he was fit to work. They knew, they said, that he had not been drinking. Their arguments prevailed and he went to hospital where he was a given a thorough going-over, including a lumbar puncture. He was there for forty-eight hours.

Freddie telephoned the studios and told them this but the man she spoke to 'sounded very strange and a bit reluctant to take the good news that Tony had been cleared. I felt by instinct that things were not quite right so I called the agent, Irving Schecter, and he moved very fast and we found that they had already replaced Tony.

'This was a terrible blow to Tony. Looking back I wonder how much damage he had done in the weeks of rehearsals and read-throughs. He turned up very belligerently, I believe, one day and had thrown one of his temperaments. These were accepted in England but they didn't go down so well in Los Angeles where he hadn't got years of good will behind him. There was also the business about the actor and his wife and some other episodes and God knows what else. It doesn't do you any good in Hollywood to be seen wandering around red-eyed, unshaven and unkempt.

'Most of the people on the Disney set were nice and normal, people who did a job of work and were fairly well-adjusted. They wouldn't have taken too kindly to someone who was living under extra stresses and strains. But I was not prepared to let Tony suffer as a result of it. I didn't want him to go back to Los Angeles. I wanted him to make them sweat it out and withdraw their replacement so we went to New York.'

The idea was that they should stay in New York while his agents sorted things out but Hancock was beyond reasoning and decided he wanted to leave, not for England but France.

'I was cross with him,' says Freddie, 'because I wanted to stay and fight it: I didn't want it to beat him.'

She was still packing when he said he was going out to get a cab. She waited upstairs for the porter to collect the cases when Bernie Lang telephoned. She told him she was waiting for Hancock and Lang said the hotel had told him that he had already checked out. He had. He had left her ticket at the reception desk, paid the bill, and walked out. All he had with him were the clothes he was wearing, and his passport and ticket. All Freddie had was all the suitcases and $20. She got to the airport as he was checking in. She went up behind him and tapped him on the shoulder. 'Have you forgotten anything?' she said.

'What?'

'Me, for instance.'

They flew to Paris together. 'It was not a happy journey,' comments Freddie.

From Paris they went to Cannes and from there Hancock telephoned Cicely so that she would know he was all right no matter what news came out of Hollywood. Cicely flew to Cannes to see him and there were some wild drunken scenes.

Hancock took an apartment with Freddie. 'I kept on losing him,' she recalls. 'He wasn't trying to lose me – he was just amiably wandering off getting drunk, drinking with Cicely and other people. It was like living on a volcano that was about to erupt any second. He was burning himself up. The slightest thing would topple him over.'

There was another row between them while they were in a car they had hired. This time it was the end. They would split. She told him not to forget his passport. Afterwards, he told her he felt that he had been in the wrong, he provoked her. At the time he got out of the car and walked into a shop announcing that he was going to buy her a present. He wanted to get her an expensive red alligator bag but she said she didn't want a red bag and they didn't have what she wanted so they left.

'Suddenly we were giggling,' she says, 'and we came out of the bag shop and walked straight into Bernard Delfont and some friends.'

Delfont was rather more than surprised. He was, after all, the head of the agency that had booked Hancock for the Disney film and, as far as he knew, Hancock should have been safely tucked away in Hollywood.

'He wasn't very complimentary about his treatment by the Disney studios,' says Delfont recalling the meeting, 'and this seemed to make him very angry. He seemed to me to be keen to have another go to get right back on top and he mentioned the Talk of the Town and said he was sorry he let me down about it the last time.'

Delfont said the offer was still open and Hancock said he would like to take it up.

'I said, "Well, fine, let me know,"' says Delfont, 'and there were some more pleasantries and off he went and I thought I'd hear nothing more about it. I duly got back to London and he rang me and said, "I'm rehearsing. I feel great."

'I thought "fine" and we set the date for ten days later. I understand he wanted to cry off a couple of times and that Freddie persuaded him to carry on. She really spurred him on. If she hadn't been around he would have cried off again, not for any malicious reason but because it became too much of a responsibility for him. Eventually he did appear and he worked. He didn't do all the new material he said he was going to do but he did his usual act. He did not do big business.'

In fact, Hancock, on a percentage, averaged about £500 a week for the six weeks he worked there. This was about half the potential of the place.

Before he went to the Talk of the Town he asked Galton and Simpson if they had any cabaret material for him.

They were too busy.

The approach to Galton and Simpson was not the only sign that Hancock was having second thoughts. In an interview with Barry Norman of the *Daily Mail* in June 1965 he said, 'I started intellectualising and moralising about comedy. All I want to do is to get laughs. That's what comedy's all about.'

It was another answer to his constant search for definitions. It came a little late in the day.

At the Talk of the Town he did the Sinatra bit, the clan bit, sang 'There's no Business Like Show Business' halfway through then stopped and said, 'I can't go on with this load of rubbish,' which was in the script and 'Nobody can get a fiasco like this without assistance,' which wasn't.

He sang 'I Feel Pretty', which was Freddie's idea, and did Captain Bligh and George Arliss, Robert Newton and Noël Coward and – something new – Eartha Kitt. He then did the Hunchback of Notre Dame and his ham Shakespeare.

'You are really getting the lot,' he told his audience. 'Tonight you are looking at Mr Showbusiness himself 1965. Born in a trunk like Judy Garland, Bob Hope, Danny Kaye. All born in a trunk.'

He sang, he had a go at pop singers. He used his Birmingham accent and his American accent. He imitated Elvis Presley and he backchatted with the band.

Mockingly he announced: 'At this moment of remembrance I feel it opportune to introduce that well-loved piece of material, first introduced by me just before the Great Fire of London, none other than your own, your very own, Gaumont British News.'

About the only thing he missed out was the stag's head joke.

No other comedian in the world has ever got away with such ancient material on such an important engagement. That Hancock did, that he still made £500 a week on percentage, is a testament to the extraordinary loyalty of his audience.

When he first opened at the Talk of the Town there was a police guard on the doors because he feared that Cicely might cause a disturbance. They were having a furious row over the divorce settlement. More important to Cicely than anything else was a gull-winged Mercedes which she loved to drive. To prevent it going to her, he sold it. As things turned out, she did not interrupt his performances and, indeed, there is no indication that she ever went near the Talk of the Town while he was appearing there.

After each performance visitors thronged the dressing room. One night there was a big crowd and Hancock was happily relaxed and talking. At 3 a.m. Freddie started flashing warning signals at him and she gradually became more restless.

'I had to open an office at nine o'clock in the morning,' she says. 'Tony thought that everything should revolve round him. I was trying to run a business as well.

'Finally, at quarter to six, he said: "If you're going to try to break the atmosphere of good conversation you'd better go. I'm not coming." I left. I wasn't happy about walking around Leicester Square at that time of the morning but I found a taxi and got back to the flat.'

Hancock had found himself a new scriptwriter called Len Costa who, he was sure, would give him the support he was looking for. And so he might have done had Hancock left him alone. It was a conversation with Costa about *The Link*, the film he wanted to make about religion, that he refused to let Freddie interrupt.

'Freddie was obviously tired,' says Costa, 'and tried to sleep on the bench seat. Tony didn't expect her to feel tired when he wasn't. Everybody else left but he wanted to talk about the film.

'After Freddie had gone home I felt a bit guilty and suggested we sought out a friend of mine I hadn't seen for years in Covent Garden to buy her some flowers. We took a taxi but it was a long time before we found my friend. Then it turned out he was in vegetables, not flowers, so Tony bought two large baskets of mushrooms from him. Then we were taken to a flower stand where Tony bought two huge boxes of gladioli. Then we went to one of the Covent Garden pubs and after that we had to find the taxi because we had left our coats and things in it.

'When we got to Dorset Square I let Tony go into the main room while I went into the kitchen. I gather the gifts were not well received though it seemed a bright idea at the time.'

Freddie takes up the story: 'About quarter past seven Tony arrived with a box of flowers. He was more than a little drunk. I made my feelings clear and said that nobody could buy my friendship and he had already told me to clear off in no uncertain language. I intended to do just that. He became very belligerent and punched my nose and ear. My nose started to bleed. He left and I telephoned my doctor who, as I had had several nose operations, telephoned my parents. I was furious at this intrusion into my private life and never used that doctor again. My parents came and were very upset. Eventually they went home and I carried on all day. I asked my secretary to stay the night with me and that evening we went to the pictures. As I came down the stairs of the cinema I saw my face in a mirror. My secretary had been telling me I should go to the hospital. My nose was twisted and swollen. We went to the Middlesex Hospital and they found it was broken. My ear-drum was pierced as well.'

Hancock had, by then, moved into the Ritz.

Leaving Dorset Square, he told Costa he was going to get a flat. They arrived at an estate agents just as it was opening. After waiting two minutes Hancock became impatient and said they would go to the Ritz instead.

'He had an old sweater on,' says Costa, 'and I said, "Just look at us; we've been up all night and we look it."

'I'd been paying for the taxis, the flowers and the mushrooms and he didn't have any money with him so with my last few shillings we got a taxi to the Ritz. Of course, he had to order a suite. We went to bed and woke up about four o'clock in the afternoon and he ordered breakfast. I wanted to go home to get some things, but Tony wanted me to stay with him. He said, "Ring your wife and tell her to bring whatever you want." I said, "She can't, there are the two children." He said she should bring them along. So she did and they stayed. Simon was six and Tony tried to teach him to play chess.'

By now Hancock was contrite. He told Costa how much he needed Freddie and he took her to lunch at the Ritz the day she was due to go into the Ear, Nose and Throat Hospital for treatment.

Hancock hated hospitals. They were kept waiting for about twenty minutes and when they were finally shown Freddie's room he decided it was too small. He said, 'Right, let's go, you're not staying here.'

He took her out and they got into a taxi. 'I explained to him that I had to have an operation that day otherwise my nose would be permanently affected,' says Freddie.

They called at Charing Cross Hospital, University College Hospital and Middlesex Hospital and Hancock could not understand why they would not accept her without a booking. The London Clinic said that most of the oil magnates were over at that time of the year. Eventually they got back to the Ritz. He had some champagne and she had some tea.

He telephoned the surgeon who was to have operated and asked for the Ritz doctor to be sent up. The two doctors said she should return to the Ear, Nose and Throat Hospital where she could have a bigger room if she didn't mind sharing with a little girl who was having her tonsils out. Freddie agreed. Hancock had got through the bottle of champagne by then and had disappeared into the bedroom.

She asked him if he would see her into hospital again. He said, 'No, I've gone to bed.' And she went into hospital on her own.

Next to the bottle, Hancock's favourite refuge was bed. When things got too much for him he tucked himself in, pulled the covers over his head and blanketed the problem with sleep. There are no problems in the womb.

While Freddie was in hospital he telephoned her at all hours. She had to go to another floor to take the calls – sometimes at 3 a.m. – in order not to disturb the little girl recovering from the tonsillectomy. Hancock visited her once, staying about two minutes.

'I had had enough,' says Freddie. 'I went into the ward attached to the room and it was full of people with terrible illnesses. I tried to make them laugh about the way I looked with sun-glasses and a plaster-of-paris nose. I had this ghastly noise in my head from the pierced ear-drum. I didn't like the food. So I thought, Right, Mr Hancock, you had better pay for your sins and so I telephoned a couple of restaurants every evening and ordered twenty-four salt beef sandwiches and Chinese food for twelve and told them to put it on Mr Hancock's bill. I thought, You dare to complain, Mr Hancock, and I'll tell them how I came to be here.'

On 6 July, while Hancock was at Talk of the Town, Cicely gained her divorce on the grounds of Hancock's adultery with Freddie. Freddie had agreed to be cited. The suit was undefended and the judge exercised discretion over Cicely's adultery. 'This lapse by Mrs Hancock,' he said, 'was very short-lived and I don't think it should stand in the way of her divorce. She admitted it to her husband and he forgave her.'

Cicely's parents, while remaining fond of Hancock and remembering him with great affection, think the divorce was the only solution.

'I was convinced it was absolutely necessary,' says Dr Romanis. 'I was very sorry about it but it had been coming for some little time.'

Chapter Eleven

Hancock's career was astonishingly resilient. Every catastrophe was followed by another chance; every fumbled chance by another offer. Like Freddie his audiences took one bashing after another and always went back for more.

'The public,' say Galton and Simpson, 'never deserted him. They suffered along with him, the same as they suffered along with Judy Garland.'

Galton and Simpson were involved, reluctantly, in the next big opportunity in Hancock's life. They had written a musical version of *Noah*, André Obey's play which makes the old water-borne patriarch a protesting, irascible, unwilling partner in God's plan to give the world a second chance. It is strange that whenever someone was required to play the lone survivor of the human race, the unhappy, harassed, weary Hancock was the obvious choice. In a neurotic age he was Everyman.

Leslie Bricusse who wrote the music enlisted Freddie's help to see if Hancock could be persuaded out of his reluctance to enter a long-running show. They would need him for a least nine months just to get the money back. Freddie read out some of the dialogue between Noah and God, putting all her long years of exposure to Hancock's timing into the task. Hancock became enthusiastic about the idea and offered himself for the run of the show.

Sean Kenny was to design the production and Delfont would mount it.

The enthusiasm was not unanimous.

'We never conceived Tony in it in the first place,' say Galton and Simpson. 'It was only because Sean said that every line of it was Hancock that we even started thinking about him. It certainly never was written for him. We thought it would be wrong for Tony to do it because he didn't like the stage anyway, even when we first met him when he was at the Adelphi.

'We thought he would not even be interested but he was. He got quite obsessive about it in fact and kept ringing us up to talk about it. If it had ever got on it is doubtful whether it would have lasted a fortnight with Tony in it.

'But Delfont and Bricusse and everybody else were very keen and we were the only ones who had any reservations.

'They took the view that his main trouble was that he hadn't done anything good for a long time. Remedy that and he'd be back again right at the top. Nobody seemed to notice that he seemed to be wandering a bit when we discussed things. But we did. If we could have done it with Tony some ten years before it would have been fantastic because he was dead right for it then. It would have been quite an event.'

Hancock became haunted by *Noah*.

Sean Kenny said: 'He used to come round to see me almost every day and talk about all the production ideas. He went on the *Eamonn Andrews' Show* and talked about the wood I was going to drop on his head.'

Kenny's idea was that when Noah looks up to the heavens and asks, 'But where am I going to get the wood from?' timber would rain down all over the stage. 'Of course,' Kenny told Hancock, 'we shall have to practise a bit so that we miss you.' Kenny told Hancock that he would leave him a little place on the side of the stage where he could act and that if he missed him with the planks he might get him with the water.

Kenny was a short, stocky Irishman with revolutionary ideas about stage décor and most other things, particularly architecture. His sets – he designed for *Oliver, Blitz, Maggie May, The Four Musketeers*, and the Royal Shakespeare Company's production of *The Beggar's Opera* – were massive and inclined to dominate the actor. It was frequently observed that people come out of Kenny-designed musicals humming the scenery.

He and Hancock grew very fond of each other. One of the essential things they shared was a gentleness of speech and a wide, loving tolerance. In Hancock's case the tolerance, at this stage, was more general than particular. He could get very ratty with individuals.

Kenny once sent Hancock a copy of the little red book containing the thoughts of Chairman Mao inscribed: 'What about this for a musical?' Hancock rang back immediately and said it was a great idea.

Kenny understood that all shows are fantasies that only begin to take shape when the contracts are signed. But he was impressed by Hancock's grasp of concrete production problems and his attention to such details as the selection of supporting actors.

It became clear to him after a while, however, that there would be no fruition. He believed that no one had the courage to say, 'Tony, they are not going to do it because they don't trust you.'

Hancock persevered with the idea long after it had been abandoned by everyone else. Even after he heard that the rights had been sold to an American company he maintained that as there was no copyright on the subject itself other writers could be found who would prepare a musical and that eventually a film would come out of it for him. He was still nursing the idea when he went to Australia and his appointment with the vodka bottle and the overdose of tranquillising tablets in 1968.

In 1965 there was no real mystery behind the failure of *Noah* to materialise. It would have cost £100,000 to stage and would have had to run about a year before any profit was shown. Delfont, who thought Hancock would be magnificent in the role, was prepared to take a chance with him on a solo engagement but he could not put up that amount of money only to find his star backing down at the last minute or prostrate through drink or stress. Hancock, he knew, would not fail him willingly, would want to fulfil every obligation. All their arrangements were on a handshake basis. But it was evident that Hancock was less and less in control of his actions.

Kenny on Hancock: 'It's a problem of every artist. Once you are accepted you are finished really because it is very difficult to explore any more. The point of being an artist is that you must progress, you must live with the sense of danger. You must be able to put your head on the block, take chances, go beyond yourself and beyond what is expected of you.

'Tony wanted to take a chance but the more he took a chance the more they laughed and the funnier he became. He was stuck, caught in the net of the clown. The sadder his face, the more people laughed. He couldn't get out of it. He wanted to become a serious artist. He was very talented. He could sketch very well, draw cartoons – fantastic cartoons – of people. His hands were good, he could dance well and he had a musical ear. He was an all-round artist in a sense but he had this bloody clown face and they kept laughing at him. All he had to do was to put his coat on and everybody would break out laughing. He was caught as a clown and he couldn't get out of it and this was what was frustrating him. So he began to drink. He never took drugs except as a cure for drink. It was purely drink to fog his mind so that he would stop thinking. And the sadness was that when he had a few drinks he would go into the old Hancock routine because the clown was still there.'

One of the more successful episodes in Hancock's life about this time was the *Eamonn Andrews' Show* in which he talked about Kenny's ark.

His appearance had been prepared for with some care. Without him being aware of it, Freddie worked on him for a couple of weeks beforehand using his comments on television shows as a basis. He thought, for instance, that the sexiest thing on television was Janet (Barbara Mullen) of *Dr Finlay's Casebook*, and he had a splendid fantasy about *Come Dancing*.

He had heard the commentator say that one of the sleek-haired, immensely serious competitors in white tie and tails was a sheet-metal worker by day and he pictured the conversation over the molten metal.

'Bert,' he would say, lifting his protective visor back for a breather and wiping the sweat from his face. ' 'Ere, Bert, I think I'll give 'em a touch of the feather tonight when I'm in the middle of me crossover.'

For a week before the show Freddie encouraged him to develop the idea and then told one of the programme assistants to get Andrews to ask Hancock what his favourite television programmes were. It came out as a superb bit of apparently unrehearsed comedy.

Taken professionally, 1965 was not a bad year for Hancock. He filmed a supporting role in Bryan Forbes' film *The Wrong Box*, BBC television repeated nineteen of his shows in a series called *The Best of Hancock* and he went to Australia.

Freddie suggested that as the decree absolute would come through while he was away she might join him in Australia where they could get married quietly and without fuss. Hancock, accompanied by his road manager, Glyn Jones, stopped off at Fiji on the way and, telephoning Freddie from there, admitted that he had had a couple of beers.

'It may sound stupid,' she says, 'but I went hysterical because one beer was the same as a bottle of vodka to him. Once the alcohol had got into his system it was just a matter of time before he was back on to it properly. So I phoned up the doctor and I phoned his mother and I tried at 14,000 miles distance to try to stop him. The doctor spoke to him and eventually I decided I would fly out earlier than I anticipated. He promised I would not have the same greeting I got in Los Angeles and he was as good as his word. There was a waiting limousine and he was clean-shaven and bright-eyed.'

Freddie was going to marry him even though, she says, he had attempted to strangle her.

At 3.30 one morning she had been pleading with him not to drink.

'You have a great talent,' she said. 'The world worships you. I love you. Yet you're prepared to let the bottle destroy you, destroy everything.'

She picked up the bottle and threw it on the floor.

He went for her. His hands were round her throat and he tried to strangle her. She fought him off and he collapsed. A doctor was called. Hancock went in for another few days' 'treatment'; Freddie was given some more pills.

On one of the occasions when she threatened to take an overdose if he took another drink, he took another drink and she could only find Ex-Lax tablets. She took five of them. The next day he was fine and she was a wreck. During the time she lived with him and was married to him she could not wear short-sleeved dresses because of the weals and bruises on her arms.

Undeflected by these experiences she was still eager to marry him. There were, after all, good times, too. When she joined him in Australia there was another period of restrained discipline.

'Discipline,' says Freddie, 'is not exactly the word for it – boredom is more like it.'

She was allowed to see his act for the first night she was there and after that she stayed in the hotel suite.

Hancock would sleep late, have breakfast, read the papers and then rest. They might watch a little golf occasionally but that was the nearest they got to the wild life. For the most part it was sleeping, eating and tea-drinking.

Hancock was appearing in cabaret at the hotel, the Chevron Hilton, so he did not even get the excitement of a taxi-ride. While he was working Freddie sat upstairs and watched television. It always seemed to be *Coronation Street*.

After about a week of this Freddie was going off her head with boredom so Hancock took her sight-seeing occasionally and let her watch him make a television commercial.

It was for a new Australian biscuit and it was rather complicated, with a number of sequences at the end of which up would pop Hancock urging, 'Don't forget to take so-and-so's biscuits.'

Only he couldn't remember the name of the biscuit. Searching desperately for the magic words, he eventually came up with a triumphant 'Silvikrin Shampoo'.

They never did show that commercial.

While they were there Hancock's solicitor cabled them to say that the decree was absolute and they were free to marry.

They bought a wedding ring in Australia and planned to return home via Honolulu where they would marry. They booked in at the Honolulu Hilton and went down to the beach where they stretched out in the sun. It started to rain. Hancock's theory was that a personal raincloud followed him wherever he went. There was also a man with a drill tearing up the street outside the window in every hotel they stayed at. Hancock often wondered how the drill operator found the money for the air fares. At any rate, both cloud and drill were there in Honolulu, as they had both been in Sydney.

Hancock planned a romantic evening. He told Freddie that they were going on a moonlight trip around the bay, two in a boat and dinner on board.

He went off to have a haircut, a sure sign that he was trying hard to please, and Freddie, knowing that he was going to appear as Ronald Colman, decided to be Loretta Young and dressed accordingly in a white dress, high-heeled white shoes and a chiffon scarf. They had arranged to meet at a quay near the hotel. The boat was a catamaran and their fellow passengers wore Bermuda shorts, Hawaiian shirts, and numerous cameras.

Freddie and Tony felt a little ostentatious but they went aboard.

They were handed song sheets of such native numbers as 'Deep in the Heart of Texas' and were offered bowls of a particularly vile-looking punch which Hancock wouldn't have drunk even if it had looked palatable, because he was on the wagon.

They drank Coca-Cola instead. Dinner was served – plastic food on a plastic airline tray. As the evening wore on Hancock became more and more cross and miserable. When they got off the boat Freddie tripped in her high heels and this cheered him up a lot.

Freddie said that she did not care whether he was on the wagon or not, she was going to have a large drink because she had never felt less like Loretta Young in her life, and Hancock admitted that Ronald Colman's mantle had dropped from his shoulders quite early in the evening.

The following day they tried to get a marriage licence. They were told that they had to have a blood test. There were a lot of people waiting – Hawaiians, Puerto Ricans, Mexicans and a dozen other assorted nationalities. Hancock reacted exactly like a comic and clutched at the cue for a piece of familiar material. 'Blood,' he boomed, 'you can have it if it's really necessary – plenty to spare of the stuff, oh dear yes, gallons of it, haven't we, Fred?'

The audience sat in silence. Poor souls, they didn't know what he was on about.

After twenty minutes Hancock had had enough. 'I came here in good faith,' he declared, 'to give 'em a spoonful of the best British blood. If they don't want it – the best of luck. I'm going.' And he went. Freddie followed.

As a consolation prize for not getting married in Honolulu Hancock bought Freddie a string of pearls. Later she lost them. They flew home.

Back in London they had separate addresses, he at the White House, she at her flat in Dorset Square. The first Saturday they were back he told her they would get married on the following Tuesday. She said it was too soon and she had nothing to wear.

He had often said that he did not know why women wanted to get married, that a piece of paper did not give them a hold on a man.

'You're right,' she told him. 'Let's stay as we are. I won't be unfaithful to you and you won't be unfaithful to me, we won't have to ask each other questions about where we have been and be possessive.'

He was frequently and unreasonably jealous and regularly accused Freddie of being unfaithful to him with the unlikeliest people. Her proposal to continue as they were did not suit him.

On Monday morning she was at her office when an *Evening Standard* reporter telephoned to say that he understood she was marrying Hancock at 11.30 on Thursday. Hancock came bursting up the stairs, disappointed that he was not the first to break the news to her.

They were married on 2 December at Marylebone Register Office. Hancock, she discovered later, had spent part of the previous night watching her flat in the belief that she was planning a wild final fling.

There were fourteen people at the wedding and one of them was Kati Hannan, a friend of Freddie's. 'Freddie was nervous and Tony was quite high,' Mrs Hannan says. 'His family were sitting against one wall and hers against the other and they were all watching him drink. There was a bit of an atmosphere. I tried to jolly things up and said, "Let's cut the cake." Tony snapped at Freddie that I was acting like a Butlin's redcoat and she fled into the bedroom – the reception was in an hotel suite – in tears.' Freddie recalls it differently. 'At least,' she says, 'my brother Leonard and Tony's brother Roger were very friendly.'

For a time after they were married the Hancocks lived near Kati. Freddie asked her for her recipe for cheesecake and they bought the ingredients together.

'I went round the next morning to see if it had been successful,' says Mrs Hannan. 'The trouble with Freddie is that she always gives too much. I had said four eggs but she thought it would be even better with six eggs and it ran all over the place. But they ate it. He was very sweet. He said it was the loveliest cheesecake he had ever drunk.'

It was not long after that that Hancock telephoned Mrs Hannan and asked her to go over to see Freddie as he had arranged for her to have psychiatric treatment and had not told her. She told him it was a terrible thing to do and insisted that he should at least tell Leonard.

He agreed to do this and Mrs Hannan sat with Freddie until it was time to go to the nursing-home.

'When they were together and when he was sober,' says Mrs Hannan, 'he was marvellous for her. For one thing, he used to slap her down and I don't mean physically. He'd say "shut up" and she'd shut up and would become soft and more womanly. In good times they were wonderful for each other. Freddie and I were having lunch one day and Tony just walked into the restaurant, gave her a watch and said, "Right, I'm going now. Goodbye."

'Other times Freddie could not go out without calling him every few minutes to tell him where she was and who she was with and to ask if he was all right.'

As a marriage gesture to Freddie he finally discarded the duffel coat she had been urging him to get rid of for years. Under her influence he was to become a far less eccentric dresser, changing his hairy sweaters for coloured shirts, his beaten-up sports jackets for neat, dark suits tailored to flatter the fuller figure. He also had his hair cut in a more fashionable style. It was combed forward and made him look like a minor Roman emperor to whom an unfunny thing had happened on the way to the Forum.

This was going to be the new, sleek Hancock and he sporadically went on crash diets to complete the image. He looked like a fat man desperately trying to get back inside a thin man's body.

The honeymoon was in Dublin at the Gresham Hotel. Months later she found out that the orange juice he had drunk there had been heavily laced with vodka and that he had filled up the bottle with water so that she would not notice. Freddie was allergic to Australian gold and they had to buy another ring. A few days afterwards they flew home.

They lived in a furnished flat overlooking the Edgware Road and ten days later there was a flaming row and Hancock marched out and went to Lingfield to see Cicely.

The following morning Len Costa was telephoned at five

o'clock at his home in Enfield by Hancock and told to pack a suitcase. A little later Hancock, accompanied by Cicely and his ex-wrestler friend, Stan Gibbons, called for Costa and took him to MacConkeys. 'We,' announced Hancock, 'are going to write.'

'Tony and Cicely were friendly,' says Costa, 'nothing more. It was a reasonable relationship. Tony had obviously had a row with Freddie. When we got to MacConkeys we worked on ideas for a television series. That night, Tony and I shared a twin-bedded room. I never slept. Cicely came in and they talked. Cicely sat on my bed and they both thought I was asleep. It was one of those absurd things. I wasn't prying but I felt it was important for me to stay awake in case anything started to go wrong. They didn't talk about anything deep or serious.

'It was clear to me that he was fond of Cicely but I am absolutely convinced that he never at any time considered going back to her. During the whole of the weekend he became unhappy every time it hit him that he was away from Freddie. I knew he would be going back to her.

'The next morning I was writing in the study and Tony and Cicely were half-joking, half-fighting. They started to spar and then it became a wrestling match. It was almost a test of strength. Then Cicely threw Tony. He landed on a small side table that collapsed just like in a film scene. Then it developed more seriously, probably because he had been thrown and it was an affront. I started clearing things up in the study; it was obvious that we weren't going to stay. They were downstairs. Cicely came in and said, "I've phoned the police." I said, "Why?" She said, "Oh, it all got too much."

'When the police arrived Cicely was, I think, regretting it and said she had called them because Tony was insisting on taking the car and had been drinking. I think she was trying to tone down the incident. They agreed that it probably wouldn't be wise to drive the car and the police left. I gather it was reported as a domestic incident.

'I also felt that Tony shouldn't drive the car and there was a big argument. Eventually, he agreed that he wouldn't drive and hired a car.

'On the way back we stopped at a pub and I rang Freddie. She asked, "Do you mean he is on his way back to me?" I said he was. It was obvious to me – had been all the time – that this was what he had to do.'

Subsequently, Cicely threatened to sue Hancock for assault and battery. The accusation was dropped during the course of negotiations for maintenance which were dragging on at the time. In fact, they were fairly speedily concluded after this incident.

Hancock returned to Freddie drunk and she sobered him up. By then there were a number of journalists around asking questions. She told them that he had merely gone back to Lingfield to collect some books, that there had been a misunderstanding which resulted in his former wife calling the police and that the police had laughed it all off as a domestic tiff. That was the version of the incident that appeared in the newspapers.

Hancock voluntarily suggested that he took an aversion cure and on 27 December, twenty-five days after the marriage, he went into a nursing-home in Hampstead. He only stayed for two weeks. He would never admit that he was an alcoholic. He always thought that one little drink wouldn't do him any harm.

The aversion cure consists of an offer of a choice of drink followed by an injection which induces violent vomiting. Hancock built up such a resistance to this treatment that he was able to wash away the unpleasant associations of the cure with more drink.

Being abroad always brought out the romantic in Hancock. There was the time they went to Rome. They had set out for Paris to discuss a possible film but on arrival at London Airport were told that Paris was closed because of fog.

'Where's the next plane out going to?' asked Hancock. He was told Hamburg. 'Right. Hamburg it is,' he said. In Hamburg they hired a taxi and drove through the night to Berlin. He wanted to see the Berlin Wall and brood a little on man's folly. They went to a beer garden and Hancock was refused entrance because he was not wearing a tie. He spoke a little German and he and the doorman exchanged insults. Then Hancock bent down, untied a shoe-lace, slipped it round his neck and said, 'Does this suit you, Fritzy?' They were allowed in. From Berlin they went to Frankfurt and from Frankfurt to Rome. In Rome the romance came to the fore. They had had a good meal and a decent bottle of Chianti. 'I feel like a cross between Rossano Brazzi and the man from the Prudential,' he told Freddie. A couple of musicians walked over to the table and started to serenade them with 'Sorrento'.

'Don't mess about with that, mate,' said Hancock, 'we're all in the same business. Sit down and have a drink.'

After the meal he asked Freddie what she would like to do. She wanted to throw some coins in the fountain.

Hancock paid the bill, over-tipped, bowed to everyone and they sauntered out into the night heading towards the Trevi fountain.

After a while he pulled up. 'Me feet!' he said. 'They're killing me.'

He spotted a horse trough not far away. 'This'll do, Fred,' he said. 'I mean, it's water, isn't it?'

So they threw a few lire into the horse trough with Hancock whinnying occasionally and shaking with laughter.

'Have you wished?' he asked Freddie. But before she replied, he said, 'I don't blame you. I'll do my best – I swear I will.'

But it was about the nearest he ever got to water. They returned to London via Paris, meeting the American film producer they had originally set out to see. Hancock quarrelled with him.

Freddie feared Paris. 'I hated Tony in Paris,' she says. 'The cafés are fun if you are with a normal person but even when he was dry he would sit in them and order endless cups of coffee because he couldn't tear himself away from them. Paris was always a threat hanging over me. It's a drinking city.

'I wasn't really so bloody-minded as I possibly seemed to so many people. But I had been terrified by what I had seen of Tony in his drunken state and by what the doctors had said, scaring the life out of me with warnings of what could happen to him. I was always tense and neurotic in Paris.

'We enjoyed the food but he would say it was not so enjoyable without a glass of wine. Of course it wasn't, but he couldn't have a wine gum without it ending up as a bottle of vodka before the day was out.'

When he came back he did a series of very funny television commercials for the Egg Marketing Board. He followed these up by agreeing to compère a weekly television variety show from Blackpool.

At the time of the Blackpool show he kept repeating to interviewers, 'I'm more mature . . . I've stopped worrying . . . I did too much intellectualising . . . I just want to make people laugh. That's what it's all about.'

He earned £1200 a show and he forgot the name of the act he was introducing on the first show. This in itself was no disaster and has happened to more sober and less talented comics. But he looked uncertain and his timing was wrong. It was as if only a great effort of will was stopping him from falling apart.

He did, however, bring a refreshing new approach to the business of compèring. Instead of whipping up synthetic enthusiasm for the feast of entertainment about to be brought to the eager viewer, he would fix him with a jaundiced eye and say, 'Well, we've got a right lot of old rubbish here for you tonight.'

Hancock travelled to Blackpool at weekends, spending the rest of the time in the flat he and Freddie had taken in Knightsbridge. Freddie had been told that she must have an operation for the removal of a growth but postponed it in order to help Hancock to get through the new series.

On 9 July 1966, Hancock was preparing to go north. He had drunk a bottle and a half of champagne and was chasing it down with brandy. It was 9.45 a.m. Freddie packed his bags for him. Then she started to take pills. Hancock sat on the bed and watched her. She took pills that had been prescribed for him and pills that had been issued to her.

'I wanted to die,' she says.

Hancock adjusted his tie and combed his hair. Then he said, 'Take enough this time. Make a good job of it. Because I shan't be calling an ambulance.'

Then he went out. Half an hour later his chauffeur returned for the cases. He saw Freddie and asked if there was anything wrong. 'Just migraine,' she told him.

The chauffeur told Hancock she was ill. He said, 'Fuck her. I'll see you in Liverpool.'

The chauffeur took the luggage up by road: Hancock went to Liverpool by train and used the car to commute to Blackpool for the show.

By now Freddie was comatose. The daily help found her in a half-wrecked flat – the furniture turned over, lamp-shades knocked down, photographs all over the floor.

'I don't know how that happened,' says Freddie.

She was taken to the Middlesex Hospital.

That night Hancock rehearsed for the Blackpool show and the following night he appeared. By then news of the attempted suicide was out. Hancock, who had always maintained that cant phrases like 'the show must go on' were a load of rubbish, said, in effect, that the show must go on.

In the struggle to save Freddie's life the doctors would have been helped if they had known precisely what pills she had taken. They were unable to get the information from the only man who did know.

On Tuesday, Hancock returned to London and went to see Freddie in hospital. He swore at her. Her mother and two women friends went to the flat to collect some of Freddie's clothes and Hancock, drunk, started throwing her things about. He telephoned Freddie in hospital that afternoon and shouted that her parents had broken up the flat. Freddie went into a nursing-home and the marriage was over apart from the formalities. When she divorced him she cited another woman but, she says, 'it would have been as true to have cited a bottle of seventy-eight per cent proof.'

A week later Hancock gave an interview in which he said the marriage was finished. He hoped he did not sound brutal but his wife could hurt him only once by doing a thing like that. He would not have gone on with the show, he said, if she had been in any real danger but the doctor assured him she was recovering gradually so 'What else could I do?' Later, he told Freddie he had been misquoted.

'I believe now,' says Freddie, 'that Tony was very angry and had genuinely convinced himself that I had phoned up all the newspapers to tell them I had taken an overdose in order to hurt his career. The last thing I wanted to do was to touch his career.'

On 25 July Hancock was out of the show and went into a nursing-home for nervous strain.

A week later he bounced back with, 'Sorry about last week. I had a touch of sunstroke or something.'

Peter Black in the *Daily Mail* reviewed one of Hancock's Blackpool shows:

To sit through it to enjoy him was rather like having to eat through an enormous round dull biscuit to get at the tasty bit in the centre, but it was worth it. For all the fits and starts it left his position unshaken as a great comedian . . .

It's not what he says or does but the interaction of the whole personality with a theatre audience that makes him irresistibly watchable . . . he seems to be living out a badgered and baffled section of his life in public . . . the watchful distrust and sense of looming catastrophe is projected with great technical skill out of his performance.

It is also very funny. Few comedians have been more sincerely willed to succeed. Instinctively one recognises the size of his dammed-up talent.

Hancock saw the piece and said, 'That was very perceptive.'

Chapter Twelve

Hancock was contrite, at least in public. He told journalist Ken Passingham in an interview: 'I am not an easy man to live with. I made my Fred suffer like mad. She is still suffering. She is, in fact, very ill and I feel terrible, so sorry at the way she has been torn apart. It has nearly creased me for good, too.

'So I sent away the furniture, all the things that reminded me of Fred. I couldn't even answer the phone. No good. I couldn't face it, living alone like some hermit . . .

'Y'see, I love Fred. And she loves me. Really she does. We were made for one another. There'll be no divorce. She's just waiting for me to, well, improve.'

Fred had, in fact, telephoned him and he had answered the phone that time to tell her: 'I have found someone younger and prettier than you.'

The new 'girl', in fact, was a married woman, older than Freddie and wife of a man Hancock had known for years. In his posthumously published autobiography, *A Jobbing Actor*, John Le Mesurier disclosed that the woman was his wife, Joan.

For all his debunking of show business myths, Hancock was hooked on the biggest one of all – the triumphant last-reel appearance of the hero in Carnegie Hall. The Festival Hall in London being the nearest equivalent, he booked himself in there. In its list of attractions for September 1966, sandwiched between the London Mozart Players on the 21st and a film of *La Bohème* on the 23rd, appeared this entry:

> Thursday, Sept. 22nd . . . Tony Hancock
> The Lad Himself Will
> Entertain You

When he set himself this challenge, the Lad said: 'It will be like taking a one-way ticket to Venezuela.'

He commissioned two young comedy writers, John Muir and

Eric Geen, who had scripted part of the Blackpool television series and were to be involved in his next – and final – British television series, to write a complete act lasting more than an hour. This time it was really going to be a new Hancock.

When he got their script, Hancock was like a small child with a Christmas present. For two months it never left his hands. He would walk about London with it, eat with it, get drunk with it and always remember to pick it up.

But he did not read it. He would open it at page one, read about four lines, say, 'This is beautiful stuff,' and put it aside. He went to Bournemouth to break in the act and used one line – the opening. It was, 'Good evening, ladies and gentlemen. I've never seen such an ornate garage.' It was, of course, intended for the Festival Hall and not for the Winter Gardens, Bournemouth. Cicely came down for a day to see him.

He had sent a message to George Fairweather telling him to take the week off while he was there so that they could both play some golf together. Fairweather was captain of a golf club. Hancock was always better at looking like a golfer than actually playing the game. He had started to learn as long ago as 1954 when he was in Blackpool where the course runs alongside a railway line. More often than not he found himself on the wrong side of the tracks.

Anyway, Fairweather must not argue; he was to make himself available for the whole week.

Fairweather, in fact, could not spare the time but hastened to the theatre between first and second houses on Monday. He sent in his name and was told that Mr Hancock could not see him because he was too busy.

Fairweather sent a message back saying that he was not hanging around for an autograph and that Hancock would not be busy at all if it were not for him. Hancock sent Glyn Jones out to apologise and explain that he had his writers with him. Fairweather never saw him the whole week. It upset him. He would have been even more upset if he had taken a week's holiday as Hancock had ordered.

The next time Fairweather saw him was in November. Hancock walked into his shop one morning 'looking like death'.

Fairweather said, 'You know what you can do, don't you?'

Hancock said, 'George, you don't know what I've been going through . . .?'

Fairweather said he didn't want to know. He had heard enough of his troubles over the years. He had his own troubles.

'You're not worried about money, are you?' said Hancock, upset at the thought. 'God, if only I'd known.'

Fairweather showed him a bill for £50 and thought that even if Hancock gave him the money it might just about square all the things he had lent him over the years that had never been returned. Then he ordered him out.

But Hancock said, 'Come on, George, you can't throw me out. I'm a customer.' And he insisted that Fairweather must cut his hair – for the first time ever. Fairweather cut his hair and gave him a shampoo. Hancock noticed that he was wearing a toupee. He called it a 'fred'.

'Have you got a good fred?' he asked. Fairweather said he had another one. Hancock asked to borrow it for a gag on a bald-headed friend. He only wanted it for a couple of days.

'If you lose it,' said Fairweather, 'it will cost you fifty quid to replace.'

'I won't lose it,' assured Hancock. 'And if I do I'll buy you a new one.'

He then telephoned a friend and talked for about twenty-five minutes.

Then, swearing lifelong gratitude for Fairweather, he left with the toupee. He did not pay for the haircut, the shampoo or the telephone call and Fairweather never saw his 'fred' again. Or Hancock, for that matter.

'But I had to laugh about it,' he says now. 'I suppose you could say that finally he scalped me.'

The Festival Hall show was looming and panic started to mount in Hancock. He tried to gain strength by summoning up ghosts from the more successful years. Galton and Simpson were once more asked if they could provide some material. They could not. Phyllis Rounce, dismissed in 1954, found herself called to the telephone at 3 a.m. and 4 a.m. in 1966 because she was, at the time, agent for Muir and Geen. Hancock kept demanding their presence during the night and suggesting comedy situations which Miss Rounce found pathetically inadequate.

Freddie's theory is that somehow Hancock always equated night work with accomplishment. To sit and talk through the night left him with a greater sense of achievement than he ever found in actually getting something down on paper in daylight hours.

Kenneth Williams, absent for ten years from Hancock's life, was suddenly needed urgently.

He was working on an outdoor lot at Pinewood, a long way from the nearest telephone. He kept getting messages asking him to ring Hancock back. He asked his agent to see what it was about. It seemed that Hancock wanted to do the 'Aeroplane' sketch – one of the funniest from the radio *Half Hour* days – at the Festival Hall. Williams was essential for it. By now it was the day before the show but Hancock still thought they would be able to do it by running through the lines in his dressing room.

Williams refused, not only because he did not want to work in such a slipshod fashion, but because he could not see how something that was essentially a radio script could be successful visually.

In *Just Williams*, Kenneth Williams says that when he returned to the studio Sid James asked him what was so urgent about the phone call. When he told him, James was 'amazed' and said: 'You'd be mad to work with him again, the man is a megalomaniac.'

But Williams adds: 'Sid wasn't given to hyperbole and at the time I agreed with him. Looking back on it now I think that the apparent selfish behaviour was only the outward sign of inner turmoil. Hancock wanted to cut himself off from the conventional concepts in search of a totally new approach to his work. His praise for the documentary-like reality of Jacques Tati's *Monsieur Hulot's Holiday* was significant. Tony was vainly seeking comedy in life itself, whereas the performer requires the alchemy of the story-teller who knows that we need art lest we perish from the truth.'

On 22 September the Festival Hall was packed. Hancock in his dressing room paced up and down muttering his lines, flexing his emotions. Kate and Terry Nation visited him to wish him good luck. They embraced and Nation said, 'Well, this is the one you've always talked about and I'm sorry it isn't me.'

Hancock told him: 'There's going to be a lot of you in it; there's always a lot of you.'

The first half of the evening was filled by singers, including Marian Montgomery. There was a lot of microphone trouble. People in the audience could not hear her and became restless. Nor, with all respect, had they paid to see anyone but Hancock. They wanted to see him; they wanted him to triumph. When he appeared an almost palpable wave of good will washed towards him and there was a great undercurrent of relief in the laughter which greeted his opening sally, a heartfelt gratitude that Hancock was still the same old lovable, laughable clown.

He looked around the auditorium and said, 'I've never seen such an ornate garage. Good evening to you all in the big dipper. I am told to say by the management that it is all acoustically perfect.

Tonight, for the price of a packet of fags, I'll be going through the card.'

Muir and Geen had, in fact, anticipated that there might be microphone trouble and had written the line about the place being acoustically perfect long beforehand.

It was a good launching, even though there was little new about the ship. Hancock did go through the card – the Olivier Richard III, Charles Laughton and all the other impersonations. He sang 'There's no business like show business', breaking off with the dismissive, 'What a lot of old rubbish.'

He also gave them part of 'The Blood Donor' and prompt boards for that and other material were held up in the wings. He tried desperately hard and the audience loved him for trying and loved him for partly succeeding and loved him for wanting to please them and there was so much love, so much good will and kindness that it became a triumph of a kind.

Of course, most of them realised that he was finished, drained, a husk of the clown they once knew.

The new, vigorous BBC2 channel had arranged with Hancock to record the show, giving him the unprecedented right to veto its transmission if he was not satisfied with it. David Attenborough, head of the channel, Tom Sloan and Frank Muir, who was then his assistant, were among the Festival Hall audience. Sloan thought the show was a disaster. Attenborough and Muir thought it was good and Hancock himself thought it had been great. Sloan's opposition was overruled and the show went out. Without the extraordinary Festival Hall atmosphere it was seen on television for what it really was – a travesty of what Hancock had once been. It was noble of the BBC to support Hancock and give him the tacit understanding that under the right circumstances there was still a place for him, but it would have done him better service to have confined the episode to the Festival Hall audience.

At any rate, the next series Hancock did was again for commercial television and the circumstances were profoundly wrong.

Before it started in January 1967, Hancock's immensely muddled private life became even more chaotic. He had a mistress; he occasionally telephoned Freddie and once he turned up at the Red Barn in Lingfield and, in a drunken, maudlin state, told Mrs Fryer that he had been a fool ever to leave Cicely.

He had arrived soaking wet from falling into a ditch and had gashed his arm badly on barbed wire. Mrs Fryer took him in and he stayed at the Red Barn that night. Cicely was away, visiting her parents.

The next day Hancock returned to London where he had an appointment to be interviewed. He almost told the truth when asked about his cut arm.

'I fell into a ditch,' he said, 'and cut it on some barbed wire.' Then he added with a laugh, 'The thing that annoys me is that I was stone-cold sober at the time.'

He told someone else: 'I'm just accident prone – but all this drama in your life doesn't half lift the audience ratings. It's like a public execution – there's never been a bigger draw than that.'

Freddie finally discarded her delusion that she could change Hancock.

'I loved Tony,' she says, 'and I never ceased to love him. But loving him and living with him were vastly different propositions.'

In December 1966, it was announced that they had parted. It surprised no one.

Hancock flew to Hong Kong for a couple of weeks of cabaret. When he arrived at the airport with Glyn Jones he caught a glimpse of a woman he mistook for Freddie. Instead of going straight to the hotel he insisted on being driven round the city. Suddenly, he ordered the driver to stop; he had spotted a giant teddy bear, more than life-size, and went into the shop and bought it.

He always associated teddy bears with Freddie. It was one of her endearments for him and, once, he had bought her four-year-old niece the biggest teddy bear to be found in the London Airport gift shop when they had returned from abroad and remembered that they had not got a present. It cost him twenty-five pounds to ship the Chinese teddy bear back to London and when it arrived he propped it up in a corner of his barely-furnished flat and sometimes gave interviews while sitting between its paws.

Hancock by now was always more enthusiastic and detailed about his plans for the middle distance, some unspecified period always six months ahead, than for today's rehearsal for tomorrow's show.

The new television series which was to be about 'swinging London' – a kiss of death both generally and as far as Hancock's particular talents were concerned – was not to be discussed. What he wanted to talk about were his plans for filming *The Link* which would show 'life for what it is'. The target would be 'accepted religion'. What was wrong with mankind was that they did not think. 'They don't use their nut,' was how he put it. And, of course, it would be international.

'Where did Laurel and Hardy live?' he asked. He supplied the answer. 'Nowhere. Where did Chaplin live? Nowhere. The world was their comedy playground.'

It is not even true. Laurel and Hardy lived in America and so did Chaplin's tramp. Their comedy was set against highly stylised but recognisably American backgrounds. The city in *City Lights* is an American city; the Alaska of the gold rush is an American frontier. It is significant that he did not ask where Tati lives. Even he could see that Tati's Frenchness is an integral part of his comedy. Hancock lived in England and was as English as a London bus.

The new series called *Hancock's* was for ABC Television and was set in a London restaurant that never was, a place where there was apparently a nightly variety show playing to about 100 people. Hancock's lifelong quest for reality brought him to a totally artificial situation.

ABC executives decided on this format believing that if Hancock were unable to sustain his solo performances, they could pad out with other acts.

After preliminary talks, Muir and Geen decided that what Hancock wanted was a return to classic music-hall routines so they gave him scripts in which the wine waiter, the gypsy fiddler and the chef acted as feeds.

ABC wanted him to learn his lines properly and were reluctant to let him have the idiot boards and teleprompts he demanded. There were shouting matches and scenes but they had to give in simply because he could not learn his lines. When shooting started he was told, very hesitantly, that he was working too slowly, that his pauses were too long. He rejoined by saying that he was not getting the close-ups that he needed. The close-up, with the camera peering into that marvellously mobile face, picking up the slightest quiver of reaction, had always been Hancock's greatest television asset. 'They've got to see the eyes. They must see these bleeding eyes.'

So they played back a show for him in the ABC offices in Hanover Square and after it ended there was a long, long silence in which nobody dared to say a word. Then Hancock groaned and said, 'I look like a bloody frog.'

It was not the *look* of the frog that mattered – many times in the early days Hancock would catch sight of himself in the mirror early in the morning and grunt cheerfully, 'Good morning, Mr Frog.'

What he had now was the stone-faced immobility of the frog. The reaction comic was not reacting any more.

The Times thought Hancock was 'sadly diminished by the script' and *The Guardian* gave him a cruelly prophetic review: 'All we get,' *The Guardian* said,

is some tired clowning: the well-known turns of the recent poor years of Hancock, the mock-Churchillian and pseudo-Shakespearian . . .

Compère and stand-up comic is his least effective role. I suppose it is some personal ambition that he is determined to fulfil. Remembering his team work with Sid James, with those scripts by Ray Galton and Alan Simpson (and even thinking of his very funny egg commercials with Mrs Cravat), it is extremely hard to see why he should continue in this particular form of suicide.

In July 1967 Hancock returned from a short visit to Aden where he entertained the troops and went into the London Clinic with 'nervous exhaustion'.

In October he went to Australia. At the Dendy Cinema, Melbourne, he was unsteady and at one point crawled about the stage on all fours. The audience voiced their objections and he made the astonishing blunder of ordering the spotlights to be turned on them. There is something shaming and threatening to an audience who find themselves lit up unexpectedly. They have not had time to compose their faces into acceptable masks and feel exposed and in danger. They booed and hooted and Hancock had to be helped off the stage by the manager. Later he gave an excuse that not even Freddie had been able to use – he was, he gravely explained, suffering from the effects of cholera injections, aggravated by his diet and two glasses of beer. One of his Australian friends, however, has a theory that some bastard laced his tomato juice with vodka.

The following night Hancock gave a free show, bouncing back with, 'As I was about to say before I fell off the stage . . .' He was cheered and loved again. Hancock's popularity in Australia was as great as it was in Britain and his audiences there were just as willing to forgive and remember.

Hancock spent the Christmas of 1967 in a nursing home in Bournemouth with another 'attack of pneumonia'. He came out armed with another theory of comedy.

'I think,' he said, 'that experience of life is more important than talent. Now, because of what I've been through, I'm a better artist.'

It was arrant nonsense. Certainly, it would never have convinced the taxi driver who, unlike the bus driver of earlier years, was not inclined to stop the traffic for Hancock.

'Can you take criticism?' the taxi driver asked him as he sat in the back of the cab.

'Yes, I can,' said Hancock.

'I thought your last show was terrible,' said the taxi driver.

'I don't like the way you're driving this taxi,' said Hancock.

The taxi driver said, 'You've no need to be personal.'

It was Hancock himself who told the story.

One afternoon about five o'clock he turned up at the Red Barn with Cicely. She had moved out of MacConkeys by then and was living in a cottage about quarter of an hour's drive away. They had been out to lunch and Hancock, as Mrs Fryer puts it, was almost sober. Cicely was unwell, though not from drink. They asked if they could come in and just sit quietly. They did not want anything to drink. They sat for a couple of hours in front of the fire in the lounge, relaxed and talking. The Fryers were hoping they would go because they had a party coming in that evening and had a lot of work to do. It must have shown.

Hancock said: 'I think you're anxious for us to go but we are going to stay a little longer.'

Mrs Fryer told him they could stay as long as they liked. Hancock told her that he was going back to Cicely.

There was a lot of talk after his death that this was his intention but, of course, if he had been serious about it, there was nothing to stop him. Freddie's divorce proceedings were already in motion. Cicely certainly would have been willing. She still loved him.

But it was about this time that he also telephoned Freddie three weeks in succession to say, 'Please come back, I need you, Fred. I miss everything, I can't go on without you.'

Fred told him: 'I thought you didn't like the Emergency Ward 10 atmosphere.'

'Ah,' he said, 'I know now it was organising.'

And he was still seeing Joan Le Mesurier.

He played an unsuccessful, unhappy week in one of the northern clubs, still using the same old material. He never saw the paradox inherent in his complaints about the boring business of doing the same thing twice nightly in a stage show for months on end and his refusal to discard routines he had used for twenty years and which were now threadbare and squeezed dry.

He had achieved greatness through television yet he was undoubtedly the last comedian able to ignore the terrible power of the medium to swallow and nullify comedy material. He behaved exactly like the old-time music-hall comics who, with one safely-established act, were able to play for years to small audiences all over the country.

In March 1968 he returned to Australia. On one of his earlier visits he had tried to persuade Terry Nation to go with him. This time he approached Duncan Wood, producer of his television shows. In neither case were they willing.

Hancock had been engaged by Sydney's Channel 7 to do a series of thirteen programmes about a British emigrant to Australia. He would be very arrogant and belligerent about the Australian way of life, very Hancockian. To supplement the Australian writers Hancock took along Michael Wale, a young British journalist and scriptwriter. Wale, who later wrote a moving account of Hancock's last few weeks for *The Times*, flew out first and Hancock followed, stopping a few days with his friends the Freemans in India. He behaved strangely and was suspicious about the curries.

The Australians were having trouble in finding a director for the series and telephoned Phyllis Rounce in London to see if she could suggest anyone. She put up Eddie Joffe, a South African who directs for Grampian Television in Aberdeen.

Before he accepted, Joffe asked her what he was letting himself in for. She told him but added that if he could pull Hancock together he would be doing something fabulous for Hancock, for show business and for everybody as he was really a wonderful person and his own worst enemy.

Joffe accepted the job with some misgivings. It had been arranged that he and his wife Myrtle should take a house and that Hancock would live with them. Joffe had commitments which prevented him from going out immediately.

Hancock first flew to Melbourne where Hugh Stuckey, the senior scriptwriter on the series, lived. He spent a lot of time with Stuckey, his wife and two small daughters, quiet domestic evenings which he seemed to enjoy. Stuckey warned him that his daughters' school sports day was about the dreariest event in Australia but he went along, was agreeable to all the back-slappers and kidders and often referred to the pleasure it had been. Once he told Stuckey, 'I'm a parochial man trying to look intelligent and sophisticated, trying to make the world a better place – and trying to find an ultimate in life.'

Hancock stayed dry for about two weeks in Melbourne while he worked on the scripts with his writers. As the pressures increased his resistance weakened and he started to drink. When he was due to fly to Sydney to begin work in earnest he was seen off by friends and, reaching the departure barrier, he turned round in a panic and shouted, 'Oh God! I can't face it . . . I just can't go through with it. Please . . . please take me back to my motel.'

The friends put it down to the drink and bundled him on the aircraft.

In Sydney he moved into the Travelodge Motel with his airline bag full of pills and Stuckey moved in next door and acquired a spare key to Hancock's room.

He was frightened that Hancock would set fire to himself as he was always falling asleep with a lighted cigarette in his hand. The sheets and his underwear were full of scorch marks.

In the past Hancock had only smoked heavily when he was on the wagon. Freddie used to get upset about the heavy nicotine stains on his fingers, and had guarded him from setting fire to himself while asleep.

Now he was drinking and smoking. He was not, however, interested in girls. His extra-alcoholic pleasures were, indeed, very simple. He liked to drive around Sydney sight-seeing with Dusty Nelson, the Channel 7 stage-manager who had worked with him in England. He would sit in the car and eat meat-pies and ice-cream – at one time he could not stand ice-cream. He had quiet domestic evenings with Nelson's parents.

There were times when he was quite childlike in the innocence of his pleasures.

There were others when he gave way to inexplicable childish rages. He was asked to appear on a satirical television programme called *The Mavis Bramston Show* but, after watching rehearsals, he suddenly rushed out of the studios. He resented the way he had been treated by the management, he said.

At the motel, Hancock spent most of his time in his room, drinking vodka and lying on his bed in his underpants. Two pageboys appointed themselves his guardians. When he wandered out in his pants and nothing else in search of more 'medicine' they gently returned him to his room. He never argued with them but allowed himself to be led back docilely.

He constantly telephoned his mother in Bournemouth.

Stuckey and Wale wanted to work. Hancock wanted full-time attention and, as usual, would call them in the middle of the night if he thought of something.

Eventually, in an attempt to avoid scandal – Hancock frequently shambled out into the corridors in his underwear to the alarm of other residents – and to allow the writers to get on with their job, he moved to another motel.

Eddie Joffe and his wife, Myrtle, arrived in Sydney but were unable to find a suitable house immediately.

Work started on the first programme. The first day was a Friday. Some rehearsals had already been cancelled by Joffe because Hancock was incapable of reading his script. The first reading had been splendid. Hancock did not merely walk through as is the custom but gave a performance. Everyone had gone home from it blithe with thoughts of success.

On the Saturday work should have started at 9 a.m. but was delayed while they tried to evict a bird that was tweeting away up in the roof. Hancock fell asleep. When they eventually started, Hancock was almost unable to speak. He had been taking anti-alcoholic tablets which tranquillised him, other tablets to wake him up and then beer. After lunch there was a scene where he was supposed to pick up a telephone, dial and speak a line. He spoke the line before he even got to the telephone.

Joffe asked the production manager to come down and see what was happening. The production manager kept saying things like, 'Golly,' and 'Gee!' But he told Joffe to carry on.

Hancock kept suggesting that they should all leave and make the series in England. Technically, this was possible, but the cost would have been astronomic. It was already the most expensive series ever planned for Australian television.

Joffe told Hancock: 'The only way to save the series is for you to dry out.'

Hancock shook his head. 'I've tried it,' he said. 'You just can't believe what agonies I go through. It's hell.'

When Jim Oswin, managing director of Channel 7, saw the first episode he ordered it to be scrapped and there was a hurried meeting of the station's executives. Hancock was called in and bluntly told: 'One more drink, mate, and you are on the first plane back to Blighty.'

Hancock decided to take the cure again. This time he really fought. He refused even to take the tapering off treatment in which diminishing amounts of alcohol are issued over a period to ease the strain. He tried bravely and valiantly and, it looked for a time, successfully. He spent his forty-fourth birthday in hospital.

Joffe asked one of Sydney's leading psychiatrists who was treating him, 'How long will it last?'

He was told: 'It could be three weeks or three months. It might even be six months.'

The psychiatrist could hold out no hope at all for a permanent cure.

If he had not tried to meet the challenge it is possible that Hancock would have plodded into obscurity, might well have ended up, as he once happily forecast, sleeping by the warm air outlet of the Paris Metro, covered by an old copy of *Le Figaro* and with an empty bottle of cheap wine beside him.

But the effort was made and when he came out of the clinic he obeyed the psychiatrist, who said he needed a home environment, and went to live with a doctor and his family in Killara, a Sydney suburb.

He resumed work. By comparison with his previous efforts he was his old brilliant self. Three episodes were made and the studio bosses were delighted.

The Joffes, accompanied in their search by Hancock, found a suitable house in Birriga Road, Bellevue Hill, a 'good' Sydney suburb. Next door they were putting up a block of flats, 'a new concept in luxury living'. The house was on a hill and Hancock had the garden flat, a semi-basement, though not below ground.

There was not much furniture in it but he seemed happy. At 8.15 every morning, Myrtle Joffe would knock on the floor to wake him and he would go with Joffe to work in the Channel 7 Studios at Epping, some fifteen miles from Sydney.

At night he would come home, sometimes buy a ready-cooked chicken and the Joffes would hear him going over his lines with a tape recorder.

On 21 June, after two years of dour defence by Hancock, Freddie obtained a decree nisi in London. She had been given permission to seek a divorce before the usual three years had elapsed because of 'extreme hardship'. The divorce was granted on the grounds of Hancock's adultery with an unknown woman. The Australian papers carried the news.

It did not seem to affect Hancock.

On 24 June Hancock finished work at the studios. Normally Dusty Nelson drove him home but this time he was too busy. Instead, Joffe saw him into a cab.

On 24 June Phyllis Rounce was in Australia with one of her clients, Rolf Harris. Hancock had heard that she was to visit the country and had given Eddie Joffe a message asking her to contact him. When she had arrived in Sydney, Joffe had taken her to lunch and said that Hancock was anxious to see her.

At that stage she only had time to talk to him on the telephone. He kept urging, 'Do come and see me.'

But she was kept busy with Harris's tight schedule which involved flying to New Zealand and back several times. Suddenly it was 24 June and her last day in Australia. The studios were too far away to reach in the available time so she telephoned to say goodbye. She could not get through to either Hancock or Joffe. She tried again from the airport but they were still unavailable.

When she reached Los Angeles, Rolf Harris, who had gone ahead, met her and broke the news of Hancock's death.

Hancock had called in to see Myrtle Joffe in the early evening and they drank some coffee. Hancock telephoned his mother – the line in his flat had not yet been connected – and chatted to the landlord who was still fixing things.

Hancock and the Joffes had been invited out that evening but he excused himself saying that he would rather stay home and learn his lines.

The Joffes went out, leaving two girls in their part of the house as the children's baby-sitters. At 8.35 p.m. Hancock knocked on the door and handed one of the girls a jar of coffee he had borrowed from Mrs Joffe.

'He looked sad,' the girl said later.

Hancock said something vague like, 'I've got to go now.'

The next morning Mrs Joffe got no response from her knock on the floor. She went out into the street and let herself into the garden flat. The lights and heaters were turned on. It was very warm. Hancock was lying on the bed in his underpants and socks. He was dead. There was a pen in his hand and two notes on the back of the yellow script of episode four of the series. Both were addressed to 'Dear Eddie'.

There was an empty vodka bottle and a scattering of pills.

Mrs Joffe ran to her husband who called the police. He told them a man had died on the premises. When they got there he said, 'You'll know who he is when you see him.' He was in tears.

The post-mortem showed the obvious – that Hancock had died as the result of taking a large number of amylo-barbitone tablets and an excessive amount of alcohol.

The notes read:

Ed – Please send my mother this. I am sorry to cause her any more grief as she has already had enough but please pass on this message to her – that the soul is indestructible and so therefore Bill, who means nothing to you, will understand.

Bill is the medium, a friend of Hancock's mother.

The other note said:

Dear Eddie. This is quite rational. Please give my love to my mother but there was nothing left to do. Things seemed to go wrong too many times.

The verdict was suicide.

It may be that Hancock eventually managed to see himself in the cosmic perspective he had sought for years, as an insignificant speck of dust in an obscure corner of the universe, end product of a long line of accidental survivals. It is one thing to talk about the need for perspective; it must be unbearable to find it.

Freddie believes – and she is probably right – that in a moment of deep and corrosive despair he suddenly caught a glimpse of himself and, with an awful clarity, realised that all the years of struggle lay drowned and that he no longer had the power to regain the lost pinnacles of his life; that ahead lay only further decline with all the admiration and love he had once commanded turned to pity. He was a man who could fight off anything save pity. Pity was a pathetic thing, to be despised and loathed; pathos had never been his style. The pills were to hand.

On 18 July 1968 a memorial service was held at St Martin-in-the-Fields, London. In January 1969 the BBC screened six of his old shows. They included 'The Blood Donor' and 'The Radio Ham'. On 11 January 1969 Cicely died at the age of thirty-eight. It was stated at the inquest that she had been a chronic alcoholic for four years. During the year after Hancock's death, Freddie spent time seriously ill in hospital undergoing major surgery. When she recovered she travelled extensively and worked on jobs unconnected with PR. She then went to the United States and now has a marketing consultancy in New York. She has never remarried.

Eighteen years after his death, millions of people still talk of Hancock. They remember him only as the funniest man of his era. Jokes become fragile and fall apart with time because the circumstances on which they comment, no matter how obliquely, vanish. But comedy based on character is ageless and unfading. Falstaff and Mrs Malaprop have lasted because they had the good fortune to be fiction; Will Sommers, Henry VIII's jester, and Richard Tarlton, Elizabeth's favourite clown, are now material for academics. Even comparatively recent performers such as Sid Field, Robb Wilton and Jimmy James are now only glimpsed on film or television because the camera was merely an onlooker at their antics, never part of them. For the great film comedians like

Chaplin, Keaton, Harold Lloyd and Laurel and Hardy, the camera was a companion and Hancock followed their example when he allowed the microphone and the television camera intimacies denied to the theatre audience. They were partners, sharing his aspirations and his desperations.

Since his death there have been more than sixty repeats of his radio shows and Hancock's television shows have been sold all over the world. When six videos[8] containing eighteen of the *Half Hours* were released by the BBC between January and May, 1985, 20,588 had been sold by July and a further 10,000 sales were confidently expected.

In September 1985 the National Film Theatre staged a seven-day Hancock festival, finishing up with a *Guardian* lecture delivered by Galton and Simpson.

On disc, no Hancock title has ever been deleted from the catalogues and nearly a quarter of a million copies have been sold of the BBC's seven records in the United Kindom, Australia, New Zealand, Canada, South Africa and the USA. There are two other Hancock records issued by Decca and Pickwick.

The Tony Hancock Appreciation Society[9] issues a quarterly magazine and has members in Australia, Canada, Germany, Israel, Italy, Malaysia and the USA. Its youngest member is twelve years old and there are other members who are too young to have been listeners or viewers of the original Hancock shows. Heathcote Williams' play, *Hancock's Last Half Hour*, is an imaginary re-creation of the hour or so before Hancock took the pills that ended his life. Actor Jim McManus, who bears an undoubted resemblance to Hancock, has given more than 100 performances of the play and reports that some people have come to see it over and over again.

In 1985 a BBC omnibus programme attempted to put together a portrait of Hancock and a long extract from 'The Wet Sunday Afternoon' radio *Half Hour* was included at the Queen Mother's request in the radio tribute paid to her on her eighty-fifth birthday.

About half the radio shows are preserved because BBC policy, until tape came along, was to record only selections of the programmes in order to illustrate their output.

Since this book was first published in 1969, Freddie has had time to take a cooler look at the turmoil of the Hancock years which, for all the pain, have left her with no regrets about becoming so closely involved with Hancock. She remains certain that his suicide came about as a result of his determination to avoid what he had always despised – pity. He had always said that pity was the worst possible motive for doing anything for anyone. But he had also always maintained that suicide was not the answer to anyone's problems. It was something they had discussed frequently after his stepfather's suicide.

'But Tony was thousands of miles from familiar places and faces and he did not like Australia,' Freddie recalls. 'He was trying to make a comeback and knew it was doomed. His self-evaluation was always tougher than any critic's because he would make no allowances for himself. I suppose it was a combination of many things, but all he saw ahead of him was the complete disintegration of everything he held precious. People were disappearing from his life and he was losing control of his talent. He must have felt that the only prospect was that he would be pitied by all those who had once admired him. He could not tolerate the idea. The marvellous thing is that no one pities him now and when I come home to England – which I do frequently – it is wonderful to find that people only think of him with laughter and love and warmth. I still laugh whenever I hear his voice.'

It is important to remember that though Hancock went through many agonies, he also laughed a lot, would roll about laughing, clutching his stomach and murmuring, 'Oh dear, oh dear, oh dear'; would shake and collapse in a shuddering heap at something that he thought funny. It is an aspect of generosity that he wanted to share with everyone this great joy that he found in laughter. For most of the time, he did.

Notes

1 (Chapter Two, page 36) The BBC's television booking manager offered the audition at the Star Sound Studios near Baker Street. The letter, dated 12 August 1948, went on to say: 'Please state by return if you accept the above invitation. In the absence of a reply within reasonable time your place at the audition will be given to another applicant.'

On 7 September, Hancock wrote from the Grand Hotel, Grange over Sands, Lancashire, saying that he and his partner, Derek Scott, had been working at the Windmill and, being unable to leave the theatre to post the confirmatory note, had given it to someone else who 'promptly forgot'.

He (Hancock) had only just discovered that this had happened and hoped that it was not too late to confirm that he would attend for the audition. He apologised for any inconvenience caused and would like to inform the BBC that his new, permanent address was 74 Natal Road, New Southgate.

The BBC index card read:

TONY HANCOCK & DEREK SCOTT (Comedy duo)

DESCRIPTION	2 pleasant young men in lounge suits. Derek at piano.
DATE OF AUDITION	14 September 1948.
PERFORMANCE	Concert party burlesque. Yorkshire comic tenor, impressionist cameo – amateur talent comp, winner, Western Brothers.
TIME	7¼ minutes.
EXPERIENCE	Windmill Th. with this act. Derek was Terry Thomas' 'Technical Hitch' accompanist in Piccadilly Hayride.
REMARKS	Not untalented, & perform with verve. Should prove suitable TeleVariety or Revue.

8

On 16 September, Mary C. Forbes, of television auditions, sent the card to Michael Mills AP (Assistant Producer) (later Head of Comedy at the BBC) with a note explaining that the cryptic '8' at the bottom of the remarks meant that they will 'either be given a camera test or recommended direct'.

There is no record of a camera test, but they were engaged for an appearance on a television programme, *New to You*, on 1 November 1948.

2 (Chapter Three, page 37) On 16 November 1950, Phyllis Rounce wrote to Pat Newman, the BBC Variety Booking Manager, saying that Hancock had done seven broadcasts that year at a fee of 12 guineas which had been raised from 10 guineas in January. Taking his last *Variety Bandbox* as an example, his script had cost him 10 guineas ('and that was by special arrangement with the writer who usually charged far more') and his band parts were four guineas. This meant, said Miss Rounce not unreasonably, that broadcasting was not an economic proposition. She asked for a minimum of 18 guineas.

Newman replied that the suggestion amounted to a 50-per-cent increase 'but from the facts that you put forward I imagine that you will feel that anything less is not of much value. Therefore I am arranging that his fee will be raised to 18 guineas from 1 January 1951.'

He also hoped that Hancock would agree that there would be no further increase in his fee 'for a reasonable time'.

3 (Chapter Six, page 94) Letter from Ronald Waldman to Stanley Dale, 25 February 1959:
'. . . I have just heard from New York that CBS have gone a bit cold on the Hancock idea . . . Hubell Robinson is still as keen as ever but in his efforts to sell the show he has run into a really tricky problem – everybody says they can't understand Tony! This matter of accent is, in my opinion, an essential part of his characterisation and yet if people in New York are having difficulty in following him what on earth is going to happen in the Middle West?

'Anyway, I have asked our New York office to bring NBC into the picture immediately and the telerecordings are now with them. It is therefore remotely possible that the NBC's suggestion has come up because of this and that Wildberg found himself caught up in the backlash. At any rate, with the position being what it is I think it would be wise to accept the NBC offer of the play if the script is acceptable to you. This may well be another version of the technique suggested by CBS of getting Tony known to the American television public.'

4 (Chapter Six, page 95) In 1959 and 1960 Hancock did ten programmes for which he was paid £1000 each. The contract stipulated a further £500 each for repeats of a maximum of five. Other income would, of course, come from overseas sales.

On 1 April 1959, Cecil McGivern, Deputy Director of Television, sent a memo to the Programme Controller and the Head of Light Entertainment. It made three points:
'(1) This is now a very expensive contract and a very expensive programme. If knowledge of this price got abroad it would considerably affect the prices we are at present paying for American telefilms.
'(2) For the amount we are now paying, we must extract the maximum in content, in placing and in size of audience figures.
'(3) In my opinion the production (as opposed to the content) is far too slow. I know the producer Duncan Wood would retort with the inevitable slowness of television as opposed to film, the changing of the clothes and set, the necessity to hang on to captions, bridging shots and all the rest of it. Nevertheless, despite that, the production must be quickened up and the writers should be told this. Live television need not be *so* far behind the speed of *Bilko*.'

5 (Chapter Seven, page 103) Ray Galton says: 'We were all reading Bertrand Russell then and talking about the cosmic.'

Alan Simpson enlarges: 'The sequence when he was reading Bertrand Russell and looking at a dictionary and then picking up a thriller and consulting the dictionary again – that's exactly what happened to me except for the actual gag. I was lying in bed just after I came out of the sanatorium when I was trying to educate myself. I had bought the blue Penguin introductions to Kant, Spinoza, Schopenhauer and Bertrand Russell. Not the works themselves, the *introductions*. I read the first page of the introduction to Kant and I could not understand what the man was talking about. I got to page two and had to go back to page one. In the end I said to myself: "I'm twenty-four years old and I'm going to be ninety before I've even got through the introduction." So I turned it in.'

Freddie recalls that Hancock, who, she says, did understand

what Teilhard de Chardin was getting at, once tried to get her to read Teilhard de Chardin's *The Phenomenon of Man*, assuring her that if there were any words she did not understand he would explain them to her. Freddie did read the book but could not get through it without the assistance of a dictionary which remained at her side throughout.

6 (Chapter Seven, page 112) Memo, 13 April 1962, from Tom Sloan, Head of Light Entertainment, to C.P. (Controller of Programmes) Tel.

'. . . Hancock was primarily interested in making television films in which he could retain full control of domestic and overseas rights. I took his brother agent to see G.M. Tel. E. [General Manager, Television Enterprises] who explained the problems and expense of such film-making and who pointed out that the BBC did not do such deals.

'Quite clearly he has found an organisation which does and he had gone there for that reason.

'His loss is to be greatly regretted, but one must remember he will be without his producer [Duncan Wood] and his scriptwriters [Galton and Simpson] – and Sidney James. The result could well be unfortunate.

'Hancock is a moody perfectionist with a great interest in money and no sense of loyalty to the Corporation.

'I am satisfied that we did everything possible to keep him within the fold but unless we were prepared to resign our production control and underwrite the project with something like £150,000 for 13 programmes and film them rather than telescreen them we could not do business.'

7 (Chapter Nine, page 131) Galton and Simpson freely acknowledge that *Steptoe and Son* was an expansion of Hancock with Harry H. Corbett's Harold Steptoe desperately aspiring to higher things such as hob-nobbing with better, even brainier, people, dating classier girls and living in a more elegant setting than the junk-yard shack he and his father inhabited. But every time there was the possibility of climbing out of the social pit into which fate had flung him, he fell back, partly through the intractable limitations of his own intellect and character and partly by the gleeful acceptance of lowly social status by Albert, his toothless old ratbag of a father. This part was marvellously played by Wilfrid Brambell who thus took over the Sid James role of implacable realist with no illusions about the nature of society and the impregnability of its

defences. It is, in short, a comedy of the English class system.

Indeed, a line that Galton and Simpson wrote for Hancock in 1954 turned up again in a *Steptoe* episode in 1970. It was a very Hancockian plot, opening with Harold bitterly complaining about the dreariness of a Sunday afternoon while his father slumped and snored near the fire. Albert wakes and decides that his son's social life will be improved by a few dancing lessons which he proceeds to give him. After a while he grimaces and says: 'I'll have toes like globe artichokes in the morning.'

In 1954, Hancock, in the middle of his solo act, would pause, look at his feet and confide: 'Cor, I don't know how they do an hour and a half at the Palladium – I've got toes like globe artichokes.'

Alan Simpson acknowledges the self-plagiarism and puts it down to sheer laziness. On the other hand, he and Galton believe that anything called a globe artichoke is inescapably funny.

It is no wonder that after Hancock's death, Harry H. Corbett suggested that the Hancock series should be remade with him in the Hancock role and Wilfrid Brambell getting Sid James's lines. (For a number of years Freddie Hancock also looked after Harry H. Corbett's publicity and organised his fan-mail, etc. She says that Corbett and Hancock always admired and liked each other.)

Simpson said: 'As the years went on and we got further and further away from the original, Harry's idea started to make more and more sense. Then Harry died.'

Later they actually did recast one of the Hancock scripts for Arthur Lowe and James Beck. Lowe was the actor who played the part of the pompous bank manager who commanded the Home Guard Unit in *Dad's Army* (with John Le Mesurier as his foil, much as he had been to Hancock on a number of occasions) and James Beck was the spiv private who could always get his fingers on such wartime rarities as nylon stockings and petrol coupons. He was perfect casting for the Sid James role of a man who would steal a church roof and swear to God he was innocent.

The BBC and Hancock's old producer, Duncan Wood, favoured the idea and Galton and Simpson slightly rewrote 'The Economy Drive' (first broadcast 25 September 1959) to establish that Beck was widower Arthur Lowe's good-for-nothing brother-in-law which explained why they were living together. This was effected on the first page or two; after that it was word for word as Hancock and Sid James had played it.

It was the episode in which Hancock decided that there must be some savings made when he returns home from holiday to find that Sid has left every electrical appliance and light turned on, had not cancelled either the papers or the milk and had even left the car engine running.

The pilot show was made and Galton and Simpson thought it was very successful. It looked as if a great many of the Hancock scripts could be recycled in this way. Then James Beck died and the idea was abandoned. A few years later, Arthur Lowe died.

8 (Chapter Twelve, page 192) The videos put out by the BBC were edited by Galton and Simpson with the aid of technician and Hancock fan Jim Franklin. The two writers decided that they had no right to make improving cuts, though there were sections which would have benefited by losing the shots that gave the actors time to change or move from one set to another, scenes where a long, lingering close-up and what is technically known as a 'slow-burn' were included, not for reason of comedy, but simply to give Hancock time to do something else. They mainly took out technical faults and fluffed lines, modern equipment giving them the chance to delete even one frame where there was, for example, an unwanted flash of light. A little of the padding also went. For instance, in 'The Blood Donor', there were far too many shots of the ambulance; it was even seen leaving its garage. Now Hancock cuts his hand and there is one shot of the ambulance. Apart from anything else, Simpson explains, the quick cutting used in television commercials has accustomed the viewer to a more rapid assessment of situation. The episodes have been shortened by about one minute on average for video.

9 (Chapter Twelve, page 192) The president of the Tony Hancock Appreciation Society is Chris Bumstead, 10 Devenish Road, Winchester, Hampshire.

Acknowledgements

This book could not have been written without the help of a great many people. It is impossible to measure their contributions for some provided whole chapters and others an illuminating sentence. But my special gratitude must go to my collaborator, Freddie Hancock, who provided both insight and masses of vital material; to Alan Simpson and Ray Galton for their permission to quote from their great treasure trove of Hancock scripts; to J. B. Priestley and Heinemann Ltd. for permission to quote from *London End* and to Spike Milligan who proves that it takes a clown to catch a clown. My gratitude to the others listed here is not lessened because their billing is alphabetical. Most of them know that is the surest way to peace. Therefore, my deepest thanks to:

Jack Adams, Peter Brough, Roy Castle, Edward Chapman, Len Costa, Stanley Dale, Bernard Delfont, George Fairweather, Eileen Fryer, Kati Hannan, Edward Joffe, Glyn Jones, Sean Kenny, John and Sally Knight, John Le Mesurier, Oscar Lewenstein, Billy Marsh, Sally Mordant, John Muir, Terry Nation, Philip Oakes, John Osborne, Ralph Reader, Dr and Mrs Romanis, Leonard Ross, Phyllis Rounce, Harry Secombe, Peter Sellers, Tom Sloan, Graham Stark, Eric Sykes, Sylvia Syms, Lynn Took, Joan Turner, Beryl Vertue, Johnny Vyvyan, Kenneth Williams, Pat Williams, Roger Williams, Dennis Main Wilson, Duncan Wood, Donald Zec, and the ladies of the BBC Audience Research Department.

My sincerest apologies to anyone I may have inadvertently omitted.

David Nathan, 1969